NEVADA COUNTY LIBRARY

W9-BEU-613

Reflections on Living

30 YEARS IN A SPIRITUAL COMMUNITY

INTERVIEWS WITH MEMBERS OF ANANDA VILLAGE
BY SARA CRYER

INTRODUCTION BY JYOTISH & DEVI NOVAK

DISCARDED

CRYSTAL CLARITY, PUBLISHERS

NEVADA COUNTY LIBRARY - NEVADA CITY

Copyright © Crystal Clarity, Publishers, 1998
All rights reserved

Interviews by Sara Cryer
Cover photo by Wayne Green
Cover design by Renee Glenn Designs
Printed in Canada

ISBN 1-56589-098-1

1 3 5 7 9 8 6 4 2

Crystal

Clarity

Published by Crystal Clarity, Publishers
14618 Tyler Foote Road
Nevada City, CA 95959
U.S.A.

800-424-1055
530-478-7600
http://www.ananda.org/CrystalClarity

DISCARDED

N.J
16.95

To:

Swami Kriyananda
for his courage, love and humility;

All souls past, present and future
who have given selflessly to the creation
of this spiritual community;

Paramhansa Yogananda,
whose love flows throughout these pages.

"Far into the night my dear friend—the first Kriya Yogi in America—discussed with me the need for world colonies founded on a spiritual basis. The ills attributed to an anthropomorphic abstraction called "society" may be laid more realistically at the door of Everyman. Utopia must spring in the private bosom before it can flower in civic virtue. Man is a soul, not an institution; his inner reforms alone can lend permanence to outer ones. By stress on spiritual values, self-realization, a colony exemplifying world brotherhood is empowered to send inspiring vibrations far beyond its locale."

Paramhansa Yogananda
Autobiography of a Yogi
Reprint of the 1946 First Edition by
The Philosophical Library, Inc.

"When I am gone, only love can take my place."
Paramhansa Yogananda
"Master"
January 5, 1893 - March 7, 1952

Patiala, India, November 1959
Swami Kriyananda (J. Donald Walters),
Founder of Ananda Village,
Dedicated to fulfilling the vision of Paramhansa Yogananda
for spiritual cooperative living.

"Often, as I stand and gaze out over Ananda's green fields, woods, and rolling hills, I am reminded of a poem I wrote...set in the legendary golden era of Lord Rama, whose kingdom of Ayodhya, in ancient India, was a place of universal harmony, peace, and brotherhood. Thus, may all men learn to live, wherever their paths take them outwardly. For now, as then, true, divine peace is possible only when people place God and spiritual values first in their lives."

Swami Kriyananda
The Path

CONTENTS

INTRODUCTION

The chapters in the book you are about to read are not the result of years of careful research, or well-reasoned philosophy, or even whimsical flights of fantasy. They are simply true stories from the lives of ordinary people who together have done an extraordinary thing—they have created Ananda Village, an enduring and inspiring cooperative community.

Ananda owes its existence to two remarkable men—Paramhansa Yogananda and Swami Kriyananda. Yogananda was one of the greatest masters of yoga ever to live and teach in the United States. In 1948 Swami Kriyananda read Yogananda's life-changing book, *Autobiography of a Yogi*, and took the next bus from New York to Los Angeles to become his disciple. Since that day Kriyananda has spent more than 50 years spreading the teachings of Self-realization which his *guru* exemplified.

Ananda was founded in 1968 by Kriyananda who, from his youth, had dreamed of creating small communities based on cooperation and high ideals. When he discovered that Yogananda, too, was committed to the concept of "World Brotherhood Colonies," he vowed to do his utmost to make this dream a reality.

Yogananda often said that what the world needs is a blend of the best qualities of the East and West: the spiritual insight of the East and the practical efficiency of the West. One without the other leads to a society barren of human fulfillment, but a balance of the two can bring peace, harmony, prosperity, and happiness. Yogananda predicted that world brotherhood colonies, based on the twin principles of "plain living and high thinking" would be the social pattern for the New Age.

Swami Kriyananda has dedicated the last thirty years to the creation of Ananda Village, which is located near Nevada City, California, and to the development of its sister communities in Seattle, Washington, Portland, Oregon, Sacramento and Palo Alto, California, and near Assisi, Italy. With wisdom, friendship, self-sacrifice, inspiration, and patience—incredible patience—he has steered the community and its now 350 residents (800 total in all communities) through the storms and trials of shaping a social prototype for the future.

The exceptional challenge of this task lay in the fact that nothing like it had ever been done before. Indian teachers had started ashrams where students dedicated themselves to the mystical search for God. Visionaries had founded small communities based on utopian dreams or economic theories. But the goal in creating Ananda was to build a community with the blending of the best of East and West—a dedication to seek the Divine balanced with the ability to operate practically and efficiently in the world.

The stories you are about to read are the experiences of people who have been an integral part of the creation of Ananda. We share them because they are inspiring, poignant, humorous, entertaining, and because they may help others to learn from our successes and our failures. Taken as a whole they give a picture not only of how Ananda was created, but how God works with infinite love to help each of us learn our lessons and make our lives something of value.

As we write this introduction, Ananda is just finishing an annual all-community workday where we devote a weekend to beautifying, cleaning, painting, planting, building, fixing, and in general, uplifting the whole Village. This morning as several hundred of us met in the pouring rain to start the workday, we saw what strength of will it takes to build your dreams. It is but a small sacrifice to rise early from bed on a rainy Saturday and volunteer for a day of hard, physical work. But this same self-offering has been repeated for more than ten thousand mornings by hundreds of Anandites. Those whose stories you are about to read, like many others, have dedicated their lives to this ideal, and the fruit born from this dedication has been incredible joy. There is a motto that captures the spirit of Ananda, "Many hands make a miracle."

It has taken great courage over these past thirty years to overcome the many challenges we've faced. Some words of Swami Kriyananda come to mind: "Dynamic courage is the strength of will not only to accept reality, but to confront it with another reality of one's own making." This labor of love we call Ananda stands as a testimony that the future is now, that we can make our dreams a reality, and that when God whispers and we listen, miracles do happen.

Jyotish and Devi Novak
May 2, 1998

"Your religion is not the garb you wear outwardly, but the garment of light you weave around your heart. Discover who you are, behind those outer trappings, and you will discover who Jesus was, and Buddha, and Krishna. For the masters come to earth for the purpose of holding up to every man a reflection of his deeper, eternal Self."

Paramhansa Yogananda,
The Essence of Self-Realization

Jyotish

Like most people at Ananda, I've always had an intense desire to find truth. I was raised Episcopalian, but my church experience didn't seem to answer my questions, so I turned away from religion and toward science, and especially psychology. In high school, I wrote a thesis on dreams, and later I studied psychology and the humanities in college. I graduated from the University of Minnesota in 1966 and immediately moved to California. The study of psychology still left me unsatisfied, so I started looking into alternative spiritual views of life, reading Native American mythology and the *Tibetan Book of the Dead*.

During this period I came across *Autobiography of a Yogi*, by Paramhansa Yogananda. Reading this book was, by far, the most profound spiritual experience I'd had in my life. But, it created a conundrum for me. I knew intuitively that Yogananda knew the truths I was looking for, but his book challenged my logical, rational, scientific viewpoint. Here were passages that spoke matter-of-factly about miracles, and *samadhi*, and a universe very different from mine. I had to choose whether to hold to my logical, scientific view of the world, or to accept that there could be something much vaster.

In the latter part of 1966, I heard about a direct disciple of Yogananda who was living in San Francisco and went to meet him on a Sunday afternoon a week or two later. I knocked on the door of the apartment building where he was living, introduced myself, and that's how I first met Swami Kriyananda.

I find it interesting that my very first contact with Kriyananda set the pattern that was to continue for the rest of my life—he asked me to help him with his work. He was doing a mailing for a class, so virtually his first words were, "Well, come in and, if you'd like, you can help with this mailing." So that's what I did. Afterwards, four or five of us went to Golden Gate Park for a picnic. The conversation drifted to the food we were eating, and he talked about the spiritual and psychological qualities of different foods. Later he sang a couple of songs and told some stories about his time with Yogananda. It was, to say the least, an intriguing afternoon.

In the years before he founded Ananda, Kriyananda's primary activity was teaching yoga classes. In March of 1967, I took one of his six-week class series. In fact, I took this same series three different times within a year, and I began volunteering, helping out a little bit with projects that he was working on.

In 1967, Kriyananda purchased land in the foothills of the Sierra Nevada Mountains for a meditation retreat. I first went there with him in September 1967 to help put up a geodesic dome that was to be the first building. We worked all day Friday and Saturday trying to construct the dome from a kit. By the end of Saturday, we had put together the various hexagons and pentagons that form a dome's structure. A geodesic dome, like any arch, is very strong once all the pieces are in place, but until that time, it's quite fragile. We had assembled all of the parts except the final pentagon that would lock everything else into place, and were working furiously to finish. But, gravity beat us. The unsupported struts gradually began to collapse under their own weight. They started falling slowly and majestically and then faster and faster until they splintered into a heap at our feet. And so, the end of Saturday saw everything in ruins.

On Sunday morning I could see that Kriyananda had distanced himself a bit from the other four of us who were helping. My assumption was, "Well, of course. We had a big failure yesterday, and he needs to be alone so he can brood." Then I heard something. He was lying in the early morning sun, saying something very softly. What I finally heard was "Ah, joy! Ah, joy!" That, more than any lecture, showed me that he had found a level of contentment within himself that wasn't dependent on outward circumstances. After that incident, I began to take the path much more seriously. Over the next year I became more involved, but I still kept my distance.

In the spring of 1968, I had a superconscious dream that changed my life. In the dream, I was walking through an open meadow in a forest carrying a fishing pole. I soon came to a cave, and in the cave was an underground stream. I knew I should fish there. I threw the line in, immediately felt a tug on it, and pulled up a fish. I've always had puns run through my mind and here, in what was the most significant dream I've ever had, a triple-pun occurred.

When I pulled up the fish, I could see it was a sunfish. As I was removing the hook from its lip, the sunfish turned into a face representing the sun with flames for hair. But, as I looked more carefully, I could see that the sun had the face of a child, and I realized that it was Jesus, the "Son" of God. As I was looking into the child's eyes, he said to me, "If you want to know what it is like to be a fish, you'll have to learn to swim in the stream." Then it turned back into a fish, and flipped back into the water. I immediately woke up and spent the rest of the night in meditation. That dream was a turning point for me, because at that time in my life, I was debating how intensely to get into yoga. The dream led me to make a deep life commitment to the spiritual path. I soon quit my job as a social worker and became Kriyananda's assistant.

In early 1968, during the time we were both still living in San Francisco, Kriyananda called a meeting to discuss the idea of forming a cooperative community on the retreat property. The meeting turned out to be a disaster. Only about 10 people showed up, none of whom wanted to live in a community. Several spoke at length about why such a crazy venture couldn't possibly work. After that meeting, seeing that people needed a clearer vision of communities, Kriyananda wrote the book, *Cooperative Communities: How to Start Them and Why*.

About a year later, in the spring of 1969, Ananda really got started, and I served as the general manager for the first ten years. In the first year, we faced three major challenges. First, we had to build consensus that Ananda was dedicated to Yogananda. The second challenge, perhaps the most difficult, was establishing a community that could actually survive. Then, in spite of the tremendous financial burden, we realized that we needed to buy land that was separate from the meditation retreat in order to start a community.

Not everyone came to Ananda for the same reasons. Kriyananda moved up from San Francisco in April 1969 and by June there were 25 or 30 of us living at the retreat. But only about half of the people were really committed to the yogic path. Others were willing to try meditation, but more as a pastime. They were here primarily because they wanted a commune in the woods, a popular concept at the time. As more people, especially families, arrived it became apparent that an active community and a meditation retreat each had distinct needs. So we bought several hundred acres about five miles away.

Within a month or two, dozens of people started to arrive at Ananda hoping to live here. Having a lot of newcomers and being split between two separate pieces of property made it more difficult to keep our original ideals in clear focus. Gradually during the first summer, we began to polarize into two groups — those wanting to be disciples of Yogananda, and those here for a communal experience. By fall the community had grown to 50 or 60 people and the differences had grown to the point where they had to be confronted. Finally, Kriyananda called a meeting and said, "We can't have it both ways. If you want a community without Yogananda, without being his disciples, then I'll leave. But if you want me to stay, then either you have to be committed to my vision or you need to move on." He didn't impose his will, but he made it clear that people needed to make a choice. I've always appreciated his non-attachment, being ready to leave everything behind if that was what people wanted. Fortunately, most of us wanted a spiritual community. After the meeting, about 40 percent of the population left.

The remainder of us got busy figuring out how to survive the winter. Our first need was for shelter, and we put up fifteen or twenty teepees, simple but beautiful living spaces. At the time Ananda was founded there were literally thousands of attempts to start communes, yet only a very small percentage of them made it past their first summer. Much to our amusement, only three months after we started, a professor from Davis interviewed people here to find out how our community had lasted so long!

In order to survive we also had to find ways to earn an income. We got some money from retreat activities and publications, but that only supported a small number of people. Over the first winter Kriyananda paid the land payments from income he earned teaching classes in Sacramento. A few of us saw the need to create businesses so people could have jobs. In the winter of 1969 I started the incense and oils business which eventually employed over 20 people. By God's grace and a lot of hard work we made it through the first winter.

The next year we started the daunting job of organizing the community. We had a huge task in front of us, needing to plan and build a small village, start businesses, and keep a deep, sincere spiritual life in spite of all the activity. We had no experience and no models to follow. But we had energy, ideals, and the blessings of Yogananda.

Community planning has always occurred on an organic level. The first year most of us lived very simply in teepees. But, for the long range, we had to build houses and all the infrastructure of roads, water, and power that goes with them. Initial community (non)planning was driven by two forces—the desire for privacy, and the need to get a road and water to your structure. Those two dynamics produced scattered, uncoordinated clusters of houses, and we soon realized that we needed more foresight. But, it wasn't until after a forest fire destroyed all our houses in 1976 that we did any serious planning. By then, both county building regulations and our own desire for a more conscious community drove us to create a "Master Plan" for Ananda.

Amidst the flurry of building homes and starting businesses, we managed to keep a very strong spiritual focus. Kriyananda gave Sunday services and spiritual classes weekly and, in the beginning, his magnetism was the primary force keeping our consciousness focused on God. Gradually, as we matured spiritually, there developed a large group of people who were unshakably committed to the yogic path. But it took some years to establish a strong spiritual magnetism.

In June of 1976 we had a forest fire that reduced Ananda to a pile of ashes. The fire started several miles from the community, and we could see smoke for quite a long time before we realized our property was being threatened. Then, the fire began moving our way. There was a road on a hillcrest that we hoped would be a natural firebreak. Having gotten myself into a warrior mood to fight the fire, I somehow had the idea that I could put the fire out, or at least slow it down. Wearing a backpack water pumper, I went down about 100 yards into a field of knee-high grass that bordered the road. The fire hit the grass and charged up the hill. I was standing there with my little backpack pumper, which was really kind of a glorified squirt gun, when I realized my folly and started to run back up the hill. When I looked back, I could see that the flames were rushing toward me much faster than I could run. So I turned around and ran down the hill and jumped through the flames into the part that had already been burned, because otherwise I would have just been caught and burned.

Much to our horror, the fire jumped the road as if it wasn't there and began to move through dense brush towards one of our housing clusters. The flames were soon 10 or 20 feet high and starting to top into the trees. My wife, Devi, and I had a geodesic dome about 300 yards from where the fire was burning, so I hurried back down to our house. I tried to save the house by cutting a trench around it and hosing it down with water. I knew I had only ten or fifteen minutes before the flames would reach our home and I was, by this time, thoroughly into battle mode, ready to fight the forces of nature.

A teenager, Dwayne Smallen, who was probably only 14 or 15 years old, came down the hill in a truck very excited. He shouted, "You've got to get out of here. There isn't a chance that you can save the house. The flames are really high and will be here in five minutes." I looked up the hill and saw this enormous wall of fire. It was 500 yards wide and 40 feet high, and it was obvious my little trench wasn't going to save anything.

At that point I went into a state of complete detachment, saying to myself, "I'm not attached to anything. This house is yours, God. If you want to take it, go ahead. Take everything." Dwayne had the presence of mind to yell, "Grab what you can and throw it in the truck." As it happened, Devi had recently boxed up everything in our meditation room to clean it, so I grabbed the things from our meditation room, took an armful of clothes from the closet, and that was it. We threw it in the truck and drove downhill through the brush and out of danger.

Devi had just given birth to our son and had taken him, now 10 days old, to a doctor for his first check-up, so she wasn't here during the fire's outbreak. By now it was mid-day and she had come back from town. On her way, about a mile from Ananda, she came to a police barrier. This was the first she knew that Ananda was burning. By the time she forced her way past the barrier and arrived in the community, it was total chaos. There was smoke all over the place, so you couldn't see anything clearly. You could hear propane tanks bursting like bombs up in the hills. Planes were buzzing over at tree top level dropping borate. It looked and felt like a war.

Devi was in the midst of this war zone trying to comfort our 10 day-old infant. She didn't know if we still had a home. She didn't know if we had a community left. She didn't even know if I was alive or dead. When I got to our little market, where people had gathered, I saw her for the first time since the fire started. I put on a big smile because I didn't want her to be worried, and she did the same for me. I was trying to find a way to break the news about our house and comfort her at the same time. Our dome had leaked like a sieve during the rains so my first words were, "Well, we don't have worry about leaks anymore."

Only days after the fire Ananda began to rebuild itself. Because of our strong foundation in meditation, there was no sense of devastation, which was so prevalent among our neighbors. We knew we would have to put out a lot of energy, but the challenge of rebuilding was exciting rather than distressing. After the fire, about 15 members left and the rest of us started rebuilding the community. Most of our neighbors collected large sums of money by threatening to sue the county, whose equipment had caused the fire. But we, at Ananda, chose not to ask them for anything. Kriyananda wrote them, "We came here to give not to take." God, and generous friends, saw to it that our simple needs were met.

As we developed, one of the issues we faced was how to make decisions. Kriyananda, from the start of the community, was the type of leader who let others take responsibility and make their own decisions. By empowering people, he was much more subject to the vagaries of human nature, but it allowed everyone to develop their own strength. Self-determination has always been a basic principle at Ananda. As soon as people were willing to take responsibility, we gave them not only responsibility, but also authority—the right to make decisions, and to experience the successes or failures of those decisions. Everyone had control over his or her immediate area. If a person was running the fruit and vegetable department in the market, then he or she decided what to buy, how to display it, and so on. We always avoided the kind of micro-management style that produces an ever-expanding manual of "policies and procedures." I would call the management style that permeates Ananda, "management by willingness." As soon as someone begins to show the willingness to take responsibility, he's given the opportunity.

Naturally, there are people who take responsibility, but aren't good at making decisions. Good leaders try to tune in to what is trying to happen in any situation. In a spiritual community we always have to try to tune in to the will of God, and try to intuit how it would express itself in any given circumstance. The more we're able to do that, the more a flow of grace and attunement comes into our work. While attunement to God's will is sometimes present in religious works, we've demonstrated that it can be there in the workplace as well. Almost everyone at Ananda is a member of our monastic order, the

"Friends of God." This is the second monastic order we've had at Ananda. The first one, in the early years, was a more traditional order, but the "Friends of God" is made of householders primarily.

One major difference between Ananda's monastic order and a traditional one is that the people here aren't celibate. To live a monastic life, the primary requirement is not celibacy but rather a dedication to doing God's will, even though it may be personally difficult. Such dedication has nothing to do with whether you're married or not. Whether single or married, to be a monastic you have to develop traits of non-attachment and selfless service.

At Ananda we define the spiritual life much more in terms of what we *do* than what we don't do. The yogic path is based upon controlling and directing energy in a positive flow. It teaches us to transmute energy wasted in worldly desires into desire for union with God. And, most importantly, it gives us techniques to do so. Spiritual success comes much more quickly through developing right attitudes than by trying to suppress desires. Meditation helps us quiet the mind so we can perceive the eternal presence of God within us.

In the past religion tried to restrain what were seen as innately sinful tendencies in mankind. In traditional monasteries, control was achieved through vows of poverty, celibacy and obedience. These vows regulate the flow of life-force in the first three, materialistic, energy centers or *chakras*, which govern security, sexuality, and power. But, unless the subconscious mind is ready for this step, such forced control feels repressive and produces a backlash.

There is a dual tendency in the psyche of American culture. Many see human nature as innately sinful and therefore needing to be controlled by rules. Others rebel. Look at the stories presented by the media, and you'll see the rebellious backlash expressed as a lust for wealth, excessive sexuality, and the anti-authoritarian hero who "won't take nothing from nobody no how."

One extreme says man needs controlling, and the other says, "there's no way you're going to discipline me." Both of these approaches are simply inappropriate ways to deal with one's life-force. At Ananda we use a much more moderate approach, trying neither to harshly control nor freely express human nature. We try simply to direct our energy gently toward that which will bring us lasting happiness.

In Ananda's monastic order, we have a vow of simplicity rather than poverty. Simplicity allows you to have what you need, but avoids excessive accumulation of material goods. Excess of any kind eventually begins to control you. Instead of celibacy, we have moderation. If you expend too much energy in sexual activity or through the senses, then you'll dissipate your energy and lose your happiness. Rather than obedience, we have what we call "cooperative obedience." Obedience forces you to obey another person whether you want to or not. Cooperative obedience is quite different. If someone makes a suggestion, you have to go within and see whether or not you want to align your will to that suggestion. If you don't, you can refuse. But, in a cooperative community, we try to have our first instinct be toward cooperation rather than rebellion.

I would say one of the most important things in our monastic order is to have an expansive, accepting attitude towards life. Accept life, accept people. Rather than seeing how other people "differ", feel how they are "similar." Enjoy their ideas, even though they may vary from your own. If the religions and the nations of the world could practice this simple concept, it could transform the world.

The benefit of living in a spiritual community is that it lets you see how God shines through a large variety of people. When you've been close to people for a long time and become friends, you can really open your heart to them. When you're having a difficult time, you can always find someone at Ananda who can lift you up and give you a model, or an example. Different people in the community excel in different things. One person might have great courage. Another may be a model of endurance, a third person joy, yet another devotion. You have all these wonderful examples to help you through the rough spots.

The essence of life at Ananda is attunement to God and to the universal consciousness that Yogananda expressed. We do this most deeply through meditation, by quieting the mind so we can hear the whispers of our own soul. That's what the yogic path is all about.

Satya

I spent my first real seclusion at the old retreat in the winter of 1968. Christmas came and everybody left. It was very quiet and it snowed until I got totally snowed-in. I created my own version of a Swedish plunge by jumping into a hot shower, rolling around in the snow, and then jumping back in the shower again. It was one of the nicest seclusions I ever had. I did a lot of juice fasts, meditated, and read. Six weeks I was by myself. Finally, someone made it up the road with a four-wheel drive. I hadn't talked in six weeks and when I finally did, I could barely get the words out.

My first job was to take care of the retreat, and later on Swami asked me to start teaching yoga, yoga postures and meditation. Yoga postures came easily to me. I had taught ballroom dancing for years and had a natural flexibility.

Working at the retreat called for me to do everything from maintenance jobs to leading *sadhanas*. In the summer time, we'd set up tents for people who came up for the weekend to take classes. Early in the morning, Swami would start out with a big drum and we'd begin chanting, going around the tents and waking people up. When Swami was gone, I'd do that. It was a wonderful way to start the morning sadhana.

Besides having morning and evening yoga and meditation, at lunchtime I'd read the *Bhagavad Gita*, then meditate for 30 minutes. We were all automatically meditating three hours a day, without even trying. I did that for about 8 or 10 years. Then I wanted to build a house and had to make a little money. So I went back to work as an officer in the Merchant Marines, and spent time in San Francisco renewing my license. I went to sea on and off while I was living here at Ananda. I'd go out for two or three months and then come back. That's how I earned money to build my little house at the Seclusion Retreat.

There was no community when I first arrived here in 1967, so I had no expectations. When I first met Swami he said me, "What do you think you want?" And I said, "The truth. I'm here to find God."

I'd heard about Kriyananda from a lady who attended my son's SRF meditation group in Reno. She told us about some records she had of Swami Kriyananda singing beautiful chants. I listened to the chanting and was intrigued by his voice. When I found out he had been the first vice president of SRF I was even more intrigued. So where was he now? This was 1965, and no one seemed to know his whereabouts, even SRF. About a year later, the same lady who gave me the recordings found out about Kriyananda buying land in the mountains and somehow she got the address and I wrote to him. He wrote me back and invited me to a retreat.

Kriyananda gave me my *Sanskrit* name when we started to become monks. I remember someone came into the dining room and said, "Swami would like to talk with you." So I walked down to his dome. He was sitting in a chair and I asked him what he wanted. He said, "I thought it would be nice if you had a spiritual name. Would you like to have a spiritual name?" So I said, "Not particularly." But after a few minutes, I thought it might be good for me. So I said, "What is it?" He said, "Satya." As soon as he said that something in my heart center jumped. I asked him, "What does that mean?" He said, "Truth."

Over time, I could see Kriyananda had a lot of depth that people could utilize. A lot of people didn't realize his depth. As an example, there was one man here with whom I became friends. He'd only been here a few years when he said to me, "Why are you so hung up on Swami? Why do you like Swami Kriyananda so well?" So I said, "I came here to find God, that's all. Swami Kriyananda gives me all the space, he never pushes me, he leaves me alone and he lets me do what I want. He gives me the space to find God." All the controversial things that have happened in this community never made any difference to me. I was here to find God and that was my main thrust. Everything else was peripheral

One of the key points to learn on the spiritual path is not being judgmental. If you become judgmental, it's spiritually selfish. When you see other people becoming judgmental, it makes you think. Until we see somebody else doing it, a lot of times we don't realize that it's not quite so good for us. Living in a spiritual community is like living in a house of mirrors. We reflect back to each other what's happening in our own soul. If people are saying this person is doing something that isn't right, it's a sin—that's being judgmental. I always try to see people in the light and not judge them, no matter what. If someone does something wrong, then that's his problem, not mine. My problem is not to be judgmental.

I think one of the most remarkable things I've noticed here over the years, is that all these people get along well together. This doesn't mean that *everybody* gets along, but what happens when people get into problems with each other is that they realize the problem is within *themselves*. Instead of pointing the finger and saying it's your fault, Yogananda's teachings show how all conditions are neutral. *He said that what we hate most about in others is really something that we hate about ourselves.* People realize, in a place like this, that they have to work on themselves. The problem isn't *out there*, it's inside ourselves.

Working and living in a group isn't easy because learning to know God requires that you learn to get yourself out of the way. When you're working with other people there are conflicts, so as conflicts come up you see them and work through them. This brings you closer to God.

The biggest misconception people have about yoga teachings is that a *guru* is not good for you. People tend to think a guru takes the place of a father or a leader or an authority. I consider Kriyananda my teacher, but Yogananda is my guru and I still have no doubt about that. Our guru said, *"God and guru, there's no separation."* Spiritually, a guru teaches you how to walk, like a mother with a child, until you're on your own. He's not going to carry you on his shoulders all the time. Once you become strong, the idea is to be free. Once you're free you realize that there isn't any separation. There isn't God or Guru; they are the same.

There's a fellow who came out here years ago, who was a good friend of Swami's when he was at SRF. His name was Swami Nirmalananda and he had an Anandamoyi Ma ashram in Oklahoma. He was a great big guy and he loved Swami Kriyananda. Nirmalananda visited here and I stayed with him for the 10 days he was here. Kriyananda is a gourmet cook and would cook for him. Nirmalanada loved to eat and it was sweet to watch them. They were like two ladies talking back and forth about old times. Just a day before he left, Nirmalanda told me, "I have an ability to see into people. I can see what they're like inside. And when I look into Swami Kriyananda's eyes, all I see there is a little child. He doesn't really know who he is. It's like a blind that's been drawn down. As soon as the blind is lifted, when that happens, he will be gone."

Satya, Kriyananda and friend in the '70s.

All the Indian swamis visited Ananda in the early days. Satchidananda, Chidananda, Vishnudevananda, and Venkantesananda (who was a real *gyana yogi*), all came. Kriyananda was always very gracious to them and they stayed for a couple of days, even a week or two. Swami Amarjyoti stayed here at the time my son was visiting me here. My son trains wild animals for movies, and used to bring one of the animals here when he visited. This time, he happened to bring a big tiger with him, and we took the tiger to visit Amarjyoti. Swami Muktananda was here twice; once he came with Rudy (Rudrananda) who was also a disciple of Nityananda. The first time he came, Muktananda was very slender looking. Later on I saw pictures of him that made me think he had gone through a spiritual change. There was a real sweetness about him.

I remember being at the retreat one night in 1968. I woke up at about three in the morning and heard this *snap, crackle, pop*. I started to go back to sleep thinking it was a dream. I still heard it, so I jumped up and ran out and saw these huge flames enveloping the retreat—the dome was a ball of pure fire. The first thing I thought was, "Ah, it's beautiful." At the same time, Swami was coming from his place. Later he said he looked at that and thought the same thing, "It's beautiful." There was no way you could put it out, you just had to keep it from spreading. The firefighters didn't get there until hours later and it was cinders by then.

Living in a spiritual community can be like walking through a fire. If you let go of things, and face your faults, it can purify you. And that, too, can be beautiful.

Shivani

My first childhood ambition was to become a rabbi. Actually it was the scriptures that attracted me, and the sound of the sacred language. At the age of six I began to study Hebrew and very soon knew all the prayers by heart. But I was never called to recite in front of the congregation, because in the orthodox Jewish tradition women are not called to read from the Torah. Nor can they become rabbis, or even, as I discovered when I was 12, can they receive initiation into the body of worshippers (bar mitzvah).

So I turned my attention to another calling: to become an advocate for truth and justice. Applying myself to my studies, I won admission into a Washington, D.C. law school. Although I had dedicated years of my life to reaching that point, I was disillusioned from the first day.

I well remember the course in criminal law, one that had a great attraction for me. In his first lecture, expounding on the theme of legality and morality, the professor remarked that anyone who believed in such a thing as natural law, or in a correlation between morality and legality, was in the wrong university: they should rather be enrolled in a seminary. Since that door had already been closed, there was little I could do but plod ahead, hoping things would improve.

In addition to classes and a mountain of homework, I also worked as a legal assistant in the offices of several private attorneys, both to gain experience and to pay for my education. Again I was disillusioned when I discovered how many and how significant were the compromises required in order to "win" a case.

Completely discouraged, I left law school after two years and began to search for some other ideal to which I could totally commit my heart and my energies. This was my real desire: to have a life that challenged me completely, that engaged me totally on all levels of my being. It became impossible for me to even imagine living in a society whose values were superficial and materialistic. I dreamed of being a pioneer, of helping create a new way of living.

I left Washington, D.C., said goodbye to my family in Pittsburgh and "hit the road" with a few possessions in a backpack and very few dollars in my pocket. I was 23 years old and it was the summer of 1968. I had enough chutzpah and sense of adventure to hitchhike across the country, picking up jobs here and there when necessary. In Colorado I met up with the hippies and flower children, and continued travelling around the country with a pet Spider monkey, Ulysses, on my shoulder.

With the approach of winter, Ulysses and I settled down in Palo Alto, where I found a job as a legal aid and secretary to a private attorney and where I continued my spiritual search at the "Free University." But what my heart was looking for I couldn't find in encounter groups or gestalt sessions. Deep down I knew that life had something special for me, but I also knew that I wasn't finding it. I wrote in my diary at that time: "I think I need a Guru to show me the way."

I first heard of Swami Kriyananda when I was in a small aircraft flying over the San Francisco Bay. My friend, the pilot, was telling me about the marvelous yoga teacher he had found in Palo Alto—an authentic yoga master called Kriyananda. I accompanied him to his yoga classes and was not a little surprised to discover that the yogi was an American who began each class by playing the guitar and singing one of his own compositions. His voice, and the way he lead the postures were very soothing. Inspired by his talk on vegetarianism, I stopped eating meat and, miraculously, stopped smoking as well.

At the next to the last class, Kriyananda told us about the spiritual community he was starting on land he had recently bought in the Sierra Nevada foothills. He had just finished writing a book about cooperative communties and he invited the students to read it and to come help him build the community.

I read the book in one sitting and immediately wrote a letter to Kriyananda's assistant, John Novak, requesting to come for two weeks in the summer. I soon received a positive reply and began to make plans for another cross-country hitchhiking journey, with a first stop at Ananda Meditation Retreat.

I arrived at 3:30 p.m. on the afternoon of Sunday, June 22. Ulysses had long since found another home; but I had again a few possessions in my trusty backpack, along with a sleeping bag, $100, and a copy of *Autobiography of a Yogi* which a friend had given me as a going-away gift. I had yet to read it.

I presented the letter from John Novak to a calm-mannered elderly man called Satya, who kindly welcomed me and showed me around the premises: the temple dome, the kitchen-dining room dome, the office dome, and the bath house (not a dome). I found a friendly pine tree to sleep under, and spent that afternoon gathering pine needles for a mattress.

Each morning Satya rang the bell on the temple deck and soon thereafter he began to lead us in the energization exercises and yoga postures, followed by meditation. All too often I wouldn't hear the bell, especially when the wind was blowing in the wrong direction. So I moved my bag onto the temple deck and slept there, to be sure not to miss the morning practices.

Having spent 22 of my 24 years in school, I hadn't learned any practical skills, other than how to pass examinations. I was given work in the kitchen, cleaning and cutting vegetables, which left me adequate time to pursue yoga practices and spiritual reading.

The few residents were mostly recent arrivals. The previous summer the buildings had been constructed, and only two people had braved the winter weather at 3000 feet. Now regular weekend programs were being offered and young people were starting to come and take up residence. In addition to Satya, there was Binay and also Jaya and Sadhana Devi. The weekend after I arrived Swami Kriyananda moved up, having finished his yoga classes, and soon thereafter his two assistants, John Novak and Sonia Wiberg (Jyotish and Seva) also came. Devi arrived about one week after I did.

Although I had studied *hatha yoga* with Kriyananda, I had not taken his course in *raja yoga*. At Ananda I observed how peaceful and happy others were when they meditated, and I soon developed a desire to learn. After some weeks I made my decision: today I will learn to meditate. That afternoon I went to Kriyananda's dome and somewhat timidly knocked on his door. A weak "Come in, please" resulted, and when I entered I realized that he was sick in bed with the flu. Excusing my intrusion, I was about to beat a hasty retreat when he asked me, "Why have you come?" I answered, continuing to back up towards the door, that I was interested in learning to meditate, but that some other time would be fine. He responded to the effect that "this seems to be the chosen time, so let's do it right now."

Even though he clearly was feverish, he got up straight away, invited me to sit down, and gave me a complete lesson in the *Hong Sau* technique, including an inspiring explanation of how the energy currents flow around and through the astral spine. I left his house with much gratitude, and with great enthusiasm I went immediately to the temple to try the technique on my own.

Looking back to this moment from a distance of nearly thirty years, I realize more clearly how much I learned that day. Beyond the precious gift of the meditation practice itself, I saw in action an example of selfless service: Kriyananda did not permit his indisposition to hinder the spiritual service he was being called upon to render. His response had been unhesitating; the state of his health had not been an obstruction.

I saw something else that day in the way that Kriyananda responded to my request that I have seen on countless other occasions, an attitude that I consider one of the hallmarks of his spiritual legacy: that when the moment is ripe, that is the best time to act. Moments of true inspiration are indeed fleeting, and when we ponder and reflect and weigh and balance, the inspiration is often gone, and with it, an opportunity missed.

I try to remember the lessons of this day whenever someone asks me for help or when something unexpectedly presents itself in my life. For me, this is one of the deeper meanings of the Indian proverb: the guest is God.

In that first year or so Kriyananda led many of the energization, yoga and meditation practices and gave all of the Sunday services. There were some special features of the Sunday program that have not survived the years, but in which residents and guests eagerly participated. The morning began with a "strolling *kirtan*," initiated by Satya after he rang the wake-up bell. Strolling through the grounds he would sing a chant and play the drums, thus calling the devotees to sadhana. The awakened ones would follow behind him, singing and perhaps playing hand cymbals. Arriving at the temple completely awake and with the name of God in our hearts, we began our morning practices.

An hour before the Sunday service was to begin, we gathered in a small clearing in the woods. Here a fire pit had been dug, with tree trunks placed all around it serving as seats. Kriyananda would arrive with his harmonium and lead us in a chant. Then he would light the fire, take a bowl of ghee, and pouring the ghee into the fire he would chant the *Gayatri Mantra*. The clarified butter, he explained, symbolized the pure aspirations of our hearts, which we were offering into the flame of devotion that they might become purer. Then he would chant the *Mahamrityunjaya Mantra*, throwing grains of rice into the flames after each repetition. The rice symbolized the seeds of our past karma which we were offering and burning in the flames of divine love and wisdom.

After the ceremony many of us stayed to meditate awhile, immersed in the vibrations of those holy mantras. As I mentally repeated these words, I remembered other holy prayers in another sacred tongue, and my soul was fulfilled.

I watched as my new friends grew rapidly in the path and as they received initiation into *Kriya Yoga*. I, too, longed to put on the white initiation clothes and enter the temple on those sacred occasions, but something was blocking me. Even though I knew I needed guidance, how could I possibly accept a Guru, someone who would be an intermediary between me and God? And how could a nice Jewish girl like me accept Jesus Christ?

Finally I sought Kriyananda's advice, half afraid that he would say I must either accept Yogananda and Jesus or leave the community. My fears were totally unfounded, and his advice totally unexpected. "Why don't you consider God to be your Guru. That should pose no conflict with your religious upbringing. Nor should it be difficult for you to accept the universal Christ Consciousness, the formless presence of God in creation. This is the real teaching of *Sanatan Dharma* and of Yogananda, and it should be even easier for you to grasp this, who have grown up with the formless God." This was a completely acceptable answer for what I had considered an irresolvable problem.

In this experience what I most of all appreciated was Kriyananda's sensitivity to my situation. He was honoring my past experience and helping me to build upon it. This respect for each person is also a hallmark of his spiritual legacy, the foundation of his teaching that "people are more important than things."

That first summer ended with a full week of classes given by Kriyananda, which he called "spiritual renewal week." Every morning after breakfast we gathered under the big oak tree next to the temple, where mats and cushions were placed on the ground and a chair placed for Kriyananda. Everything he talked about was new to me, much of it way over my head; yet it was all somehow familiar. Even the outdoor setting and the summer heat were familiar. I had heard these teachings before and done these practices. I had come home. Sitting there, listening to these wise discourses, I knew I had found the Truth and Justice I had been mistakenly seeking in the field of jurisprudence.

I spent the winter of 1969-1970 at the Meditation Retreat, while most of the others accompanied Kriyananda to the Bay Area to find work. At the outset it was Kriyananda who had earned the money to make the down payment on the land, and he continued to make the mortgage payments, inviting others to share this responsibility with him. It was at this time that Jyotish did the ground work for the incense business and Binay for the flower jewelry. I was among the very few who stayed and looked after things at the retreat.

Actually, there was very little to be looked after, and we had a lot of time at our disposal to lead the life of forest hermits. The larder was scant indeed, with a preponderance of powdered milk, whole wheat, barley and prunes. Since there was no income and no savings, we got by on bread, yogurt with prunes and grains.

Having been so accustomed to studying, I thought to delve into *Sanskrit* during the long winter months. When I asked Swamiji if he had a Sanskrit text he would lend me, he suggested that I rather read *The Gospel of Sri Ramakrishna*. I spent that winter in a tiny trailer a guest had left for our use, parked way out on Sunset Boulevard, absorbed with Ramakrishna and his disciples, meditation and hatha yoga practices and long, long silent walks in the woods. I spent days, sometimes weeks at a time in silence, which I found very comfortable and comforting. I was never lonely. Although part of me was thinking that I too should be in the city earning money for the mortgage, another part of me was very grateful for the chance to construct a spiritual foundation on which to build the rest of my life. As for the mortgage, my tree-planting days still lay ahead.

I had been at Ananda two years and the summer guest season and Spiritual Renewal Week were over. Kriyananda was enjoying a time of retreat and silence in his dome. One day as I was taking his mail to leave outside his door, I found him standing on the porch. When he saw me he asked: "What to you think about monasticism?" I was so surprised to hear him speak, and even more so hearing what he said, my mind froze and I couldn't immediately respond. After standing there dumbly for a moment, I said: "You mean living like a monk?" "In your case," he answered, "it would be like a nun."

Even though I was shocked, I was not unprepared. I had been reading *The Gospel of Sri Ramakrishna* and had been thinking seriously about the monastic life as a possibility for myself. Kriyananda said that I was welcome to think about it and speak with him privately if I wished.

Just at that time I had an interesting dream. I was working with others and we were making a wide road, using shovels to dig down and flatten the area. Someone approached me with this advice: "If you really want to make progress on this road, you need to cut off your right arm up to the elbow." I replied: "But then I could only work with one arm and the work would be much slower." He responded: "Actually, if you want to make really fast progress, you should cut off both arms." At that point I awoke and began to meditate on what the dream could mean. The answer didn't come quickly, but eventually I understood it to signify that I could make more rapid spiritual progress through a dramatic act of cutting off my ego, the thought that "I" am working. I took it as an indication that I should seriously consider joining the monastery.

I went to speak with Kriyananda and he told me about the monastic order he evisioned at Ananda. He explained to me the three traditional monastic vows, and how he saw them in the context of our community life. The one that gave me the most pause for reflection was obedience. I had never been very good at it, and I was always getting into trouble with "authorities." He was very understanding and I've always remembered what he said: "I'll never ask you to accept any spiritual advice I may give you, for I could be wrong. I would ask only that you hold it up to the light of your own conscience. In matters pertaining to the organization of the community, however, I would expect that you cooperate with me."

Having understood that, I asked to be accepted into the new order. Some days later, seven of us met in Kriyananda's dome for a simple initiation ceremony. There was Seva, Sadhana Devi, Satya, Binay, Jaya, John Blake and myself. In blessing John, Swami gave him the spiritual name Haridas; and when blessing me, he gave me the name Shivani, which he said means 'renunciation'—a good name, I thought, for a nun. The order itself he called "Friends of God." During the ceremony Swamiji explained that of all the relationships that we can have with God, friendship is the most freeing. Even

Master, he said, who worshipped God as the Divine Mother, said that friendship was the highest relationship, because it is completely unconditioned by the responsibilities inherent in other relationships. He mentioned Yogananda's relationship with Krishna in the incarnation when Yogananda had been Arjuna.

This was in September of 1971, perhaps even on the 12th, which is Swamiji's spiritual anniversary. He invited us to move our trailers and teepees onto his private land, which he called Ayodhya, the name of Lord Rama's enlightened kingdom in ancient India.

After we had moved, we went to ask him for the guidelines of the new order: At what times should we meditate? Should we have a temple in common or a separate one for the monks and the nuns? In answer to all our questions, he responded: "You decide. Find within yourselves the way that is most suitable." As he must have anticipated, we did not always decide wisely, and we had ample opportunity to learn through our mistakes. Although he never actually participated in these "practical spiritual" decisions, his energy and his prayers were obviously guiding the work on a higher level.

Even though I was adverse to authority, there many times I wished that Kriyananda would set down some guidelines. It would have been easier to get up early and meditate long hours knowing it was required of us. Easier in the beginning, perhaps, but apparently that was not the kind of spirituality Master and Swamiji wanted from us. We needed to learn to meditate and serve because we loved doing it, not because we were obliged to do so.

And this is perhaps what I appreciate most of all about Swamiji and how he trains us: he creates the situations in which we can grow, and then throws us into them, knowing that we'll either sink or swim according to the energy we put out. In all situations that I have observed, he gives each person the freedom to grow without the stifling weights of restrictions, or rules or conditions. He often quotes Master, saying: "Too many rules ruin the spirit."

And so the monastery and the community grew without too many rules, and with a great spirit. Swamiji invited the monastics to his house every week, where we meditated together and then listened to him speak about the spiritual qualities we were trying to develop. We tried our best, we struggled, and for the most part we swam. We worked hard to build up the community, and after work we came back to Ayodhya to meditate, study and get ready for another day of service. Others joined the order and soon there were 30 or 40 of us, serving in all of the areas of the community.

My early Ananda experiences and spiritual growth are inextricably linked with our organic garden. Until I arrived at Ananda I had been undoubtedly a city girl, with very little experience of the great out-doors or, for that matter, of physical hardship. Yet even a short while of living amongst the ancient oak trees, walking long distances through the forest, swimming in the Yuba River and seeing the dis-tant high mountains had a remarkable affect on my consciousness. I realized that my first spiritual lessons would come to me through nature.

In 1970 Kriyananda invited Haanel Cassidy to move to Ananda and develop an organic, biodynamic farm on our new land. Haanel was already in his sixties, a long-time *Kriya yogi* and had considerable experience with biodynamic gardening in Canada and in Chile, where he had attempted to retire. Kriyananda offered him Ananda as his retirement spot, where he could practice Kriya and serve Yogananda by teaching us youngsters how to develop a self-sufficient farm.

I had never in my wildest dreams imagined myself working on a farm, slinging manure, driving a tractor or cultivating earth worms. Yet one cold day in January I presented myself to Haanel—which took considerable courage given his somewhat ascetic appearance, white hair, noble bearing and piercing blue eyes, and asked if he would accept me as a student worker in the garden he was to start that year. Skeptically he looked me up and down and, as was his wont, with a few well-chosen words, he bade me meet him at the water tower (at the Meditation Retreat) at 7 a.m. on Monday morning. That was the first lesson: gardeners start at sunrise and yogis should be finished with their practices by then and ready to work.

It was a bitter cold Monday and Haanel took me to the apple orchard that we had inherited with the Farm. The trees had been neglected and hadn't been pruned for years. He patiently taught me how to look at an apple tree and see the ideal form that God had given it—its main, or leading branch through which it grows tall; the best number of lateral branches to support its current size and the load of fruit it would bear. Then he taught me how to cut away everything that was extraneous to that essential form. And not just to hack away the unnecessary, but to liberate the tree from its burdens in a gentle and scientific way—each cut was angled so that it would quickly heal over and permit the life force to flow in a new direction. There was real poetry in Haanel's approach to gardening and to life, and indeed he himself was an accomplished photographer, writer and singer.

We worked together that morning, he showing me which branches to eliminate and how to do it. Then he left me on my own for the afternoon, expecting me to do as much as possible. Not only were my hands frozen and barely functional, but also my mind was sluggishly trying to grasp the concept of helping the trees by eliminating a great part of each of them. By the end of the day I had begun to understand not only that the trees needed and were grateful for this work, but that I as well needed to be pruned of many useless ideas and habits if I wanted vigorous, new spiritual growth. In later years, when I began to study the New Testament, I could resonate with Christ's words, "Every branch in me that beareth not fruit he taketh away: and every branch that beareth fruit, he purgeth it, that it may bring forth more fruit."

Eight years I worked in our gardens, sunrise to sunset, spring, summer, fall and even into the winter, learning more about life and spirituality than books could teach me. Perhaps the most important lesson of those idyllic years was the recognition that growth is cyclic, and we need to work in harmony with its rhythms, irrespective of how we feel or what we want. How nice it would have been to take a summer vacation and go hiking in the high country. But in the extra-ordinary heat and dryness of Ananda summers, even one day without water would have been the death knell for the plants.

I clearly remember the year of the exceptionally long Indian summer. We had a large winter squash crop, and it was happily ripening, gaining more vitality with each passing day. But we had to closely watch the weather, knowing that we would have to harvest them before the first hard frost. A long rainy period ensued, with warm temperatures. But by then it was well into November and the frost could come any day.

It was in the middle of Sunday service when the skies suddenly cleared. A starry and freezing cold night lie ahead. As we were filing out of the temple, I whispered to the other gardeners: it's now or never—let's skip lunch and get those squash inside! We worked well past sunset, but we didn't lose a single one of them. When in later years I read in the Bible, "the harvest truly is plenteous but the labourers are few," I remembered that day and could well imagine the labour needed to reap the harvest of God-consciousness.

While the garden provided us with unpolluted, tasty vegetables, it didn't bring money into the community, which was needed to meet the monthly mortgage payments. And so began the first phase of economic development and responsibility at Ananda, which can be called the "cottage industry phase." The first of these small industries was the incense and perfumed oils business that Jyotish had developed in the Bay Area and brought to the community. At the same time Binay developed the wild flower jewelry business, and soon thereafter was added a macrame plant hanger endeavor.

Most of the gardeners spent half of the day in the fields and the other half day, as well as the winter months, in the incense business. The "cathedral building" had been erected, next to the barn—a simple construction of curved wooden supports covered with heavy-gauge plastic, which kept the inhabitants dry but did little to keep out the wind or the cold. Winter mornings in the cathedral building are especially memorable. After having usually spent a pretty cold night in the teepee, we arrived to find the building no warmer than the teepee. The incense paste that the imported sticks were to be dipped into was solid enough to cut, and the perfumed oils were too sluggish to be poured. A good part of the morning was spent standing near the stove, warming ourselves and our materials. The building itself never really got warm, so we worked with old gloves that had the finger portion cut away. My most welcome acquisition of those early years was a pair of L.L. Bean felt-lined boots, which made a remarkable difference in my joie di vivre level.

While this indoor, repetitive work was not nearly as enjoyable as being outside with the plants, it was part of the challenge of being a pioneer. I had long lamented the materialistic and, to me, meaningless life that had been created, no doubt through untold sacrifice, by previous generations. The physical hardships were of little consequence to me, for I was now able to live one of my most cherished dreams — with my own hands and the sweat of my own brow to build a new way of life.

One winter in the early '70s our financial situation was so dire that we had to find outside employment for many of the residents. As Master often said: "Circumstances are always neutral; it's the way we respond to them that makes them positive or negative." This seemingly catastrophic circumstance gave me and many others the chance to do what Sister Gyanamata called "testing your spirituality in the cold light of day." We were forced to leave our nest of spiritual security and measure our inner growth out "in the world."

We learned that the Forestry Service was offering contracts for planting sapling trees in areas that had been clear-cut and burned. Anyone could enter a bid. Ours was the lowest bid to replant a large number of acres in northwestern California in an area called Happy Camp. We had, I believe, 12 weeks in which to complete the job. If we didn't finish on time, we would be subject to a daily fine.

We were all tested during those weeks, which, while they got somewhat easier, were never a stroll in the park. As we were approaching the end of the time limit, and it became obvious that we wouldn't make it, we called back to the community for reinforcements. By that time our bodies were exhausted and wounded, and divine intervention needed to come through other bodies. It's hard to describe the relief we felt when four men arrived to help us finish the contract. Our spirits soared, our bodies felt renewed, and we finished on time! And we came back to the community with money in our pockets to contribute to the mortgage payments, and some hard-earned spiritual strength under our belts.

My favorite time of the year was Christmas, and especially the period leading up to the long meditation. There was little work to be done in the gardens, because in most years they were buried under a thick blanket of snow. Life slowed down and everything got very quiet. Many of us took seclusion at this time, and remained in silence until the long meditation. The atmosphere at Ayodhya was remarkable—deeply peaceful and deeply joyful.

I used this time to learn more about the life of Jesus and his teachings. Yogananda's commentaries on the Bible, published in the old *Inner Culture* and *East West* magazines, I found deeply inspiring and thrilling in their universality. The nice little Jewish girl was learning to be a Christian as well.

The Expanding Light didn't exist then; all of the Christmas activities were at the Seclusion Retreat. Many years the snow was so heavy that the cars couldn't make it up the final hill. So we would walk in, dry off, meditate, then walk out again. Swamiji, of course, was right there with us, holding his orange robes above his boots and plowing through the snow.

The social side of Christmas at Ananda was in those years touchingly simple: on Christmas day we met with Kriyananda in the temple and listened to Händel's Messiah. Then we exchanged gifts we had lovingly made for each other, which resulted in a temple full of discarded wrapping paper and ribbons. After the Christmas banquet, as had been Master's tradition, Swamiji spoke to us, right in the dining room, about the deeper meaning of Christmas.

A conversation I had with Swamiji that especially stands out in my memory occured in the mid '70s while we were at a spiritual conference in Vancouver, Cananda. Swamiji had been invited and introduced as "the father of spiritual communities," an honorific he gently rejected with this interesting comment: "I don't care all that much about cooperative communties; it's people I care about, and their spiritual growth. That is the only reason I've created Ananda. And if ever in the future it is not helping people in this way, then it should not be perpetuated."

Later, as we were walking together, I asked him what he did see in the future for Ananda. His answer was unexpectedly specific. "For a while longer," he said, "there will continue to be an implosion of energy, a building of our base at Ananda Village. But at a certain point there will be an explosion, and people will go out in small groups to start communties around the country and on other continents." He mentioned, I believe, groups going to India, Australia and other places. "Ananda Village," he continued, "is the model community, and it is taking my energy and presence to get it started. But once the model is established, it will be easier to reproduce it, and others will be able to do so." I wondered if I would be sent out to some distant country, but at that time I was so content with my present that I didn't really want to know about the future.

Shortly thereafter our city centers began to be established, first with Sacramento, then San Francisco, and, more than a decade later, also in Europe and then in Australia. Looking back to this conversation, I see that it was more prophetic than casual.

The spiritual magnetism of the community was growing stronger all the time, and many devotees were being attracted, like bees to the veritable honey. An exceptionally large group arrived in 1974, and amongst them was my future husband, Arthur Lucki. He was already years on the path, a Kriyaban and, praise God, a building contractor.

I was very happy in the monastery, although I had my fair share of struggles. Never had I thought of leaving it, and certainly I had no desire to ever marry and have a family. Yet when Arthur proposed marriage, I referred the proposal to my spiritual father. I was absolutely and terrifyingly shocked when he suggested that I accept the proposal. His reasoning was straightforward and simple: spiritually I would grow more in a relationship than by staying in the monastery. There were other lessons I needed to learn now.

Arthur and I were married six weeks later, on the 25th of April, 1975, under a full moon and extremely auspicious planetary aspects, in a very simple evening ceremony presided over by Swamiji. In his talk to us that evening, Swamiji broke the ice of solemnity by remarking: "This union should bode well for everyone, for is it not said that peace will come on earth when the lion of Judea shall lie down with the lamb of Christ?" And when during the ceremony he gave Arthur the spiritual name Arjuna, prince of devotees, I felt that Master himself was blessing our marriage. His talk that evening was about renunciate marriage, of living for God first and serving Him in the spouse, who should be considered a channel of God's divine love.

For me, not very much changed in my life. I had the same work, the same dear friends, the same purpose and goal. And, in addition, I had a wonderful companion to serve and grow with. I have always considered this marriage a spiritual gift and a great blessing. It has never been the center of our life, but rather another part of our life which is dedicated to God. We consciously decided to forego creating our own family so that we would be able to serve Yogananda's greater family, wherever that might take us. In 1985 the call came, and Swamiji asked us if we would like to serve in the newly-established center in Italy, where we have been ever since — living together with 50 other devotees in our European community.

Binay

It is interesting that I felt most strongly about resisting the Viet Nam War when I was taking a class on the *Bhagavad Gita* in college. We learned in the Gita that Arjuna was told by Krishna to fight, even though Arjuna did not want to fight. The whole lesson of the *Bhagavad Gita* is to stand by your principles and to do what's right. The battle of Kurukshetra was a *dharmic* war. I've never felt like I'm against war. But the Viet Nam War did not seem to be a righteous war. It was good for me to resist the war; it taught me to not worry so much about what other people think of me. And it taught me that a few people can make a difference by taking a stand for something they believe in.

I had been drafted out of college by mistake, and had received a notice to report for a physical in Oakland. I remember going to Oakland carrying in my pocket a little copy of Yogananda's book, *Metaphysical Meditations*. I constantly referred to his meditation on peace and could feel Yogananda's energy with me quite strongly, guiding me as I attended a demonstration against the war. The police declared the demonstration illegal and they were prepared with 500 troops, and helicopters. There were several thousand of us. The troops swept the streets and clubbed people and maced them to disperse the crowd. In many ways, we were able to help change the course of the war by publicly committing ourselves.

During college, a good friend of mine, Tom Hopkins, introduced me to Yogananda. I began taking the SRF lessons and wanted to become a monk with SRF but I was told I would have to wait at least a year. Tom told me about a place called Ananda, where a disciple who had lived with Yogananda was starting a community. My vision of Ananda was of a place with a stream flowing through it where I would meditate and get spiritual teachings. I thought I'd stay with Ananda until joining SRF.

When I first arrived, there wasn't much of anything here. Kriyananda was in San Francisco earning money to help pay for the land. We all needed to earn a living, so I started Ananda Flowers, which was a flower jewelry business. One of the first things we made were pinecone flower designs that sold in Cost Plus stores. We also collected pearly everlasting flowers, curlydock, chia seeds and moss and made intricate designs that were set in resin and made as pendants. We sold them to large department stores and gift stores.

Ananda has changed a lot over the years. In the early years, you knew everyone well because there weren't so many people here. Now, we have circles of friends around our work or in those parts of the community where we put the most energy. It's in these smaller circles that I feel we can be more comfortable with people and share common experiences. As Ananda becomes larger, it's very important to have smaller groups of friends that can help foster a closer sense of community.

For me, being part of the early monastery was one of the best periods of my life. The monks used to visit SRF every year to attend Convocation, which I always enjoyed very much. At one Convocation there were so many of us from Ananda that SRF invited us as a group to Mt. Washington. But when we got there, an SRF nun gave us a stern lecture about how SRF was the only true Yogananda organization. In fact, she was much more blunt. She said there was a pattern for Yogananda's work in the ether, and that they knew it and we didn't. She said the pattern was for SRF, and did not include Ananda.

What flashed through my mind as she spoke was what Yogananda's guru, Sri Yukteswar, had said about spiritual pride and the little meannesses of the heart. I felt as though we were being slapped in the face. As I sat and listened to the nun, she told us things that I knew were not true. At another meeting we were also treated very disrespectfully. An SRF monk shouted and pounded his fists warning people about false teachers. We were all stunned at their behavior and wondered why they were speaking so negatively. To this day, I've always felt that these petty jealousies have hurt Yogananda's work. I was reminded of the Master's words: *I will take pride in being humble. I will feel honored when chastised for doing God's work. I will rejoice for any opportunity to give love for hatred.*

I think gossip can be very destructive. Master always warned against gossip, especially malicious gossip. It's in the world but it's in spiritual groups as well. Yogananda said that it's all right to see other people's faults, but to not hold that to them and to see them in a higher light. Jealousy, pride and gossip can be spiritually destructive. Though I had loved going to Convocation, I never went down again. Interestingly, after the nun had spoken to us, we all went to meet Kriyananda for a visit to Lake Shrine and to see Brother Turiyananda. Everyone from Ananda felt welcomed by Turiyananda, who had been close with Kriyananda when he was the head monk at SRF. Turiyananda was a very dynamic monk who loved everyone. When he saw Kriyananda, he said "I saw you in a dream last night." I could see they were deep spiritual friends.

After several years, my own life in the monastery was taking a new turn. I started to feel a bit trapped in being a monk. I enjoyed it, but at the same time I didn't want to reach the end of my life and not fulfill my karma. So I left Ananda for a while to work in the forest with a fellow monk. I went to the forests near Ft. Bragg and worked as a timber faller for a logging company. It was quite a contrast from living in the monastery. I needed to make money and be apart from Ananda to do some things I wanted to do. I was still connected with Ananda and would visit regularly.

I started a meditation center and had about 15 people who would come for meditations and services. We had several buildings on our property and we had one set aside for a temple. There were several marriages there and it was a sweet temple. We had a restaurant and cabins, and many people from Ananda came to visit.

In the same way that I left Ananda, I also came back in 1986. It was like coming to Ananda for the first time. I felt blessed to have two entries into Ananda. When you first come to Ananda, you're filled with spiritual enthusiasm. It's like Divine Mother gives us a few blessings to entice us on our spiritual journey. So the second time I came, I was asked to be part of a membership program for new members. I met my wife through this class. She had just moved here from Stockholm, Sweden. I entered the next stage of my life and became a householder.

Before returning to Ananda, I prayed deeply for guidance, and what I felt to do was to work with astrological stones and healing. I didn't have any money or training, so I took a job to earn money to buy gems and equipment for making jewelry. Little by little I grew my business. Today, I travel to Sweden once a year to sell craft jewelry. We have a small storefront located right in Ananda Village for our astrological stone and jewelry business, and we also attend many craft shows throughout California and Sweden, selling our jewelry.

When you go in one direction, you build up a lot of energy going that way. But people can change directions. It took a lot of willpower to come back to Ananda. I've never regretted the decisions I've made. The time I spent away from Ananda gave me another perspective on life here. Ananda has room for people in many different situations. But what holds us together is our spiritual bond—and that is very precious.

Devi

My first conscious connection with Paramhansa Yogananda took place when I was about five years old. I was looking at pictures in a magazine, and I remember seeing Yogananda's face in what was probably an advertisement for *Autobiography of a Yogi*. I gazed at his face and wondered what kind of person he was. Years later when I saw the *Autobiography*, I recognized him from those moments in my childhood and began to discover who he was.

When I was older and in high school in St. Louis, Missouri, my world literature class studied the *Bhagavad Gita* and other selections from Eastern literature. My teacher was a member of the Vedanta Society, and she suggested we all go to hear an Indian swami who was giving a lecture there. I felt a deep familiarity and joy at hearing Eastern teachings expressed, even though the Indian swami's English was almost unintelligible.

During my college years in Madison, Wisconsin, I became lost in social, academic and political activities. I majored in cultural anthropology because I was fascinated by how the religion and culture of small groups molded the world view of the people that belong to them, and how dramatically these views of reality differed from each other. In retrospect, I can see how my interest in the dynamics of small groups and my attraction to Eastern religion led me to dedicate my life to building a cooperative community based on the teachings of yoga.

During my last semester in college, I took a class on the mystic poet, William Blake. One of my fellow classmates was a member of Self-Realization Fellowship, and he gave me a copy of *Autobiography of a Yogi* to read. When I told him I wanted to learn how to meditate, he gave me a little folded up piece of paper that a friend of his in Boston had sent him. It was a very early copy of the Ananda Meditation Retreat brochure. This was in 1969—the first year the Retreat had been in operation. The fact that a brochure from California was mailed to someone in Boston who mailed it to someone else in Wisconsin, and finally found its way into my hands has always struck me as evidence of how well-planned are the ways of God.

With my degree in anthropology, I had been accepted to graduate school at the University of Washington in Seattle. I was pretty tired of school, however, and wanted to take a break from education. I thought I'd go to Ananda Meditation Retreat for the summer and learn how to meditate. I arrived on July 4, 1969 which was the day Ananda first took possession of the farm property where Ananda Village is now located. Then there was just a handful of people, one old farm house, and 500 acres of undeveloped property. Yet somehow I could feel an incredible potential for something to be created there.

I think Master's blessings were present from the beginning, guiding the creation of this World Brotherhood Colony. Years later after we had developed to a certain level, when we'd take visitors around the community, drive them on the dirt roads, and show them where the outhouses were, we had to remind ourselves that guests didn't always see Ananda with the same vision of future potential as we did. Now after thirty years, the potential is more manifest, but we still have a long way to go before we can say we've accomplished what Master envisioned.

But in that first summer, the sense of new beginnings was very strong. Everyone I met was practicing yoga and meditation, and their inner joy impressed me tremendously. I thought to myself, "Whatever these people have, I want." I decided I'd stay for the summer, and unrolled my sleeping bag on the hill where the school campus is now, and lived there.

My first meeting with Swami Kriyananda took place the day I arrived. I was standing on the front lawn feeling somewhat bewildered and looking like a hippie, wearing old cut-off jeans, a faded shirt, sandals, and very long hair. A man came up to me, and his first words were, "You look like a Phi Beta Kappa." In fact I was, but no one would have known it to look at me. I stared at this man who was wearing Bermuda shorts and a colorful print shirt, and said, "Yes, I am." There was a little cooperative kitchen where the market is now, and at that moment somebody came out and said, "We're having hash browned potatoes for dinner." With transparent enthusiasm the man said, "Oh good, I love hash browned potatoes." And in he went for dinner. Later someone told me that that was Swami Kriyananda.

A lot was conveyed in those few moments. He had seen who I was on a deeper level, and had expressed child-like joy in the simple things of life with complete naturalness. There was no pretension, no spiritual role-playing. He wasn't afraid to be himself with joy and freedom, and at the same time, with a deep attunement to other people. As the weeks went by, and I attended the weekly Sunday services he gave at the Meditation Retreat, I felt my mind being opened to sublime truths that I'd been seeking. The things he spoke of were a reflection of the things I'd read in the *Bhagavad Gita*, yet it wasn't the same as being taught by a scholarly college professor with an academic approach. I'd never met anyone in my life who inspired me as he did. He clearly had personally experienced and was living the things he talked about.

My parents were Jews, and my mother was a person of tremendous compassion and purity. I didn't appreciate it at the time, but while I was growing up, I never heard her criticize anybody. Sometimes I'd come home from school crying because somebody had teased me, and instead of instantly defending me, she would say, "Let's try to understand why that person did that." She was always trying to look for the deeper truth in all things. Being born after the Second World War, I met people who had survived the concentration camps in Germany. I was quite aware of the fact that this world is not always a great place to be, and that there's a level of human suffering here that is very profound.

Being surrounded by a Christian culture also made me aware from an early age that I was different, yet I learned to be happy in my difference. I lived in a predominantly Jewish community with wonderful neighbors, schools, and educational and artistic opportunities. It was like an island amidst the sea of life of the city. Consequently, it was an easy transition for me to feel at ease in a "counter culture." After being at Ananda for a few weeks, I thought, "It's a different way of life, but it's great. I can finally be myself in *this* community. I can be who I really am, and people will understand that."

In the environment where I grew up, there was always a strong trend towards materialism that I couldn't relate to. I didn't care about material things like cars, clothes, and things one could buy. Ananda was a place where people were motivated by ideals, selflessness, and the challenge of creating a new way of life. I felt at home here, I loved the people, and I knew that Kriyananda could teach me things about the search for God that I wanted to know.

I stayed at Ananda through mid-October, and when the weather started changing, I began to question what I was doing. I had never camped out before, I had no place to spend the winter, and my savings were almost gone. I went back to Madison, Wisconsin where I thought I had friends, a job, and an apartment all waiting for me. When I got back there, everything fell through. My friends had left, the job had ended, and the apartment had been rented to someone else. It was a quite a blow, and a lesson in how to tune into inner guidance. Everything was saying, "These doors are closed. This life is over. What are you going back for? There is nothing here for you." I went through that winter pretty unhappy and confused.

When the following spring came, I started thinking about Ananda and the possibility of going back, but California seemed so far away. I didn't even know if Ananda still existed because I had had no communication with anyone there. One day as I was trying to decide what to do, I went into the library at the University of Wisconsin, and picked a *San Francisco Chronicle* off the newspaper rack to read. In that day's edition there happened to be a big article about Ananda with a picture of Swami Kriyananda, Jyotish Novak, and others I remembered. Again God was guiding my steps, and I knew that I should go back.

A month later when I returned, I was received with great kindness by everyone, and particularly by Kriyananda. This surprised me because I didn't even know if he knew who I was. I could feel that he was welcoming me on a deep level and trying to reach my soul with the understanding that this was what I was yearning for. The first SRF lesson I got that week had a poem by Yogananda that said, "You left your soul-home to go out into the world and seek happiness. Now you realize you'll never find it anywhere else." Finally I understood what was going on, and I thought, "Okay, okay, I do get the message."

In the early years we all did many things to try to earn money so that Ananda could survive. There was never a large benefactor, so everything was done through our own efforts—sometimes effective, sometimes ridiculous, but always with the goal of building Ananda. I worked at many jobs including in our incense shop which Jyotish started, and in our health food candy business which Anandi and another woman, Mukti, founded. The incense business is still running today, but the candies were a disaster though lots of fun.

The job I enjoyed the most was working in the garden under the direction of Haanel Cassidy, which I did for three or four years. Haanel was a man in his mid-seventies, a remarkable person, and a cherished friend. Working in the garden under his training was a life-changing experience because everything was done with deep love and understanding of how to work with the plants and soil, how to harmonize with the cycles of nature, and how to tune into the life-force of the garden. After spending a whole day concentrating on weeding rows of new little carrot plants, I'd come home at night, try to meditate, and all I could see were those rows of little carrots. But it was wonderful training that has helped me in everything I've done since. When he died of cancer in 1980, we scattered his ashes in the gardens and orchards as he requested.

I remember the first time I went to a kirtan at Ananda. I went into our Farm temple which was a teepee, and I heard people chanting with devotion to God. I was overwhelmed, and had never experienced God's presence like that. Someone once told me that when you first come on the path, it's as though you're cashing in your spiritual savings account from other lifetimes. By this they meant that very often we have powerful experiences which get us on the path but which may take years to become a regular part of our life. There was a particular vibration of grace on my meditation then. It was as though Yogananda was saying, "Come home. Come quick. Here I am."

How would I describe the feeling of Yogananda's presence as I first experienced it? It was an awakened or heightened energy with clarity, purpose, and momentum. And behind it all, there was an incredible sweetness, kindness, a sense of security, and strength. Who is Yogananda? He's not a personality—he's a soul so totally connected to the one universal spirit, to God, that he reflects God back to us.

My marriage to Jyotish has been inextricably linked to my spiritual life at Ananda. I met him the first summer I arrived at Ananda, but I can't say I felt any kind of immediate personal response or recognition. I did notice that every time he would come into a room that I was in, I felt at peace. It was as though something that had been lacking was now present. I didn't think much about it in a personal sense because he was always very involved with helping Kriyananda get the community started, but I always felt great respect for his humility and spiritual depth.

The first summer I was there, I became friends with a woman named Haripriya who was a disciple of Anandamoyi Ma and had spent many years in India with her. Haripriya, which means "beloved of Hari, or God," was also a dear friend of Kriyananda years before Ananda started. She knew Jyotish, and she and I had developed a close mother-daughter relationship. A day or two after I returned in 1970, she walked up to me and said, "You and Jyotish are going to get married." This took me totally by surprise, and I said, "What are you talking about? I don't even know him. We've never said more than 'hi' to each other." She calmly replied, "You just wait and see." Years went by and there was no personal interaction between us, though her words remained in the back of my mind.

In 1972, a monastery called "Friends of God" was started at Ananda, and most of the single men and women in the community joined. All of my women friends joined, but I felt hesitant to make this choice. They asked me, "Aren't you serious spiritually? Aren't you committed? Do you want to get *married*?" I just knew that I couldn't see myself being a nun for the rest of my life, so I said, " I don't feel it's honest for me to do this. I don't know enough of what my life is going to be like."

It was a hard decision because it meant that I was somewhat isolated from my friends who all lived, meditated, and ate together in the convent. I lived by myself in a little trailer and meditated alone. I was lonely a lot, but at the same time there was an inner understanding that this was what I was supposed to do with my life. It was curious because Jyotish made the same decision not to join the monastery, even though all the other single men who were spiritually committed did. In the back of my mind there lingered the thought of what Haripriya had said.

Though Swami Kriyananda rarely gave people personal advice, I sought his guidance on this issue and asked him, "Do you think I should marry or become a nun? He simply said, "Your karma could go either way." Two years later I asked him again, and he gave me the same answer, "It could go either way." It was curious because although this was a struggle for me, I knew that it was right. I was learning that if we live our lives in accordance with what God wants us to do, He will give us everything we want.

In 1975 I began to feel I was entering a new period of my life, and knew that this problem of being married or being a nun would be resolved. I went to Swamiji a third time, and asked him again, "Do you think I should be married or become a nun?" This time because I believe the time was right, he said, "I think you should marry. Let's see what Divine Mother brings."

Jyotish didn't know that I had spoken to Kriyananda, but the very next day he came up to me and said he wanted to talk about something. We'd been working on a project together with a group of others, and I thought that's what he wanted to discuss. He said, "I'd like to get to know you more on a personal level." I was amazed. Still because I had such respect for Jyotish, the first thing I said was,

"Let's talk to Kriyananda about it." So Jyotish went to talk to him, and Swami gave his blessings and encouragement. As it happened we were married less than a month later.

Though everything happened very quickly, I felt a calmness and deep assurance that this relationship was a wonderful gift from God. In fact, I remember when we were buying our wedding rings at a local jewelry store, the saleswoman said, "You're kind of different from most young couples. You're so calm. Are you two already married?" For Jyotish and me, our personal lives have always come second to the needs of the community. It wasn't something we had to think about, but it just felt natural to us.

In serving the community, we've learned how to work with people by watching the example of Swami Kriyananda. He has consummate consideration for other people's realities and has never tried to make people fit into any mold. He tried to help everyone, not based on their personality or if they were well-liked, but if they were sincere spiritually. I've used him as a role model of how to relate to others with wisdom, patience, and dispassion. I would watch him at community meetings and be amazed at the tolerance he had for accepting people, even though the person was being disruptive. Kriyananda was a remarkable channel of unconditional love for others through his acceptance of their mistakes and flaws, and through his ability to see God in them.

In working with people, I try to follow his example of helping people to see their own strengths and to realize that the answers to their problems lie within them. There's a particular joy that happens when people begin to experience their own potential for happiness and for directing their own lives successfully. Over the years Ananda has developed into a beautiful community with houses, gardens, schools, job opportunities, businesses, and roads, but I've never seen Ananda as a place. To me it's always been an opportunity for the spiritual growth of the individual. The job, the house, the social experience have been secondary. Without a sense of your own inner reality, nothing outside of you can make you happy. When people come with problems, I never try to make all the details work out right, but try to inspire them to get energy moving in their lives that will draw to them the things and the solutions that they need.

Once I asked Peggy Dietz, who had been a direct disciple of Yogananda and served as his chauffeur, what advice Yogananda gave his disciples on how to counsel people. She said, "He told us to be gracious and hold them in the light." That was all. Hold them in the light, and realize the answers to their problems lie within themselves.

Our son Kalidasa was born in 1976, and being his mother has greatly helped me to understand other people, and to accept and love them unconditionally. Our son, who's now in his twenties and goes by his English name, Mark, is a wonderful person and a good friend. When some critical newspaper articles were written about Ananda, I asked Mark why he thought people had negative opinions about Ananda. He said, "Of course people won't like you. You're trying to do something different."

It's true. We are trying to do something different. While many people are seeking only personal gain and are willing to compromise their ideals to get it, Ananda is trying to live by its ideals — of love for God, of selflessness, of simplicity, of helping others outside one's immediate family, of consideration for friends and neighbors and their needs. To have a way of life that's based on reaching out to others from a core of love for God isn't going to be widely popular or even well understood. One of Yogananda's guidelines for spiritual communities is "plain living and high thinking" — to live for God with few material possessions, but still with a sense of graciousness based on the desire to share with others.

What advice would I give others, drawn from my experience of Ananda? Listen to the voice within that wants to reach out to become more, that wants to try to accomplish goals that seem impossible. Have courage and joy to go forth to find your highest potential and live your dreams. God's grace will guide you and bring you fulfillment.

Jaya

The idea of being a *sadhu*, living simply, living in the wilderness, was a romantic ideal that was very strong for me. The first winter I lived here, I basically lived on bread and yogurt for five months, and there were only a few people here. It was just a wonderful winter.

In the early years, Ananda was mostly single people who had come here with a lot of energy and a lot of enthusiasm. The strength of the community was the idealism that underlined everything that we were doing. People were extremely motivated, energetic, and devout in their ideals of finding God, trying to express God in their lives, trying to meditate deeply, and trying to become good disciples of Paramhansa Yogananda.

I had first heard about Ananda in 1968, shortly after graduating from the University of California at Berkeley with a major in anthropology. One Sunday morning I heard Swami Kriyananda speaking on a radio program. During the program, I heard that he was a disciple of Paramhansa Yogananda. I had recently finished reading Yogananda's *Autobiography of a Yogi*. Hearing Kriyananda's reference to Yogananda stimulated my curiosity. He was offering a six-week class on Raja Yoga and Hatha Yoga, which I decided to take.

I began to visit him at the weekly *satsangs* that he held in San Francisco in the late '60s. There would usually be about 20 people gathered together for meditation. Kriyananda would give a little talk and perhaps do some chanting. He had just finished writing his book, *Cooperative Communities, How to Start Them and Why*. I attended a few meetings he held for those of us who were interested in spiritual communities.

Concepts like moving to the country, being in nature, and Eastern philosophy all appealed to me. By this time, I had begun a focused practice of meditation and wanted to pursue the spiritual path more earnestly. I had always wanted to move out to the country, to live simply, to live close to nature, to be on my own, to camp out.

I first visited Ananda when I was only 22 years old and didn't have many practical skills. I moved up in 1969 and began helping create Ananda on the physical plane. The first thing I did was work as a laborer. We were trying to complete the shells of the buildings that had been started in 1968, trying to get them finished to accommodate the retreats we were doing. We were building dome structures, and one of them was earmarked so that Kriyananda could move up to Ananda and live there permanently.

When I arrived, I was one of nine people living at the retreat. As people began to come for weeklong retreats, we began to have live-in staff, organized meal schedules, and regular *sadhanas*. When we didn't have organized classes during the week, there was a work-study situation for those wanting to stay at the retreat. Gradually, more people began to come to Ananda and the idea of a spiritual community started to develop. We all aspired to be a spiritual community, but what did that mean? There were people here who were attracted to the spiritual path, but they were attracted to many different spiritual paths.

Through what seemed like disorganization, there was also a strong sense that something was going to happen, something was going to work. I had a lot faith in what we were doing, and I had a lot of faith in Kriyananda. I also had a lot of faith in the people who were here then. It was a very good group. If you took 50 people, put them in a room together and said "let's make a community"—you can imagine what might happen. There were all different ideas.

There was also no economic base here, so there were no jobs. In the late sixties, Nevada County was a logging county. If you went to Nevada City during those times, many of the stores on Commercial Street were boarded up. It was an economy in decline. In contrast, today Nevada City is a thriving tourist destination. So a lot of changes have taken place in 30 years.

Once we bought the new land, which today is known as the Village, more people began to move here. The first thing we did was create places to live. This meant fixing up spots, putting up tents if you were living outside, digging outhouses, cleaning the area up, and getting rid of the junk. We were working with neglected land.

Most people lived very simply. Individual living expenses were paid for out of people's own pockets, whatever they could do. Some basic expenses came from the income earned by the meditation retreats we had during the summer.

How do you get people to work together to build a community? Honestly, as the years have gone by, I have become more and more perplexed by that question because I don't know the answer. But I do know that when we started, the first thing we were forced to deal with was creating a physical environment and creating jobs. From here, it became apparent that you need to have people who can work together cooperatively. I would say you need to have people of good will who can work together harmoniously and cooperatively.

It also became quickly apparent that we needed to have a central spiritual focus for our community. Within the first year we decided to become a community dedicated to Paramhansa Yogananda. We were trying to express Yogananda's ideals of World Brotherhood Colonies as he talked about in the original *Autobiography of a Yogi*. He had envisioned this concept, and we were trying to live it in our daily lives, and share what we were doing with others.

In 1971, Kriyananda invited a group of us who were interested in starting a monastery to his dome. We saw a little slide show of his stay at New Camaldoli, a Roman Catholic hermitage south of Big Sur, California. He talked about his stay down there and what we might do. He looked over at me and said, "Would you like to do this?" I answered yes. Then he had me kneel before him for a blessing, and he gave me a little piece of rose petal from one of his monastic initiations. That was one of my prized possessions until it burned in the 1976 fire.

The early monastery had a wonderful spirit, and it's something that I think all of us who participated in it will always cherish. It was something that was very special, but it just didn't seem to be the *karma* for us. The community ended up evolving towards a householder community. Our new challenge was to be married without giving up what it meant to be a *devotee* or a renunciate.

For us to live here as single monastics in yellow or orange robes wouldn't have had relevance to society at large. It may have inspired society, but by becoming householders we had to learn to "be in the world but not of it." Kriyananda saw what was happening and tried to adjust his focus accordingly. And so the first monastery passed into history, and we began to focus on what would be relevant to a householder community.

I think there is a place for people to go off and live the traditional monastic life. I honor and admire that and find inspiration from people who do that. I would even like to see them encouraged. But for most people, that is not going to be their path, or their karma. There needs to be an alternative model for people who can take these monastic ideals and put them into practical, everyday practice. I don't like to think of myself as being a model—I think one falls into a trap when thinking, "Well, I'm going to be a model for other people," because then you're living from the *outside* in. We need to be living from the *inside* out.

In 1976 a forest fire destroyed many of the homes at Ananda. After the fire, people wanting to go in other directions left the community. We were also evolving and growing as a community, and this was all part of it. Once the new Master Plan was completed, it was as if we started building the community all over again, but in a more societally "real" way. Everything needed to be brought up to code; we couldn't just continue camping in tents. We had to have real houses, real roads and real water systems. Many people in the community were starting to create families. People needed to have incomes, housing and a place to send their children to school.

In the early '80s I began working for the community as the community planner. We were doing a lot of work on our Master Plan, which enabled us to have the proper zoning for Ananda from Nevada County. We had to help Ananda comply with zoning for the Ananda schools, The Expanding Light retreat, the business park and residential areas. There was lots of construction work, and more jobs began to develop within the community.

I think there was much more broadness of personality here during the first ten years, at least on an outward level. For instance, the apprentice program was a spiritual boot camp. People lived on rice and beans, got up at four o'clock in the morning, probably meditated way beyond their capabilities, and loved it. On the other hand, you had people trying to start businesses and become accustomed to wearing suits and ties. There's a funny picture from the early days of Binay wearing a suit and tie, with this big head of hair and a beard. And all this is merely a charming expression of who Kriyananda was in those days—the spiritual anarchy blended with the uniformity of vision that we had inside. Outwardly we must have seemed like very wild characters, but inwardly we were all on the same wavelength.

My relationship to Swami Kriyananda is probably consistent with that of everyone else in that we have a unique relationship that is singular to who we are. Over the years, his characteristics have begun to shine in their own right. Initially, I was very much attracted to him as a disciple of Yogananda; to me he represented a very good disciple. He is a direct disciple of Yogananda, and has more experience on the spiritual path than most people. He once told us that he thought of himself as being an elder brother. In the Eastern Indian Hindu tradition, one regards with great respect the elder brother as being in charge of the younger siblings. To me, he's my spiritual teacher, my spiritual mentor, and my spiritual older brother. I feel that's a healthy relationship to have.

One of the hardest things for me at Ananda has been that it's extremely difficult for me to work publicly with people, in an outward way. I realize that through my own personal karma, I've been forced to do that. Although it's been painful at times, I recognize that it's also been helpful. I tend to be a private person. If left to my own devices, I'm not honestly sure if I would have the inward compulsion to get out and serve as I do here. I've been involved in a community work, a work reaching out to people. Serving in this way has forced me to help other people. As Yogananda always said, "If you want to be in tune with me, serve my work."

Jaya working on the Ananda Village master plan.

Seva

I loved San Francisco and the life I was leading, yet underneath it all, I always felt out of place. In 1966 I was working with an architectural firm doing accounting work, and really enjoyed my work and the people I worked with. But there wasn't any great magnet in my life that was holding me. There didn't seem to be a reason for me to be there. I had a few boyfriends now and then, but no great love relationship. I didn't really enjoy the thought of family and children. I also didn't have a religion. So I would go to parties and socialize with my friends, just trying to find some kind of meaning to life.

At one point I got very despondent and took a few aspirins too many, but I knew it wasn't enough. It just made me very sick. That episode woke me up to the fact that I was skating on the edge. I thought, "Well God, you've just got to do something here because I just can't live this way. You've got to show me that there's some kind of meaning to life." That was the first time I realized that I was searching for something.

Soon after that, my friend Arlene heard that Swami Kriyananda was coming to the area to give a lecture on yoga and meditation. We went to his class, and that was it. I fell in love with the teachings of yoga. I realized that there *is* meaning in life, after all! This was 1967, and the way Kriyananda presented Yogananda's teachings was so clarifying to me. I began to realize that I could find God, but that I had to search for that within myself. That was exciting to me.

I started attending his yoga posture classes and assisting him with typing the books he was writing. I also took his meditation classes and came up to Ananda for visits. Arlene and I came up to see what Ananda was all about. There was hardly anyone here and nothing in the form of buildings. It had a very peaceful vibration even then. Kriyananda started building that year, and he would give classes on the deck of the dome, which was the temple at that point. It was summer and it was wonderful.

Very early in the morning he would walk around playing his *tamboura* and singing chants to wake us up. We camped outside or slept in sleeping bags on the deck of the temple dome. We'd all begin to join in the chanting, playing bells as we walked together. It was hard to get up that early, so it was a very sweet way to start our day. Then we'd do *sadhana*. Often Satya would lead the early morning sadhana and Swami would lead *Energization Exercises*. After meditation, he would give a class, then we would have breakfast outside. After lunch he would give an art class, or some kind of class where everyone would go off on their own and be quiet, either to draw or come up with a poem or something like that. During this time, he would be inside dictating his Fourteen Steps to Higher Awareness home-study course. He was always busy writing books.

When I moved here in 1970, my choice of living accommodations was a trailer or a teepee. I thought I'd be different and go for the teepee. It was quite an experience. There were tarantulas running around and mice trying to camp with me, and here I was a city girl. So I got Binay and others to help me move to a trailer.

About a year after I moved here, Kriyananda said he felt guided to start a monastery. About seven of us were the first to join: myself, Shivani, Sadhana Devi, Jaya, Haridas, Satya, and Binay. We took conditional vows of *brahmacharya*, so they weren't full monastic vows. I had already worked through a lot of the sexual energy that I had, so that just wasn't important to me. What was important to me was following Yogananda's teachings and helping others.

After several other nuns began to join, they started looking to me as the head nun, probably because I was older. The nuns each lived on $50 a month, which was nothing, even in those days, and yet it was a wonderful time. We didn't feel any lack. It's interesting, but I don't feel any different today than I did when we were first starting Ananda. I still feel that I'm living in a monastic atmosphere and I've never felt drawn to be in a relationship or anything like that. I'm still giving what I can, even though I'd like to give more.

Swami had always intended Ananda to be a householder community. He saw it as a village where householders could be with God, as a primary focus in their lives. It took a long time for that to happen. Early on it was just impossible. The householders were all trying to build their houses, bring the wood in and take care of the children. Eventually, with the concerted effort of a few people and the monastics, we were able to build businesses and get things going enough so that the householders could start taking over. I think the whole idea of the monastics helping the householders while living together in a small community was much different from traditional monastic orders.

By following Yogananda's teachings the community was embracing a new expression of renunciation, where through meditation and yoga individuals could find God within themselves. Householders need an atmosphere that supports their spiritual search. We try to create ways that allow families to have the time and energy to find God, so they don't feel like second-class citizens.

Yogananda's techniques for finding God within oneself have given me a strength and understanding that I never knew could exist. The

Seva means "service" in Sanskrit.

realization that I could find happiness in my life was a revelation for me. When I was working in the city, I had no support and nowhere to go. I was really outside myself, and I was very moody when Swami first met me. So he told me, "Well, that's from past lives." He said, "Be even-minded and cheerful. Work on that." Those little hints were very helpful for me. Knowing that there was karma and reincarnation made so much sense to me.

When the forest fire swept through Ananda in 1976, we all got together and tried the best we could to save the community. We went immediately to the top of Rajarsi Ridge, which is where the flames were coming from. I did fear the monastery might burn down, although there were only our teepee temples and our little trailers. Afterward I was concerned with trying to find places for people to stay and rebuilding the community.

After the fire, a lot of people who didn't seem in tune with what we were doing here left. It was like a huge purification fire, because people really needed to examine why they were here. When it came down to having a nice home in a comfortable village and then, poof, it was gone, reality set in. Many of the people who left wanted Ananda to give them their money back for their houses. Ananda had lost a lot too, and didn't have much. So for many years, we paid them off, even though we never got any money for those houses. We learned the fire had been started by a county vehicle with a faulty spark arrester, so some neighbors who lost homes sued the county for huge monetary awards. Swami said, "No, Ananda would not sue the county." We had sustained the largest loss, yet I think he was trying to show us how *adharmic* it is to file a lawsuit.

I've seen things happen here that force us to face our limitations and learn from them. If we have old fears, attachments, and judgment of others, we seem to attract those opportunities necessary to help us grow. Many years ago, I lost my job here and wasn't able to be near my friends or Swami. It was just a real wrench. I realized, "Boy, I'm not the kingpin around here anymore; I'm not anything, just totally nothing." I had to really work on that. That's what we need to do to get rid of the ego and to stop blaming others for our predicament. I had to really understand over a period of time that I couldn't blame others. What was wrong with my own situation wasn't anybody else's fault. When those realizations started coming in, then it was easier to say, "Yes, I have karma here. It's my fault on some level, somewhere. Maybe not now, and maybe not even in this lifetime, but at some point I created all of this, and I've got to just live through it and work it out in the best way."

That's when you start really embracing the path of yoga—when you're able to go through the fire of your own limitations, face them, and come out of it. You realize God has given you an opportunity to grow. When you start thinking of life's events as opportunities for growth, then grace just comes in. It's so powerful.

Throughout Ananda's history, I've seen many major issues here that test people. And what I've seen is that some people fall away, and some get very strong. Beautiful things are happening. Now, I think people are truly here because they want to find God, and they will help that process for others.

Haridas

My early introductions to this path were memorable; my family lived in Manhattan Beach in southern California and we'd often take the old Highway 1 down to San Diego to visit my grandparents. We would pass by the Encinitas towers, which is where Yogananda had his seaside hermitage. The towers were so striking and unique that I would always ask my father what they were. My answers didn't come until I got on the spiritual path. In reflecting back, I loved the symbolic thought of the guru coming in at an early age.

During my youth and teen years, the thing that helped me establish my spiritual life was my frequent visits to Mexico. I was struck by the devotion and simplicity of the Mexican people. Being raised in a home where there was no television, I was a bit of a curiosity in my own southern California neighborhood. We did other things for entertainment: Sunday drives and symphonies, plays and special events. Since I wasn't constantly being saturated by media, I had acquired a taste for simplicity—a quality that my parents emanated and for which I'll always be grateful.

My first very powerful spiritual experience came during a High Mass I attended one Christmas in Guadalajara, Mexico. It was the power of love and the simplicity of the people there that moved me so deeply. I had to tell myself that someday I wanted to come back to the feeling I had there. It was a very heart-opening experience. Being raised half-Catholic, half-Jew, I could have had my Bar Mitzvah at 13 if I wanted to, but I didn't think it was fitting because all my friends were going after the toys which you'd get in superabundance at that event. So, I decided it would be a sacrilege. I had too much respect for the mystical side of Judaism.

During my last year of high school I became interested in Yogananda's teachings. A friend that I was close with gave me a book, *The Master Said*, which is now called *Sayings of Yogananda*. I opened the page, saw Yogananda's photo, and read, "If you want to find God, yearn for Him like a drowning man yearns for air." That little saying took me right onto the path. I wanted to be a monk. But I was a bit taken aback, because I still had my band of friends, and we were having lots of fun. This was during the late sixties and I was going to Griffith Park with friends who were into alcohol and drugs. I had to process my desire to be a monk, and I did, usually under the influence. I knew if I gave up alcohol and drugs I would lose a batch of friends, and I knew it was going to be a very lonely journey. But what on earth was I going to do with my life? Be a rock star? Open a large, non-profit veterinary complex with my girlfriend? I thought of all the things that we think about when we're free of responsibility and yet can dream. As I dropped out of the social scene more and more, my friends started to wonder if I'd gone a bit overboard.

Finally, I decided I didn't want to mix Yogananda's teachings with drugs and alcohol. So, for discipline, I also embraced a Buddhist path for two years. Basically, what you did on that path was to chant for things in order to get the things you wanted and to be able to put material desires aside. I chanted for all the things I wanted, and it worked. And the last thing I chanted for was that I would be free of the things that were encumbering me: the alcohol and drugs—not that I was addicted, but they were hanging on. I wanted to be free of them so that I could concentrate on Yogananda's path exclusively. And it worked like magic.

After this, I saved up money from working in a gas station and began a journey to Vermont, where I had this dream I would spend the winter determining whether to be a monk in Self-Realization Fellowship, or whatever. While I was hitchhiking across the country, I had a very interesting experience in Redding, California—a psychic picked me up. I had a real good feeling about his integrity. He explained things about the Bible that were of interest to me; being half-Catholic, half-Jew I was trying to figure that one out! So then I asked him about a place I'd just recently heard of called Ananda. And he said, "You'll like it there. That'll be your home." And that was it. The first night I came to Ananda Village there were all these joyous people greeting me. And I thought, "They have something I want." Soon it became apparent that they had an inner joy I really hadn't ever seen before. I had found it in a few individuals: a postman would have it, a grocery clerk or teacher—but it was very infrequent.

In 1970, it cost $30 to spend a month at Ananda on work-study. If you wanted to eat, it was an additional $15, for $45 total. I still have a little slip of paper from Satya when he first signed me in. I worked as Satya's sidekick, painting beds and helping out with the retreat. When I first came, all the tents were reserved, so for three weeks I slept on top of a picnic table out by Kali Lodge near the fire pit. I worked a lot in the kitchen, and in the late evening some of us would sneak into the kitchen and eat cashews like raccoons. Shradda Ma was the cook in charge, and we were afraid of her because she was so tough. But we loved her dearly. And we were always keen on helping her out to make amends for our evening's jaunt into the cashews and dates.

I had met Swami Kriyananda that first night I arrived, and he was a young man, in his early forties. Right away I had a deep appreciation of who he was and a glimpse of what he had attained on a spiritual level. To be with a direct disciple of a great master was a dream come true. But it didn't mean that it would be easy. In Swami, I saw a man of extraordinary energy. Just being in his presence challenged us to wake-up and begin the race to God-realization.

After I had been at Ananda for about a year, my first big opportunity to grow appeared. Swami asked if I would build something to house our cottage industries. I couldn't believe he'd ask me. I was just barely out of my teens and my construction expertise was sorely lacking. Nevertheless, I tried. My first day on the job found me sitting on a tree stump, completely overwhelmed and paralyzed with fear. As it worked out, a friend, who was about 17, took the project over and the building went up, much to my astonishment. Though greatly relieved, I knew my work was cut out for me. I would have to tackle my fears while following Swami, our fearless leader! I have always appreciated his "go for it" spirit of adventure, especially when I have seen him tackle projects which I consider beyond the scope of what most people can do. I've learned a lot by watching him come through many different experiences with grace, regardless of a project's success or failure.

After being at Ananda for some time, I began to pray for some way that I could earn my membership money. The answer to my prayers came in the form of a little jewelry shop Binay had opened, which was located where the bakery is now. This had been an old chicken coop, so I had to clean out the chicken manure and fix the place up before we could begin to produce flower jewelry. That was my first formal employment at Ananda. Prior to that it was three months of honeymoon; those three months stick in my mind to this day as a time of just pure joy. Even though Ananda was challenging on the physical plane, it was a very happy time.

In the fall of 1971, Swami founded the monastery and I was asked to join. I'll never forget taking our first monastic vows at his Seclusion Retreat dome. The power of those few hours is with me still. The monastery grew rapidly, and we were all very committed to our spiritual life and the need to roll up our sleeves and help out with the various businesses.

The monks built platforms for teepees and mine was equipped with an outdoor refrigerator, so there were a few comforts of home. The main thing that I enjoyed about the monastery was the esprit de corps and the support of the monks. We had many group *sadhana*s, and one of the highlights was that Swami would have satsangs with the monks and nuns at his dome. He would read to us the transcripts of the different books he was writing; we would look forward to that immensely. It was a tremendous experience for us.

I remember a particular instance which was a lot of fun: I decided to take a peek at the monks and nuns while they were meditating with Swami, because I thought it would be interesting to see how people were doing. All of the monks looked like women; their spines were kind of bent over, and they looked sweet. And all the nuns looked like men; their spines were straight and they looked like they were going to burn up the universe! I nearly burst out laughing, because of the contrast. The monks were trying to balance their energies, because all of us have a strong will, classically the masculine will. We needed to develop the more receptive, intuitive, feminine aspects of ourselves. If they needed it, the nuns were working on developing more masculine aspects. Everyone is different; some people are more masculine, some people are more feminine. That image of the monks and nuns meditating never left me. And I see those same things here at Ananda today.

For the monks, it was very austere in the early days because we weren't focused on building up the comforts of the monastery. We were focused on building the Village. We'd work on trying to renovate the chicken coop so we could get the jewelry shop in, or remodel the incense shop or build the publications building. Our foundation was all about meditation, in the morning and in the evening when we returned from work.

One time we rented what we called the "Monkmobile," which was a nine-seater brand new stationwagon, and we all went down to the SRF Convocation. In the early years we all went with Swami, but he didn't go into the Convocation. We'd spend time with him though, then we'd all roar off to Disneyland for a brief respite. I enjoyed Convocation immensely, except for the political aspects between SRF and Swami, which were very unpleasant. There was one time when a particular SRF monk came and spoke against Ananda in a disguised fashion, but so thinly disguised that the energy was very polarized against Ananda. As Ananda's Spiritual Renewal Week grew and became a very strong force, the need to go to Convocation fell away.

After 12 years of living as a monk at Ananda, I left the monastery. A few years later I met my wife, Eilleen, and the next exciting chapter began. It was time to embrace the life of a householder. The transition from monk to householder was an easy one for me in many respects. I saw before me vast opportunities to serve selflessly, coupled with increased joy! New people who come to Ananda and the spiritual path will see in a glance what the householders' path is about. When you've got a kid tugging on you, there it is in front of everybody to see. Kids are great for that. They put out the message as no one does, in my opinion, because they let you know where you're standing spiritually every moment.

Many of the kids here are very strong-willed, like their parents. And they push us to our limits. And yet, I've appreciated the experience, because I also feel that these little souls are deeply sincere, and in their own way love God. So, though I've gotten a good run for my money being a householder, I've loved every minute of it, because it's exactly what I needed. It's conceivable that those who have the calling to be householders could burn out a lot, if not all, of their karma in one lifetime because it's like being in those control towers: if you fall asleep, the planes crash. So you can't fall asleep as a householder. You've got to have a strong meditation, and you have to lead a balanced life.

The thing that I've often appreciated is that there is a depth of spiritual feeling here that I can still remember from when I first visited. All the buildings and all the outward things, the extracurricular things we do, that's all fine, but it's not really where our hearts are. Becoming a bit more affluent has been helpful for us, because in the early years everything was suspect: the first telephone—is that simple living? Our first toilet—is that simple living? Everything was looked at in that way, which was a bit overboard, but we didn't want to get tricked into getting knocked out by materialism. I felt that God wanted us to make this community as beautiful as we possibly could, so that people could come and see that the spiritual life was a balanced experience; devotees could raise a family here, and they could exist in a way that was reasonable. At the same time, if it's time to go back to teepees and forming communities from scratch, is there the willingness to do that? I've always felt there was, and I think there are many who feel the same.

For others who want to form a community, they would do well to do what Swami Kriyananda did here: start a retreat. By starting a retreat, right away one begins thinking in terms of service to other people. And then as you feel the bliss of that experience, you begin to realize that God will take care of your own needs, too. I've always appreciated what Swami Kriyananda says, "Those who try to just get *their* trip together never do, and the people who work hard with the thought of living their life with God and learn to trust in God, always find everything coming." And I've found that to be so true. I've tried, and obviously the community has also tried, to learn the art of self-lessness. The more selflessly we live for God, the more we grow in our faith.

In the early years we did our best with faith, but we didn't quite know what it was all about. Now that we've been in a community for some time, we've seen so many colossal things, whether it's being able to go on a pilgrimage when there was no money, or getting buildings built, or getting projects completed with scanty resources. We're at the point where we trust that Divine Mother will provide. And so I think that I would share with people to court a daring spirit. Be willing to live on the edge, putting all of your energy possible into God's hands and allowing Him to pick up the pieces. Do all that you can, in a balanced way, to be selfless.

I'm constantly experimenting with ways to keep my heart open. If I do anything throughout the day, I try to remain inwardly centered while working on keeping the heart open at all costs, whatever it takes. Even though I've been hurt, and whatever happened was unfair, I still think that has nothing to do with it. Just keep the heart open.

I feel a yoga community is a group of people dedicated to exploring what it is to have an inner life and sharing that with anyone who would care to benefit from that experience. The trick is to learn to apply the experiences that we feel inside to all that we do, whether it's business, being a homemaker, or whatever. That's what has made this community so dynamic; it's the experiential process of living the spiritual life. We have as many experiments as there are people. Over time we've become natural, as Yogananda always encouraged, with our inner and outer life.

It's good to think in terms of who we really are on a soul level and our vast connection to all other souls. When I'm meditating or praying, I can often feel this wonderful wave of unity with the rest of humanity. I am a great fan of prayer, because it's transformed my life. Prayer has really helped me when I was in dire need. For many years I was just hovering around myself, and I didn't know what to do, until prayer came. Through praying for others, I am actually blessed by the experience.

There was an instance at the retreat when for some reason a guest really bugged me. And I guess I bugged him too; there was tension. We didn't even say two words to each other. Well, I embarked on dynamic prayer for some days, and out of nowhere, toward the end of his stay, he came and gave me a very warm and spontaneous hug. And again there were very few words that were spoken. That's happened again and again. Prayer works. Ananda has always encouraged people's interest in prayer and how dynamic prayer and meditation are, as you might say, sisters on the path. The inner life for us is everything. I feel that incredible things have happened here because truly that's our focus. If we didn't have a dynamic inner life, I don't think we would have such a successful community.

Sadhana Devi

When I was 24 years old I heard that my friend Binay was living in some kind of intentional community in the Sierra foothills. The idea of a community that was created consciously was intriguing to me. I was young, out of college and wanted adventure. I had been a social worker and was looking for other ways to serve. Ananda was a social experiment that was fascinating to me.

I was interested in yoga and had learned to meditate through TM before I came here. TM was a great start and taught a lot of people how to meditate, but it didn't take me very far. I was looking for something other than just 20 minutes of meditation, say your *mantra* and then get up and go about your day. I thought there must be something more.

A friend of mine had a copy of Yogananda's *Law of Success*. I was a smoker at that time, when nobody really thought it was bad for you, but I decided I wanted to quit, so I read the *Law of Success* and practiced all the things it tells you to do to change a habit. It took some energy and effort, of course, but I was able to stop smoking. Once I stopped I never started again. I was impressed by the idea that I could do something in an internal way. Drawing on my own resources seemed so sensible. I didn't need to go anywhere, buy fancy equipment, attend classes, or follow a teacher everywhere. There was something profound to this whole discipline that Yogananda was offering. After following his teachings for about a year, I began to feel that he was my guru.

There were only nine people living at the Ananda Meditation Retreat when I first arrived in the spring of 1969. Kriyananda was living in San Francisco and would come up on weekends to teach meditation and *hatha yoga*. He gave the same *sadhana*s that we're still using 30 years later at The Expanding Light—an hour of yoga postures and an hour of meditation each morning and evening.

The idea of gurus was fairly new at that time. In the late sixties and early seventies many of the Indian swamis were starting their work in the United States. Some stayed and started yoga groups while others didn't find it conducive and returned to India or other countries. Ananda invited a number of different spiritual teachers to come visit. The one I remember best was a woman swami named Hridayananda from Shivananda's ashram. Satchidananda came at least twice. Yogi Bhajan came here and was very entertaining. Swami Chidananda of the Divine Life Society in Rishikesh also visited. He was wonderful. In the beginning we were not quite so focused on requiring members to be disciples of Yogananda. Sometimes different groups of people tried to pull the energy away from Yogananda, who is an avatar and a true guru. So, at one point Kriyananda said something like, "Look, I don't care what you do with this community, the only thing I care about is that this community be dedicated to Yogananda's teachings."

I think if everyone could have agreed on a few core concepts, people on different spiritual paths could have all lived here harmoniously. But at the time, we were all beginners and nobody clearly understood the underlying principles of all religions enough to see the similarities. Maybe we could now. I think we can grow in that direction and at some point be able to transcend sectarianism.

Sadhana Devi and Jaya's daughter, Shyama,
demonstrating the "Tree Pose".

We also didn't have a clearly defined common purpose like we do now. Kriyananda's original idea was to have a small place for people to learn yoga, meditation and adult seclusion. He had bought land together with the poet Gary Snyder; Dick Baker, a roshi from the San Francisco Zen Center; and Alan Ginsberg. They formed a small group called the Bald Mountain Land Association. One of the agreements of the organization was that they weren't going to use the land for commercial venture.

We didn't expect the Meditation Retreat to become so popular in such a short time. More and more people wanted to come here, including some with families. We were bursting at the seams, and had no facilities for children. That's why we bought the property where the Village is now. It was once a hog farm that had been abandoned for several years and was quite a mess. The market building had been there since the 1860s, and most of the other buildings were also old. There was quite a lot of cleanup work needed to beautify our community.

At first there was no housing or any way to earn an income. People would come with whatever money they had, which usually wasn't much. We would pool our money for food. As winter approached, we started making teepees, working together to gather and prepare the poles. I sewed 12 of the 15 teepee covers myself. I lived in a teepee for four years, where there was no electricity or running water. I tried building a fire in the floor, which is the authentic Native American way. It lasted about two nights! After the first rains came I got a wood stove and found a way to put the vent through the canvas without burning the teepee. Someone built a wood platform for my teepee, and it became quite cozy. We had no running water, but carried it in containers. I used to fantasize about things like a hot bath. Now, Jaya and I have a simple home and, yes, we even have a bathtub. Every time I think of leaving here, I try to think why. It never comes down to anything more than money or material comforts. Not a good enough reason to leave.

Jaya and I both lived at Ayodhya and were part of the monastery when it first began. We got married after we had been here four years. Jaya once read statistics that 85-90% of the population is married at some time or another. I think as a community, Ananda needs to be something that people can relate to. A traditional renunciate community, where everyone is a monk or nun, doesn't seem realistic. Although we renounce a certain amount of individual preferences for the larger goal of living our lives for God, outwardly we face the same challenges as others. A person can find God in a householder community as well as in a monastic setting. The challenge is to find God anywhere! Most of the nuns I met as a child of Catholic upbringing were quite bitter, yet their lives were sheltered and everything was provided for them. I wonder if they may have needed the challenges of the world as well. While traditional monasticism might be good at a certain time in one's life, probably most people need to learn to support themselves, raise a family and be productive in society.

The vows we take at marriage are as important as monastic vows. The traditional Hindu way of living through the four ashrams of life would be a healthy way to approach life in a spiritual community. The first ashram is the student or *brahmacharya* stage where you're learning discipline. The second ashram is a *householder* stage where you learn the responsibilities of marriage or raising children. The third ashram happens after your children are grown and you can spend a lot of time in service outside your immediate family. And the fourth ashram is the renunciate stage, where you "retire to the forest" in traditional terms, and spend time in meditation and with God. I think Ananda offers a way to experience all four of these ashrams.

Satsang has been the greatest benefit of living here—the support of people that are doing the same thing that I'm doing. Living in a spiritual community has helped me grow, with all of us keeping up meditation and *Kriya* day in and day out. Living simply, I meditate an hour in the morning and evening, work during the day, and relax a little after dinner. If I am going to be teaching a class the next day, I study in the evening.

It seems like Ananda has always been controversial. By some we've been viewed as irresponsible hippies, others have seen us as big developers. We've always been different, and people often have a hard time seeing us as individuals; they tend to generalize after meeting one person here, and assume everyone is alike. Since the spiritual teachings are subtle, it's difficult for people to see these things unless they actually come and spend some time here.

Sometimes I feel like a pine tree in the sense that whatever happens, I keep standing. Something may happen that pushes me this way or that, or snow may fall on me, but it just slides off. I try to face fear by looking it in the face, imagining the worst that could happen in any situation, then asking myself what I would do. This is my version of surrender to God's will. Because of my roots in this community I can keep standing like the pine tree. This is what yoga does for you—it helps you to become flexible, yet firmly rooted.

Nakula

In the mid-sixties, I was studying architecture at the University of Illinois. Though my father had been a lieutenant commander in the Navy and we were very close spiritually, I did not agree with the war in Viet Nam. I moved to Boston to work as a conscientious objector in the surgical ward of the New England Baptist Hospital. When I was in Boston, I was living in a communal house with a small group of people. Even with the peace and love movement, I saw misunderstanding and ego, even with those who were trying their best. Around Thanksgiving of 1969 I remember crying out in frustration one night, "I just want to live in a place where everybody loves each other." Within one month someone had given me a copy of *Autobiography of a Yogi*, and nine months later I had arrived at Ananda.

I hitchhiked across the country to join Self-Realization Fellowship. I walked in to the SRF headquarters at Mt. Washington and asked them if I could take the SRF lessons. They said they had to mail them to me, and I didn't have an address. So with one month's worth of SRF lessons, I began to hitchhike up California's scenic Highway 1. I wanted to build a log cabin in the mountains and study Yogananda's teachings. On the way up the coast, I stopped in the Big Sur area and backpacked into the mountains. I heard there was a Zen monastery 30 miles back in, and decided to hike there. It was the Tassajara Zen

Center. I still remember my first experience of meditation. I was sitting in Strawberry Valley amidst the wildflowers of the pastoral Big Sur mountains, reading Yogananda's lessons and trying to meditate. When I first arrived at the Zen Center, they were surprised to see someone hike that far. Most people took the road.

I stayed at Tassajara a week on a work exchange program, working in the kitchen and the garden. My first real meditation experience was meditating with Roshi Suzuki and the monks for 90 minutes each morning and each evening. It was wonderful. I knew that this kind of a life, dedicated to God, was what I wanted. I met a monk there named Ruvane who said he'd always wanted to meet certain famous writers, thinkers and philosophers. He said he let go of that desire when he entered the monastery. He was surprised to find that all the people he had once desired to meet had eventually come through Tassajara and he had that chance to meet them. I created a little saying about this monk: "Ruvane, weathervane, it's all the same to the man who knows which way the wind blows."

While talking with one of the other guests, I revealed that I loved Tassajara, but Yogananda was my guru. And he said, "Oh, you should go to Grass Valley, he has a community there." And I said, "No, he's dead," and he said, "No, he's there!" So by July, 1970, I had arrived at the Ananda Seclusion Retreat with my backpack, bedroll, about $1.50, ten pounds of brown rice, and a frying pan. The first people I met were Lakshmi and Satya. They suggested I come to the Sunday service. I camped out in the forest nearby and came to the service the next day. Kriyananda performed a vedic fire ceremony and chanted the *Mahamritunjaya* and the *Gayatri* mantras right before the service started. To this day, I say those same *mantras* every day. Afterwards, he kindly offered me a ride to Edward's Crossing where I was camping. He asked about my life and I was struck that he could be so normal; yet I could see his great spiritual stature, which was all the greater because he was so normal. He had no pretentious dress or talk. I knew, without any doubt, that Ananda was where I belonged.

Over the next year I made a living of various endeavors—picking berries, baking bread, and for some time I ran a small granola business called Kali Oats. Ananda Products distributed the granola, which sold in health food stores throughout Northern California. I would make the granola then drive all over in a little truck distributing it to the stores. I was happy to be earning my way to stay at Ananda, but I was seeking to be more involved with the community. In the spring of 1972, I took part in the infamous tree-planting episode at Happy Camp in the Klamath Mountains. I knew we were in for a hard time, because I was called in as part of the reserves. It lasted about six weeks, and it was an important event because the community had few opportunities to make money. We made hardly anything, but for us it seemed like a fortune. It was also a way for all of us to go out and bring money back into the community, just as Swami had been doing. In fact, this is where I got my seed money to start the dairy.

At this time, a number of the families at the farm were buying milk from a man in Grass Valley and we were dependent on him. In the spring he told us he was going to sell his two cows and wouldn't have milk anymore. In my meditations it came very strongly to me, "You should buy those two cows." The more I tried to shake this feeling, the more I felt Master coming to me and saying, "You should buy those cows." To add to this, a small paper was circulating of Master's recommendations for starting world brotherhood colonies. He recommended things like buying your own cows so you could have your own milk. He, of course, recommended meditation and spiritual practices. He also said people should work half a day every day in the garden, and spend time writing or doing music and art. And he suggested people grow their own food and pool their money to buy land in the country together.

The more I tried to put the cows out of my mind, the more they came in. So I went to all the families who were buying milk from the farmer and I got them each to agree to pay for 200 gallons of milk in advance. Half the milk would go to the families who contributed and the other half would be sold to buy hay and grain and to care for the cows. It seemed like a good plan. So I went to Swami to ask for his blessing on buying these cows and starting a little dairy. He said, "Well, I was thinking that you might like to start a little market, but if you feel guided from within to do a dairy, you should go with that."

The first two cows were registered Guernseys named Goldie and Shortie. I put them in a little lean-to shed that had been used for a burro, right where the old dairy barn stands today. This was fine for the summer, but I realized as winter was approaching that I needed a small barn. So I borrowed $1,000 for lumber, sketched out a small plan and organized a workday to help build the dairy. It was a good old-fashioned barn raising. Everyone showed up to help. I ordered the cement for the foundation and started to build the forms myself, but got only about 10 percent of it done. When I called to postpone the cement trucks, they'd already left. At this time a crew of carpenters were working on the publications building, and they heard of my dilemma with the cement. They all came to help me finish the forms. It was probably the fastest set of concrete forms we ever built. Unfortunately, the cement truck driver had to wait three hours before he could unload the cement!

Over the next few years, the dairy herd grew to a dozen cows, a bull named Nandi, and four young heifers. We gave the cows names like Tara, Lakshmi, Asha and Rosebud. We provided milk and also made farmer's cheese, yogurt, buttermilk, and ice cream. We eventually added a small goat herd for goat's milk, and also had about 100

Nakula feeding the cows at the dairy in the '70s.

chickens. Over the years, we got a small hay baler to make our own hay. We grew fields of corn and comfrey to make our own feed. Once Master's Market got started, all our dairy products were sold there.

As with most jobs at Ananda, the dairy paid very little. We each made about $200 per month—plus all the free milk you could drink!

We had a small dairy staff that would milk the cows, do dairy chores and help make the dairy products. The dairy operated from eight in the morning until ten at night, seven days a week. This is where I learned that I was a *karma yogi*, by feeling God flowing through my hands in activity. Many times the dairy work felt like a *tapasya*. I was not able to join the monastery and meditate several hours a day. But I was able to serve. My *sadhana* was strong but not long. Through all those years I never missed meditating morning and evening, even if it was a short time. The discipline of having to milk the cows every morning and evening had also helped me keep my sadhana strong.

One of the milkers was a young monk named Richard Salva. When he would walk to work in the morning from Ayodhya, Nandi would see him and start bellowing and running around in the pasture. Then Richard would sing to him and Nandi would come over to the fence and lick his hand. As the years passed, Nandi grew to be a strong bull and his horns grew. I had raised him from a calf like he was my son. As he came to full size he learned he could break out of the fences and toss hay bales high in the air. One of the scariest times I've ever had was having to approach him with a can of feed and pinch him between the nostrils in order to lead him. I had to hang on and pull him back into the pasture without him shaking free and tossing me high in the air. Once, someone made the mistake of putting a young horse in the pasture with him. The young horse wanted to be playful but Nandi wanted none of it. With the shake of his head, he tossed the horse high in the air. That was when I knew it was unsafe to keep him in the community with so many people around. I took him to the cattle auction and turned in his registration papers to make sure that he was sold as a breeding bull. As I watched the auction end, I saw no one wanted him for a bull and it broke my heart. I knew what happened to bulls that no one wanted.

The dairy taught me interesting things about working with energy. It was always muddy in the winter and the cows would sometimes get mastitis. I found that the typical dairy solution was strong drugs, which I believed were harmful to the animals. And when drugs were used, their milk had to be discarded for one day. I sought to find other natural solutions so we could have organic milk. In searching within for the right solution, I found that gently massaging and practicing Yogananda's healing techniques with my hands on their udders was more successful than any other treatment. As we got more cows, I got a small milking machine. But some of the milkers were unskilled in using milking machines, and I found that the machines did more harm to the cows, so we decided to stay with hand-milking. Years later, Richard Salva won the hand-milking contest at the California State Fair in Sacramento.

The dairy was very hard, demanding physical work. When the evening chores were done at the end of the day, sitting at the door of the barn, looking out over the farm, the presence of peace was immeasurable. One evening near Christmas time, as I listened to the cattle, I could feel the presence of Christ as if I was at the manger the night he was born. We decided to have a live manger scene right in the dairy barn with all the animals. A couple with a new-born baby posed as the holy family. It was held Christmas Eve, after all the community festivities. To this day, Ananda still has a manger scene at Christmas.

I ran the dairy for almost 10 years until I moved to our Ocean Song community in the early '80s. The dairy continued until about 1987 when the health department requirements made it too expensive to keep open. Ocean Song was a smaller community located on the Sonoma County coast on a ridge about a mile inland, overlooking the ocean. A small group of about 20 devotees of Yogananda lived there. We had a small garden, a one-cow dairy, a school and a temple. We all lived in canvas yurts that we built on platforms. It was one of the most peaceful sites I've ever lived in. When the fog would roll in it would be so quiet and still you could hear nothing but the silence of your own thoughts. It was an idyllic place for deep meditations. I wanted to stay and work in the Ocean Song community, but I had done that for so many years at Ananda Village, I was encouraged to take a job in town. I worked at the Traditional Medicinal herb tea company in Santa Rosa with a few other devotees. The owner and several employees were also devotees of Yogananda and it was a very uplifting working environment.

All my years of working at Ananda and in the dairy gave me the strength to go out from Ananda into the world and gain experience that I could then bring back to help build Ananda in a new phase. I moved to the East Coast and worked for an architect and for a large construction firm, eventually starting my own construction company. When I moved to Virginia, I felt the same guidance from within as I did when I started the dairy. But it seemed unusual to go that far alone, away from Ananda. I knew when I arrived and found I was a few miles from the SRF Greenfield Retreat Center, that Master's hand was there guiding me. I attended the SRF meditations and services on a regular basis. I lived in Virginia nearly four years. Every year I would return to Ananda for seclusions and *Kriya* initiations and to visit my friends. It was uncomfortable to live so far away, and I always knew Ananda was my home.

One year, I was back for a friend's wedding and heard about Ananda's pilgrimage to India. I knew that was the next step for me.

Many of my friends from Ocean Song were on the tour that went to all the sacred sites where Yogananda and the great masters had lived in India. It changed my life, yet another time. To be immersed in the holy vibrations of India brought me to the realization that those same vibrations were what I'd always loved about Ananda. Within months after the trip to India, I had closed my business in Virginia. I returned to Ananda to join the Ananda Builders Guild and to marry a fellow devotee.

I remember a letter I once wrote to Swami Kriyananda, which summed up my gratitude for all he had done for us in founding Ananda. It said, "I have long been loyal to you and to your vision of Master's work. I have always tried as a good disciple, not to imitate you in what you do as a disciple, but to absorb into myself how to be a disciple, how to know Master's work for me. Not to take on your personality, but to take on your vibration of being a devotee—to take on your commitment to the path, and your commitment to build Ananda. I try to do the work that is given to me with the same commitment to *dharma* and righteousness as you do with your own work. Not from thinking, 'how would Swami do this,' which would assume separateness, but from that same place of dharma that you come from, in always reviewing my actions to see if I am on track."

Ananda and Swami Kriyananda have taught me tenacity, perseverance and to always strive to the highest level of perfection that I can reach. My path is through action, doing things like creating the dairy and manifesting buildings.

I always lived at the farm in the family areas, and I have always been close to Lahiri Mahasaya who was the ideal householder yogi. I've always felt that Ananda's path and the world brotherhood colony mission was to follow Lahiri's example of the householder yogi. To me, that means having the responsibilities of maintaining family, job, and home while keeping an inner life connected to God that is untouched by this world. To live in the moment, fulfilling the duties of this world, but retaining the consciousness of God's world.

Looking at the people here now, I see the same things I saw in Swami Kriyananda when he gave me that first ride to my campsite. On one hand, these are unusually dedicated people who have devoted their lives fully to God—yet they're just normal people living a normal life and going through the same trials and tribulations that people everywhere in the world go through.

Arati

One thing I've found out over the years is that when you need them, life will present you with new friends to help with your next step along the spiritual path. My first spiritual friend was Michael Deranja, a fellow senior at UC Berkeley in 1968. I was majoring in Fine Arts, and he in Eastern Philosophy. We would spend hours talking about the meaning of life, knowing that there had to be more to it than what appeared on the surface. I had always felt something happen to me when in nature; he felt inspired by reading Alan Watts and other philosophers. What was this mystery all about? Did anyone really know the answer? I had once asked a science teacher what makes the atoms move around in the molecule. He looked up, smiled and said, "We don't cover that in this class."

I will never forget one very beautiful evening Michael and I and some of his roommates spent in Tilden Park pretending we were each petals of one flower! Each petal shared his thoughts with the others. I didn't define it at the time, but this was our way of expressing a truth that we are in fact "one" with each other; a very sweet legacy of the '60s and the permission we gave to each other to be together in new ways.

We graduated. Michael left for a trip around the world, and I went off to work in a summer camp, on to a year of teaching in an outdoor school, and then the Alexander Lindsay Junior Museum in Walnut Creek. I was in nature much of the time, but still not getting to its essence.

I was living in a group house in Berkeley, when Michael entered my life again. He handed me a paperback book that he'd picked up in New Delhi. It was called *Autobiography of a Yogi*. He said it had given him all the answers to what we'd been talking about.

And I started, then, on my own journey. Not around the world, but into the adventure of reading the book that has changed my life. I read slowly over several months, savoring every chapter, feeling my heart open to Yogananda's presence emanating from every word. I knew that he knew Truth. I knew that the path of meditation, of yoga, was mine.

It was another three years before I actually moved to Ananda. I had some personal exploring I needed to do: I learned yoga postures from wonderful devotees from the Integral Yoga Institute, Swami Satchidananda's group. I became a vegetarian, explored a new relationship, and traveled to Australia.

Michael had moved to Ananda in 1971. When I went up to visit him, he was living in a tiny hut (which is now the mailroom) with a sleeping bag, a little propane heater and all his books. It was freezing in the little room, yet he was so happy! He'd been given a new name, Nitai. It means "dispassion."

In 1973, upon returning from Australia I visited Nitai again. This time the community was in the middle of the most powerful week of the year, Spiritual Renewal Week. Swami Kriyananda, a direct disciple of Yogananda, was speaking all week. His classes touched me on a very deep level. I could almost feel Yogananda talking to me, through him. I knew that I had come home. And I knew that here again, life was giving me my next spiritual friend. This time, I had been given someone who had traveled much further on the path than any of us. And he had devoted his life to teaching us what he had learned. At this writing, I have studied with Kriyananda for almost 25 years. To say what he has given me would take books.

Those early days at Ananda were very special. It was a perfect environment for a young, creative woman to expand and grow and learn with others of like mind. The membership committee consisted of a few people who met with me for about a half an hour, decided I was sincere, and said I could stay. The housing "committee" was one man, Nakula, who told me it was ok to get a trailer, and when it arrived helped me park it out in the field near the neighboring horse pasture. I had two jugs for carrying water, and a little outhouse shared by my two neighbors out in the field. I was in bliss.

For the first year I worked in the garden. Haanel Cassidy was our mentor: an expert in biodynamic gardening. We hoed long, long rows of irrigation trenches, tied up what seemed like miles of tomato vines, picked aphids off the leeks, and built huge compost piles. The first time I ever heard Yogananda's voice was at the end of a long garden row. A powerful, booming voice was being projected out of the incense shop at the end of the garden. I'd seen pictures of Yogananda looking loving and kind. I was stunned to feel in that voice another aspect of the Divine: Power and Will and Cosmic Energy!

In the early days, there was a very active, wonderful monastery. Swami suggested to us that if we were serious about the path, and not already married, we should try to live there. I felt very committed to this path, and after a year moved my trailer over the hill into another part of the forest: Ayodhya (named after Sri Rama's mythical kingdom). Monastery! Well, a group of trailers and a teepee with a wood stove to meditate in. It was perfect for me. And, I was surrounded by a group of loving sisters. These women, to this day, are my dearest friends. Although our lives have taken us to other Ananda colonies, even other parts of the world, when we get together, we resonate on a deep level with one another. I know that it comes from meditating together those seven years. We have experienced "oneness." Not imaginary, like the petals of the flower back in Berkeley, but parts of our souls are one.

Life in the monastery was simple. The bell rang at 5:30 am. (I am not a morning person, but luckily I had an arrangement with Parvati that she would come and knock on my window to get me up.) We'd meditate for half an hour, then go back to our trailers and meditate on our own. A simple breakfast, then a walk together through the forest and to the Publications Building to work. We all worked together, helping to produce Swami's books, tapes, tour publicity, etc. I'd studied fine art, but six months after I started to help, the graphic designer left and I was it. It was really a crash course in design, while running full speed ahead, trying to keep up with Swami's prolific writing.

In those days, "Pubble" was the hub of the community. We had the one phone and answered all the calls. We took turns preparing steamed veggies and rice for each other, and meditated together for a half an hour every noon. In time I became the production manager for the building: overseeing typesetting, graphics, and printing of the books. We worked together, lived together, meditated together. And, yes, learned to tolerate each others imperfections too.

Evenings at the monastery were quiet: no phones, no electricity. Quiet, that is except for when we had to go on a porcupine hunt. There were two porcupines living in the monastery with us. I remember coming home late one night and hearing this humming sound in the grass. I shined my flashlight and there was a porcupine humming happily while he was eating his dinner. Here was a little creature showing happiness just like humans do, by humming a tune. The porkies were fine for awhile, until they began to gnaw on Asha's wooden trailer supports. We were afraid that the trailer would fall apart, so we decided to move our spiny friends to another part of the forest. One evening Asha heard one chewing, snuck out, and got me and Anandi. We surrounded him with our flashlights on, plunked a huge wooded box over him, uprighted it and drove him off to another part of the forest. In time we had to cart off some raccoons too (they are very ingenious in getting into any place that has food). I loved sharing the forest with the animals. I used to see bear, fox, skunks, red fox and, of course, lots of deer living at Ananda.

As time went on, and Ananda grew and changed, it was becoming clear that the community needed to have a more integrated feeling to it: That those who were married and committed to the path, those who had children too, could also feel that they were as much a part of Yogananda's mission as were the monastics. If the ideal of "cooperative communities" was to "spread like wildfire," as Yogananda had put it, a little monastery would not serve that purpose. So, Swami entered into a relationship, and others of the monastics followed the lead. Our monastery changed and people left.

With the changes, came new areas to explore for me. I've spent a number of years living in different urban Ananda centers on various assignments. Many of them had to do directly or indirectly with music. I play guitar and sing, so have often been involved in singing and leading choirs. What a blessing for me that Kriyananda is a composer and musician. Here I was in a spiritual community, and not only was the leader of it sharing with me what he had learned from his years of spiritual experience, but he was writing hundreds of new chants and songs and choir pieces which flowed out to us all from the love he felt inside himself. I marvel again at how the universe provides us each with a spiritual friend, perfectly tailored for us. New, fresh music was coming to me, and as I sang it, I was literally "vibrating" with the love that created it. I had wanted to feel from Nature Her essence. Now, as I sang, I could feel Her essence of love flowing through me. *"What is Love, is it only ours...or does Love whisper in the flowers...Surely we, children of this world, could not love by our own powers..."*

So much beautiful music. Even for children! One year I had the opportunity to work with another woman on the production of a tape of Kriyananda's songs for children. All the pieces were written to reinforce and affirm positive qualities inside oneself. *Move All Ye Mountains* is about courage; *Its Time to Go to School* is about new possibilities in learning; and the theme song, *All the World is My Friend* is about what happens when one shares one's love. A wonderful group of Ananda school children and musicians sang and played guitars, drums, flutes, trumpets, piano and alarm clocks to make a fantastic music tape of affirmative positive qualities for children.

Ananda is one big creative experience. To me, it's an on-going experiment in living and changing and sharing and loving together: in making just what the name says, a "cooperative spiritual community." Take any one of those three words, and go into it, and think of the possibilities. Who knows what the years will bring or where all of us will be? I do know that the Love that is Yogananda is inside each of us, and looking for new ways to express Itself.

Asha

When I was about 18 years old, I began to study Indian Vedanta philosophy. I had become very engaged with Vedanta through the teachings of Ramakrishna and his disciples. For the first time in my life, I felt like I was reading something that was actually relevant to what I'd always felt. I had attended Stanford University, and although I was always good in school, it never answered my questions about life. I gradually worked myself around to reading the lives of the great saints. In retrospect, I see I was trying to figure out how someone actually *lives* these great spiritual teachings.

My family is Jewish, but we weren't particularly religious. There was nothing about my childhood that was overtly spiritual, however, nor was I an atheist. Once I began to study concepts from the East, I recognized that through my entire life I had lived as a yogi—which means I had lived with the understanding that my inner consciousness was all that mattered.

When I began studying the life of St. Francis, I had a desire to bring my daily life into conformance with higher spiritual ideals. I was married, living in San Francisco, and working as a legal secretary. My life seemed to be an endless cycle of paying the rent and paying the bills. I was becoming really desperate for more meaning in my life. A friend of mine, Lakshmi, who was also a student of these kinds of teachings, had met Kriyananda through yoga classes he was giving in San Francisco. She called me on the phone to tell me about him. I'll never forget the phrase she used. She said, "I have met a real teacher."

In the fall of 1969, Kriyananda was giving a program at Stanford University. It was a very odd, chaotic evening. I remember Kriyananda later described it as one of the worst nights of his life, because it was an environment that neither understood nor respected what he was talking about. For me, it was the first time in my life I felt I had met someone who actually knew how to live in a way that brought inner satisfaction.

My interest in Yogananda was clearly due to Kriyananda's ability to offer an experiential way to live Yogananda's teachings. I had tried to read Yogananda's *Autobiography of a Yogi* several years earlier, but for some reason just couldn't get through it. The miracles were just too much for me! After I learned that Kriyananda was Yogananda's disciple, I went back and read the book. This time I found it a perfectly reasonable book with such natural explanations of truth that I didn't know why I had rejected it earlier.

One of the reasons that Kriyananda inspired me so much was that he had so much understanding of things that really mattered, and his life was about helping people. My main desire has always been to help people. But I needed to help them with something that would really help them! From the moment that I met Kriyananda, I became determined to learn from him. However, it wasn't until 1971 that I was able to move to Ananda Village, which is where he lived.

My first impression of Ananda was intuitive. I arrived at the Seclusion Retreat, I opened the car door, and as I stepped onto the land, I actually spoke these words, "This place is true," meaning the teachings were true, the consciousness was honest, and what was asked of people was honorable. It was very undeveloped, almost like a campground. Fortunately, I grew up in a family that was never very materialistic, so the entire primitiveness of Ananda just didn't matter. In fact, I adored it.

When I eventually moved to Ananda, my husband and I sold everything we had and bought this wonderful tent that we lived in for six months. We arrived in June. By January, we were separated. And in the spring I joined the monastery. I was grief stricken at the loss of a marriage to a wonderful man to whom I was very attached, yet I had to make a choice because he didn't want to live at Ananda the way I did.

My life at Ananda was physically very simple. It was very much like the ideal of India with very little concern for the material level of things. People were mostly young, in their twenties. There were very few couples, and very few children. We lived in trailers, teepees, and small cabins. And we served. I lived in a trailer that was so small I had just enough room for the things I needed to live there: a bed, a table, a hot plate, a place to meditate, a heater. I made fifty dollars a month. I couldn't buy anything beyond food and heat, but through this simple living I found so much freedom and liberation from the endless preoccupation with material things. For the first time in my life, I was really doing something meaningful by serving the world through our publications, or through the guest retreat. The message we had truly helped people. They were inspired by our books and guests loved staying at the retreat. As renunciates, we drew our security from our relationship with God and from our faith that we were doing what God wanted us to do. By comparison, material security meant nothing.

When I was growing up I had a very deep desire to lead a meaningful life. In fact, I always had this fear that I would end up being trapped in some perfectly ordinary life in a little house with a little husband and a little job—I used to be terrified that I might end up with what most people were striving for. I didn't want to drop out, I wanted to live by truth. To live the teachings of Yogananda is to experience the fact that life is joy, because God is joy. If I were to describe 27 years of Ananda, I would call it *ananda*, I would call it *joy*. Once you have that inner joy, that's all you're looking for in everything else anyway.

I learned from Yogananda's teachings that I *could* be happy. In fact, joy was my very nature, and by constantly adjusting my mental attitude, I could always be joyful. If I lost that joy, it was because in some way I had moved away from right consciousness and right attitude. Through the extraordinary example of Kriyananda, primarily, and through the group of people that lived at Ananda, there existed a powerful sense of security that came from our common goal of living a spiritual life together. Living within Ananda I had the perfect opportunity to discover my own potential. It wasn't that the community itself was perfect, but it was perfect for those whose priority was personal spiritual growth.

As individuals, we understood that we were responsible for our own state of mind and our own consciousness. Even though people were very compassionate and very sympathetic when you had difficulties, you were in an environment where everything was feeding you true solutions of personal responsibility and self transformation instead of saying, "Indulge your selfishness."

For instance, there was a time at Ananda when I had seven jobs in fourteen months. I just kept getting moved around from department to department. I thought, either I'm a fast learner, or I'm just a hopeless case! I remember once I got fired from the retreat staff. I was surprised, because I thought I was hot stuff. There would be this feeling of rejection, and then I would think about karma. I knew God was looking out for me. I could feel bad or I could just hold my head up and go forward. I remember there were days when I felt somewhat snobby and disconnected from life at Ananda. I'd just lie at home feeling miserable and nursing my wounds. I had become so much more concerned with my own opinions and my own preferences that I was just no fun to have around. Suddenly, I realized, "Honey, you got yourself into this by wrong action. Well, just decide what right action is and start acting right." And I really did. I just got up, and I went out, and I started behaving properly. To live by these yogic principles sincerely, you have to accept that God loves you, you are a beloved part of creation, but you yourself are responsible for your own consciousness, and you can't blame the world.

When Kriyananda invited me to help him with his secretarial work, I was very interested because my most profound interest was in learning from him. Through his example and also through deepening my own meditations, I learned to be much more intuitive and much more relaxed about life. When Kriyananda wrote *The Path*, which was over a period of a couple of years, I typed and retyped his manuscript as many as 50 times. It was an extraordinary opportunity for me. What I learned from Kriyananda, above all things, is how to relate to people. I have never encountered anyone who is so selflessly conscious of the reality and the needs of others, and so self-sacrificing in regards to those needs, as he is. I was often present for personal counseling sessions and meetings, and I just watched him for hours and hours. I watched how he worked with people. He always knew that a person had to arrive at truth at their own speed. He was masterful at giving you the confidence to go on, no matter how badly you were actually doing, and I always left his presence feeling encouraged, rather than diminished.

Kriyananda himself states that he is not a fully Self-realized master. But through these years, what I've seen him express is a level of selfless concern for others, and unconcern for himself, that I never even imagined was possible until I met him. He is very intuitive, and in some way his intuitive abilities wake you up to your own intuition. He also taught me the attitude of a minister. I remember him scolding me once, saying, "You go too much by your likes and dislikes. You have to respond to people's spiritual needs. Whether you like their personality or their behavior is not the issue. If someone comes to you who sincerely desires spiritual help, their sincerity is all that matters, not your opinion." From my point of view, people would often impose upon him, and I would tell him so. He would listen politely to me and always totally ignore me. If there was some sincere potential for him to help someone, that's all that mattered to him. Even if a person was completely out of line and not able to respond to his subtle way of trying to guide them, he would just endure them.

I lived at Ananda sixteen years before moving to Palo Alto to help start our first urban community with my husband, David. Prior to that time, and in the last four or five years before we moved, I was actually traveling out from the Village and lecturing throughout the country. In the early years, I was only able to maintain God's presence and my inner joy as long as I was in the supportive environment of Ananda. If I spent too much time in an environment that was too contrary, it was easy to gradually lose contact with that inner experience. But after enough time had passed, my inner life was strong enough for me to live in a non-supportive environment and still influence that environment with my consciousness without having that environment overcome me.

No matter where you are, both in and outside of Ananda, the entire issue is that you must be working with your consciousness. The benefit of being in a spiritual community or something like it, is that a vibration is created by the group energy. You can learn from other people's experience. What is said in a general way in a class also has to be individualized. In a community like Ananda you get to practice applying yogic principles to the ordinary experiences of life, such as dealing with a child who suddenly becomes rebellious, a sick mother, a personal health crisis, or relationship conflicts—it's all here. It's hard to transfer theory into practice without a supportive environment in which to try things out. Living in a spiritual community year after year, through both example and instruction, you can begin to transcend problems and spiritualize situations more readily.

Spirit is more important than form. If you make too many rules, it destroys the spirit. The secret of Ananda's success is the individual spiritual sincerity of everyone. People are more important than things. The way Ananda is structured fosters sincere spiritual effort. Those who are not self-motivated have a hard time in a community like Ananda.

I believe we're proof that old forms of living in spiritual community can change without diluting the essence of a deep, spiritual life. What we're working with now, because we're moving into a new age, is an expression and understanding of Yogananda's saying, "Your religion is not the garb you wear outwardly, but the garment of light you weave around your heart." Spirit *is* more important than form. At the same time, because we live in a human society, a certain amount of form and organization facilitates the spirit. We may see things coming into our culture that appear at first to be very exaggerated—the garb of Buddhist monks, or Indian ashrams, for example. But it only looks affected or extreme because it's not American. It is perfectly natural if you're in a different culture.

Whether the form you adopt helps you or distracts you depends on whether it's a living expression of your inner consciousness or whether it's a substitute for that inner consciousness. And it's a fine line, which is why Yogananda said, "Don't make too many rules. Rules destroy the spirit."

At Ananda we try to be very attentive to the form so that it doesn't become empty or an end in itself, no longer serving the actual needs of the individuals. I think as the age progresses, as we move into a higher age, the forms will get much lighter.

Those of us who belong to Ananda's monastic order call ourselves monastics, but it is more clear to say we are renunciants, since we are mostly householders, not monks and nuns in the usual sense. In many ways Ananda is still a pioneer work. We understand the *inner* point, to be attached to God, and detached from the world. How that manifests is something that we're still working out because the form changes as our understanding evolves, as our stage of life changes. We haven't yet been through a full generation at Ananda. At one time Ananda residents were almost all the same age—young, single people. Then there were couples, and then there were families with children. Now we're beginning to have people dying. What will retirement years be like at Ananda? We don't know what those forms will be yet.

I think Ananda is an idea whose time has not quite come. Soon, however, it will be more obvious. People will say, "But of course. Why did I ever think I had to have my own $500,000 house all by myself with just my two kids?" It'll occur to people that excess isn't the answer, and they'll see that places like Ananda, and others, have just quietly, persistently worked through a lot of the bugs and are able to provide an alternative. Right now it's still a little too new, a little too scary, and the other system is still working, though imperfectly. Many people in today's society, especially in the cities, feel lonely and disconnected. There's also lots of drug and alcohol abuse, divorce, workaholism, and over-satiety on the material level. I do think that cooperative spiritual communities solve many of the problems of our culture. Personally, ever since I was a young child I've wanted to live a true and meaningful life that would serve others, and now Ananda has provided me with this opportunity.

Nitai

Starting the Ananda School was an organic process. From the very beginning I've had a strong karmic connection with the kids here. I had first visited Ananda in 1970 after graduating from UC Berkeley. After spending a summer at the community, I decided to go back to school to get my master's degree in education. Two years later I returned to Ananda and began teaching. I desperately wanted to approach the school differently, because everything I had studied in education emphasized that things were presented as being external to the person; getting educated meant learning facts about some topic that you might or might not be interested in. Besides all the discipline required in public classrooms to keep kids from hurting each other, there was no time to get to know them and find out what they needed to do for their lives to become more integrated and more dynamic.

During my years in the study of education I found that the Montessori and Waldorf schools exhibited the most promising approaches. When I asked Kriyananda about going off to study these systems, he said, "No, don't do that. Your answers need to come from within." So in addition to meditating, I flipped back through all the old SRF magazines looking for education ideas Yogananda had written about. I came up with two articles: one was called "The Balanced Life," and the other was called, "The Psychological Chart." Essentially,

Yogananda had outlined his ideas of education in those two articles. So through Yogananda's guidance and by working with the kids, I began to focus on the core philosophy for our school.

It was never Swami Kriyananda's style to guide me through the experience of creating an Ananda school; he wanted me to figure it out for myself. He was modeling for me the style of teaching I needed to learn. When Kriyananda wrote his book *Education for Life*, he did it all from intuition.

Education for Life (EFL) isn't supposed to be teacher-led in the sense of now we do this, and now we do that. The idea was to get the students to the point where they feel like they have some of the reins in their own hands in regards to their education. He showed me the way to do this with the schools, and later on with the monastery.

A major problem in most schools is motivating the children to learn. Yet if you approach education with the EFL method, the child provides the motivation. They are eager to learn if it's the right time and the right subject matter for them—which means that children go at their own pace, in their own style. This holistic approach is more exciting because the student feels involved; she feels that it is she herself that she is exploring. There is a joy to learning.

So the job of the teacher is to get to know the child, and find out what the child is ready to learn. You can then help him become connected with the materials he needs. If this is done correctly, the child will not resist what he's being taught. In the process, the child will become well-educated; he will cover most of the usual academics, but in a much more organic way.

Yogananda challenges you to step back from your own ego, your own list of priorities, and to try to stay centered in your soul and become aware of what is actually happening in front of you, rather than what you're *projecting* onto what is happening in front of you. In her book *The Flawless Mirror*, Kamala describes her guru, Yogananda, as a perfect mirror—flawless in that he reflected back to her exactly what she was going through. You don't have to be a perfect mirror to be a good teacher, but the more flawless you are, the better the teacher you are going to be. The whole idea is to stand in front of the child and let the child show who they are. As a teacher, you're there to read him or her.

Yogananda said there are physical, mental, social and spiritual aspects to a child, and the teacher tries to become aware of all four of them. Then, in "The Balanced Life," he says the idea is to balance those four qualities for optimum growth. Every child learns in a unique way. That's what makes teaching at Ananda so exciting, because you're constantly being enthralled by this kaleidoscope of life. Whereas with traditional education you're constantly bored because you have to teach the same things to kids over and over again; and the kids don't want to learn it.

It took me two years of teaching at Ananda before I felt this new system was a completely constructive experience for the kids. There were so many things that *I* needed to learn. Being a trained educator, I had all this programming to unlearn. Yet from the very beginning we incorporated an altruistic element into education—the idea of having children reach up in their consciousness for higher things. Last year was one of the best classes I've ever had; it was a fourth and fifth grade class. They were excited about the Hindu classics, the *Mahabharata* and the *Ramayana*. We spent a whole year working on those two epics, which give a picture of life from a higher octave, in storybook form. Ideals of right living like selflessness, integrity, truthfulness, and courage all come into play. By sharing stories or plays or having discussions or ceremonies, the teacher opens a window for the kids and lets them see this higher dimension of life.

EFL encourages teachers to keep a steady flow of uplifting things happening in the classroom. This doesn't mean that everything has to be inspirational, but I try to eliminate things that have a downward pull. An awful lot of television programs undermine positive values by accentuating the gross, the crass and the negative. Kids see these negative values expressed in the cartoons and other TV programs, the videos, music, and the newspapers as well. Some kids are going to find negative stuff on their own; they just have that kind of magnetism. And that's OK; everybody has their karma to work out. But I think one job of the teacher is to weed out negative material from the classroom.

At the same time, there is also a huge space in education for things just to be fun. The right kind of fun is uplifting, in a wholesome way. Jokes and funny little stories are things I look for, where the main benefit is humor.

When we began in 1972, there was no money for the schools. I went to Seva, who was in charge of finances and she said, " The community is going to give you a budget, and out of the budget you've got to provide your salary and supplies and buildings, everything." I said, "OK, how much is that?" And she said, "$50 a month"! Obviously, we didn't have a lot of funds for creating our school, so a lot of the parents pitched in to build the original building, which is now the Aspen building.

You just have to live here to see how much grace there is at Ananda. One story that stands out is from my junior high school class in the late seventies. We had no recreational facilities, just a building for the classroom and that was it. It was February and we were having an extremely wet winter; the kids were jumping off the walls with all their pent-up energy. We couldn't go outside, but I did know it was snowing further up in the Sierras. I came in one day thinking we *have* to do something, we're going to kill each other if we stay in the classroom any longer.

The kids were all asking, "What will we do, what will we do?" And I said, "Let's go snow camping." I can't remember how I even got the idea. They asked, "What's snow camping?" And I said, "I don't really know. But I know that there's snow, and I know that people camp in the snow somehow. We'll find out." Well, earlier that afternoon there had been a knock at the door of the classroom, and a lady came in and asked if she could observe the class. So she was sitting there observing the discussion about snow camping, and when I told the kids that I didn't know how we'd learn about it, the lady raised her hand and asked if she could say something. She said, "As far as snow camping goes, I'm probably the nearest to a professional snow camper that you'll ever find. I take people on trips and I teach them how to snow camp." And I said, "Come right up here!"

She gave us a complete explanation of snow camping, including how to dig the cave so that you can keep the heat in. Then she left and we never saw her again. We went up and had a beautiful experience. We didn't freeze to death, and the kids got the exercise they needed. Over and over again things like that would happen. A book would appear on my desk, and though I could never find out where it came from, it would be just the book I needed for the next lesson with the kids. That must have happened twenty or thirty times. Materials would appear, people would appear, opportunities for the kids would appear.

I remember the first time we did a puppet show, I was trying to make it a big deal, but here we were, way out in the country, with nobody around. I wanted the kids to have an audience to show their work. Well lo and behold, the day we were ready to do our dress rehearsal, a TV crew pulled up from Canada! They had come down to do a documentary, and Ananda was part of it. They happened to arrive while we were doing the puppet show, and so the kids had this experience of having TV lights and everything. These kinds of experiences have happened at our school over and over again.

I've always felt that there is a flow of grace happening at Ananda, that there was something that God wanted to have happen in the school. And if I could get in touch with that in whatever way I was capable of, then I could facilitate the process. I encourage the teachers to have lesson plans, but I also encourage them to be able to drop them if they feel that the flow is going in a different direction. When you're in that "flow" then the right things come at the right time, and the kids get the experiences that they're supposed to have.

I've tried to describe flow learning in different ways. Sometimes it's like the feeling of being on a raft, floating on a river. As long as the raft stays in the middle of the river, then you're carried along with the current. It doesn't mean that things are effortless; you might have to paddle and do different things, but there's an energy that you become a part of. If the raft goes too far to one side or another, then you get into rocks or eddies and things that slow you down. In my experience of teaching, I've had the most problems when I was too tense, too fixated on some particular thing that I thought should happen, or I wasn't willing to see that something else was trying to happen here. In developing the school, part of my training over the years was to learn to just listen more and more. Through real listening, you find that when you follow and stay in the flow, good things happen. And when you fight it, they don't.

I've always emphasized that, for teachers, the most important thing is to find time to connect with each child on a regular basis, so that they know right where that child is and are able to come up with a plan for his or her growth. From there on each teacher is going to have his or her own particular style—which is one of the real strengths of the school. Two of our best EFL teachers have completely different styles of teaching.

My own life goal is to try to develop something that's not available in our society right now. I want to train children who are ready to become *kshatriyas*, a Sanskrit term which stands for people who give selfless service to the broader society. That's basically what we're doing in the Ananda high school right now; this high school is about service, adventure and self-discovery. The high school this year has been fantastic. You can't coerce teenagers into joining a school like this—they have to self-select to be part of it. When you get a group of kids together who have chosen to be part of something that aspires to higher values, you have an incredible time.

One of the highlights of our high school year has been a play about Mother Teresa of Calcutta that the students wrote and produced together. Telling the story through the eyes of a girl, the play embodies the essence of giving your life in service to others, and giving it to God in the way Mother Teresa did. We performed the play around town to different groups, mostly young people but to some elderly people as well, and it really touched people; you could tell they were getting a message from it.

I've always thought that the teen years could be the greatest decade for personal growth in one's life. Now I'm starting to see that it's true. Between the ages of 13 and 18, students are able to introspect and identify unhelpful tendencies before they become deeply rooted. Later on in life, these tendencies are much harder to change. I've seen teens make radical changes in just three months with the EFL method.

Yogananda had a strategy that I think is one of the keys to EFL. He said to identify what changes need to happen with the child and then only talk to them about it once or twice—don't harp on it; don't nag. If the teacher is then able to hold the positive quality in their mind very vividly, they will gradually draw those situations that will help the child change. With most parents and teachers, if they've got the insight to figure out what a child needs to do, they nag them, which causes the child to end up rebelling and shutting down. When a student has a problem, we try to hold their positive qualities in mind and when the situation arises, we encourage them to draw on those qualities.

When I was first teaching in the Ananda schools, there was a six year-old boy, who, as far as I could tell was a compulsive liar. The boy was causing all kinds of problems in the school and I wondered, "Gosh, what do I do?" I thought the child needed a counselor or a psychologist but, of course, there was no one available. So I thought, "Well it's obvious what he needs to learn to do is to tell the truth!" I needed a solution, so I thought, "What do I know about lying?" I remembered the story of Pinocchio! And at first I laughed and I thought, "Oh, what a stupid thing." But I realized that's all I knew about it, so I had to start there. I sat in a circle with the children so that I could see this one boy out of the corner of my eye, and I read the story of Pinocchio. And as we got deeper into the story, the little boy's eyes got bigger and bigger—he was transfixed by the story, and I knew he was having a really strong connection with it. It was exciting. So we finished the story about the long nose and the ears, and I sensed the boy was ripe for discussing his problem. I found the time later that day to talk with him, and we just talked about the difference between lying and truth, and how it was really important to learn to stay in the truth.

For the next step I realized that I needed to be in a situation where I could observe what he did and then talk to him about it. So for the next two weeks I would go out for recess and follow him around from a distance. Then I would call him in five minutes early and ask him what happened at recess. And he would start to tell me. Well, at first it was just off the wall and I would say, "No, I was just there. That didn't happen." Then he would tell me something that did happen.

"That happened," I would say. So I was a mirror for him, and that allowed him to learn to tell the truth. In six weeks he wasn't telling lies anymore. I was stunned at how we could deal with something like that in such a seemingly primitive way. It gave me the confidence that God would provide the tools—that I didn't need to go out and get an advanced degree in clinical psychology in order to help this kid. What I needed to learn was that if God was giving me a problem to solve with these kids, then he would also give me a solution, if only I would just open up and trust in that process. This was a powerful step for me.

When I joined the monastery in 1974, I found myself in a similar situation of having to rely on God to help me organize the monks. I remember Keshava saying to me, "Swami wants to know if you would be the head monk of the monastery." I went down to see Swami a week or so later, to ask him what he wanted done. He looked at me and said, "Nitai, I organized one monastery in this lifetime; I'm not going to do another one." And that's all he would say to me! I didn't know just what to do with that, but it was very similar to how he worked with me with the school. He wasn't going to tell me anything directly.

For the monastery, the thing that seemed most important was to have group meditations. I thought it would be nice to help everybody get up in the morning, so I found an old propane tank and hung it in a tree. I'd go out every morning at 5:30 a.m. and ring the "bell." Then I would go down to meditate in the teepee temple, but no one else came. I was having great meditations because I had to get up and ring that bell every morning. It was good for me so I continued for several weeks.

One morning I thought that since it was a little bit out of my way to go ring the bell, I'd just walk down to the temple—nobody would be listening anyway. So I walked on down, sat in the temple and had my meditation. As I was coming back up the hill, there was Swami out for a walk. Our paths crossed, and he said to me, "Nitai, I didn't hear the bell this morning." I said, "Oh Swami, I just decided that there was no point in ringing it; nobody ever comes. So I just came down on my own." Well, he said, "Keep ringing the bell. Eventually they'll come." So I went back to ringing the bell, and sure enough, over the next few months, people started coming to the group meditations. We got a strong group sadhana going, and eventually there were 30 men living at the monastery. We would go and ask Swami every year if we could take life vows, because we were so gung-ho about sadhana and our spiritual life. Sometimes Swami would give us one-year vows, but he would never give us life vows.

In retrospect, it seems so clear that the dharma of Ananda was to be a householder community. Master already had a monastery at Mount Washington; and Swami would talk about that too, that Yogananda's vision for the next age was to establish world brotherhood colonies and communities. At the time, I could never envision spiritual communities as Kriyananda described them—nobody at Ananda seemed inclined to be householders.

So I would wonder, why is this happening this way? It doesn't make sense. But there was nothing one could do about it, so I just kept doing what was in front of me. In the spring of 1980, I think it was, my excitement about the monastery just dried up. Here I was the head monk, leading the monastery, when all of a sudden I started to lose my inspiration. And I thought, well, this is just temporary. It's just a dry spell. But it went on for about eight months.

Then my life changed, because I got together with Kalyani and went through a lot of inner questioning about what was the right thing to do. When we got to the point of thinking that this is probably the right direction to go in, we went to talk with Swami about it. He was flying in from Hawaii at the San Francisco airport, and we're thinking, "Oh my gosh, what is he going to say?" So he came out of the entryway holding Parameshwari's hand. And I thought, "Well, this isn't going to be so hard after all!"

At that point, it was as if a wave of new energy came through Ananda. What always had happened with householders in Yogananda's time was they could never get the point that the spiritual life had to be first, and the relationship second. So in retrospect we had a whole generation at Ananda getting deeply ingrained in the experience of knowing that the spiritual life, *sadhana*, was first. Then when they got into a relationship, they brought that with them. It helped set the tone, so that when new people came in they could feel that. It makes real sense now, but at the time it was a mystery why everyone seemed to be leaving the monastery for relationships. I can see that it would have been a distraction to have a strong monastery here while we were developing our householder order.

Ananda has given me the experience of having men and women in my life who have shared my spiritual goals and provided role models for me in many, many different ways. It has given me Swami Kriyananda, a spiritual teacher who has personally shown me a deepened and broadened experience of what it means to be a disciple of Yogananda. Kriyananda has incredible enthusiasm, perseverance and commitment to the spiritual path. I haven't met anybody else in my life who has had the same commitment to the spiritual path, or intensity, that Kriyananda has; although there are other people at Ananda who certainly come close.

Kriyananda has never been a guru to me in the sense of an infallible source of instruction. I've gotten enormous inspiration from him and guidance, but it's never been in any kind of automatic, unthinking way. He respected my own need to feel like I participated in the process and could check it out: do I really agree with that direction, with what he said, and that model he has given? And most of the time, I certainly have. But there have been times when I've thought, "It's OK; I'm happy he wants to do that, but it's not my particular direction." He never did the work for me.

Ananda is one example of the higher dimensions of society that are manifest on this planet. To me, Ananda has been a laboratory for people to pull back and work on their inner life. When your inner strength is developed, you can come back out into any situation in society. But it doesn't happen in six months; it can take years, and everyone is different in how long they need. In my own life, I've had a gradually evolving and growing sense of peace and harmony coming from within. And that's what Ananda is all about: it's each person finding his or her own dharma and learning to live it. To the extent that each person does that, then Ananda becomes a better place, a more dynamic place. We're a reflection of the people who live here and their inner growth.

Nalini

I was living in New York City and getting my Masters at Columbia University when I read a newspaper article on Ananda and thought how fascinating it all sounded. A few years later, in 1970, I began living in Berkeley, an open-minded place, and heard about Ananda again through a hatha yoga class I took. At the time, I was working at a place called The Center for Research and Development in Higher Education. A woman I worked with had been to Ananda several times and was a member of SRF. She was from South America, where there is a very strong group of devotees of Yogananda.

I had split up with my husband and, during several months of turmoil, had been praying to God to guide my life and show me my next step. One day, my SRF friend invited me to visit Ananda with her. I said "yes"—intuitively I felt something wonderful was about to happen and my prayers would be answered. After only one weekend at Ananda, I fell totally in love with the place...it was the spiritual family I had been looking for my entire life. I moved here to the Seclusion Retreat on January 5, 1971, with three feet of snow on the ground, during a very cold, snowy winter.

My first home was a little teepee with no running water. At that time, a few people were participating in nude swimming and gardening, which I felt was a hangover from the hippie days of our generation. In the fall of 1971, Swami changed the energy by creating Ayodhya, which was our first monastery.

I hadn't learned about Yogananda or his teachings until after coming to Ananda. In the early days, part of being a member of Ananda was taking the SRF lessons. I attended a number of SRF convocations in Los Angeles, and we were encouraged to visit the shrines. It was only after SRF started saying negative things about Swami Kriyananda that we began to rethink visiting there. Certain SRF monastics would say very little, but a few couldn't seem to restrain themselves. All of this contention was a very disheartening thing. I reconciled it mainly on an inner heart level through a couple of major experiences, one being my trip to India with Kriyananda in 1974.

I had always wanted to visit India and in 1974 the calling for me to go was very strong. I was fortunate to be able to travel there that year with Swami Kriyananda, Jyotish, another man, and Shraddha, (a woman who died about 10 years ago). The five of us all fit in one car, so it was very convenient. Since everything at Ananda was much more Indian in the early days and women wore saris at special occasions, it was easy to feel right at home in India.

The trip over in the airplane was incredible. I remember walking down the aisle and thinking how grateful I was to be on this trip with Swami, that it was such a blessing, and right at that moment Swami opened his eyes and smiled in acknowledgment of my thought. These sorts of things happened throughout the trip. The feelings of shakti power coming from Swami were understated and sweet. I had many very powerful experiences of Divine Love while in his presence. To me, he has a divine sweetness just like Yogananda, and he acts as a channel for that love and sweetness.

Our plane landed in Calcutta, which for a Westerner is the most shocking place in India, yet it is also where Yogananda grew up.

Yogananda's brother, Sananda Lal Ghosh, who wrote *Mejda*, met us at the airport. Master's family welcomed Swami with open arms, totally loving and embracing him, even though he was no longer with SRF. As he walked off the plane, Swami's whole posture and demeanor changed; he became Indian. He seemed more in his spine, and he was vibrating with the idea that this was his home, the land where he belonged, and his joy was apparent with every footstep. It was interesting how a body could say so much, with just a footstep.

Part of my reason for wanting to go to India was to see the woman saint Anandamoyi Ma, who was still alive in those days. Even though I had taken Kriya initiation there was a part of my mind that thought maybe she was my guru, not Yogananda. When we visited Yogananda's boyhood home at 4 Garpar Road, we met many of his relatives. It was here that my concerns about the differences between Swamiji and SRF were resolved in a very profound way. I had a chance to meditate in Yogananda's little attic meditation room, and while there I received a very strong message to "forget about Anandamoyi Ma. Yogananda is your guru and Swamiji is your teacher—your channel for Master—and it's an incredible blessing for you to be here in India with him." After that experience from Yogananda, I didn't even care about other gurus. It was the outward sign I needed.

We did meet Anandamoyi Ma in Hardwar, India, at her beautiful ashram there, where we stayed for three days. She wasn't feeling well at the time so there was some question as to whether we would see her. When we did get a chance to have *sat sangha* with her, she put a garland around Swamiji and gave him some gifts. He likewise showed his love and respect for her. I remember when we had asked spiritual questions of Anandamoyi Ma she answered, "Why are you asking me? Ask your teacher," and she pointed to Swamiji. It was amazing to see the respect and reverence the Indians showed Swami on our visit. Many of them knew him from years before when he used to teach on behalf of SRF in India, and you could tell that he was their major source of inspiration from Yogananda's path.

Through the years, I've served the community in many different capacities. In the early years, my main job was typesetting Swami's books in the publications department, which was in the building that is now Master's Market. The print shop was upstairs, where the healing offices are now. I worked there in small offices with Seva, Lakshmi, Jyotish and Nakula. Around 1972 the new publications building was built. Personally, it was sometimes difficult working there after the monastery formed because I wasn't a nun and a close group of nuns ran Ananda publications. There was no overt conflict between the monastics and householders, but there was definitely a wide divergence in views.

Nowadays it is much easier to be a householder and to be active in the community while still living your life for God. Before, there was a strong sense that if you wanted to find God, you had to be a monk or a nun. Now there's much more emphasis on the family ministry at Ananda, as we've evolved to a householder community. However, the monastery was important because it really helped to cement the spiritual focus of the community.

In my life now, I consider it a blessing to be able to visit Ananda meditation groups and to give by sharing these teachings, leading chanting or working with a choir. When I am serving in this way, I experience firsthand the effects of what Swami Kriyananda means when he says, "The channel is blessed by that which flows through it." When I served as a minister in the Ananda Seattle community, I was put in charge of the choir. It was a lot of hard work—most of it volunteer—but so much Divine Grace came to me as I showed my willingness to put myself in that position.

One of the things I have learned from living at Ananda is that joy exists, goodness exists. I feel the joy we have here is genuine; it is not put on. People here are not motivated by selfish issues. There's a song that Swami Kriyananda wrote that always reminds me of this concept. It goes:

> Is there anywhere on earth,
> Perfect freedom, sorrow's dearth,
> Selfless friendship, blameless birth?
> Cherish these, naught else has worth.

After my sister died, I invited my nephew to visit Ananda. I tried to have activities for him that were as normal as possible: pizza night, a trip to the river, a video. My nephew's comment was, "What's wrong with all these people? They seem to be smiling all the time and always happy; they must be weird." That's just a small example of the cynicism of some when confronted with a place like Ananda. However, at the end of my nephew's visit, he was smiling himself!

Whenever I even imagine living away from Ananda, I'm left with a feeling of stark emptiness. Before I was on the spiritual path, I was a pretty indecisive person, not very centered, and without much sense of who I was. Through the years of working and serving here, my intuition has developed to the point where I can experience it tangibly in my life. For me, the chance to develop friendships with others seeking God has been very important for me. Through the service we all give here, my life has meaning beyond anything I've ever experienced in society.

Keshava

I was attending a university in Vancouver, British Columbia when I became drawn to the whole hippie scene of living in communes. I was attracted to living with other people with similar interests, but most of the people living in communes back then were into drugs. I had a girlfriend who practiced Transcendental Meditation. She was calmer and happier than all my other friends. On a trip to the country to visit other communes I became attracted to living away from the city in nature. While on this trip I contracted hepatitis A and became quite sick. I lay in bed for a few weeks and my life passed before my eyes. I didn't like the way my life was heading. From the moment I came out of that experience I had a complete change of personality. I became a vegetarian, then in a few days I took Transcendental Meditation instruction. Next, I went to a yoga postures class and moved into a living situation with new friends who were all meditating. After about a year, I took a seclusion on a deserted beach and came to the conclusion that my next step was to live in the country with a community of people who were all doing meditation and yoga. I barely knew if such places even existed.

I had heard of Yogananda through a friend I was staying with who was taking the SRF lessons and encouraged me to read *Autobiography of a Yogi*. Then, in 1971 I visited Swami Sivananda Radha's ashram in

Kootenay Bay, British Columbia. After visiting her ashram a couple of times, I became serious about searching for a spiritual community. I returned to Swami Radha's ashram for a three-week stay. It was quite small, about 20 full-time residents, and most of the committed people were socially conservative and much older than I was. While I didn't feel a real connection there, I did see the value of group meditations and being in satsang. Swami Radha, seemed to me very mental and intellectual, but also seemed spiritually evolved and doing something that I admired. I respected her sincerity and courage. I had an interview with her and asked her if I could live in the ashram. She said that many had to work outside and send money back. She suggested that I work and save $1,000 and then return to live in the ashram.

Coincidentally, exactly one year later I came to Ananda where the membership fee was $1,000 and you were asked to bring it with you when you came. I had heard about Ananda while I was staying at Swami Radha's ashram, and it was on my list of about a dozen spiritual communities to visit. I had also picked up Swami Kriayananda's yoga postures book and his book, *Cooperative Communities*. While I was in San Francisco visiting different ashrams, I went to a birthday celebration for Sai Baba at his ashram and one of the two speakers that day was Swami Kriyananda. I felt a subtle deep attraction to Kriyananda, the tone of his voice, his graciousness and his love.

I still remember my first image of visiting Ananda at the farm — there was this beautiful cooperation of people working together. It was as if the people seemed to work together harmoniously, without anyone telling them what to do; they just did it. Jaya, Shivani and those who worked in the garden all seemed so willing to serve. There was a strong sense of selfless service in action. I didn't see a lot of egos clashing as I had in other places I visited.

My first job at the Village was working for the incense business. We would buy the unscented sticks, dip them in the scent of essential oils mixed in alcohol, soak them in cake pans, then "teepee" them to dry out for a few hours. I also worked for the macramé business, which was quite popular for a while. In 1977 Swami Kriyananda had asked Jyotish if I could become his secretary and get used to writing correspondence under his signature. It was an incredible experience for me to be Kriyananda's secretary for eight years. I learned from him by osmosis, seeing him in action with other people. He was always consistent, either alone or in a crowd of people. He was selfless, even-minded, always gracious and reaching out, never showing anger or desperation or retreat, even when others were draining him. He always talked to us about understanding others, and being sensitive to their needs.

My fondest memories of the early days of Ananda are of just being with Kriyananda, though it was not always easy. His energy level was very demanding and he never slowed down. I tried to tune in to his vibration as I wrote letters for him, and I learned subtly from him each time. I lived in the monastery, in a little trailer that had a small altar and meditation area. I was just about the last one to leave the monastery when it began to dissolve in 1981. In 1984 I went to Italy to help start the first Ananda community in Europe.

Inwardly, I have found all the different Ananda communities in which I have lived spiritually the same. People's souls, Yogananda's presence, the lessons we all need to learn are the same everywhere, just as it was when I first came to Ananda in 1972; only the outward trappings are different. Living at Ananda's community in Assisi, Italy was the most different and challenging outwardly, for me on the physical and mental plane, because you were always a foreigner, and there is a barrier to overcome before you can relax with people. However, I found the Italians marvelous to work with because they are always on a heart level, so it is easier for them to focus on Yogananda's teachings from a devotional aspect. They also seem to attune to spiritual teachings without a lot of intellectual questions. I felt a natural attunement to Italy and it was easy for me to make friends there.

In the 1980s Ananda also had a spiritual connection with Peki, another spiritual community in Italy. Peki started as a charismatic Christian group whose members were attracted to Yogananda and to Kriyananda. We felt an immediate bond with them. During the first months in Italy both Ananda and Peki members worked together to run our retreat in Como. I fell in love immediately with a woman in the Peki group. When Peki and Ananda went their separate ways, it was traumatic for both of us. We separated as our spiritual paths diverged.

In 1990 I returned to Ananda Village and then moved to Ananda's Palo Alto community in the San Francisco Bay Area. This is the right place for many people. There is a balance here between individual privacy and group living in a thriving spiritual community. It has a wonderful sense of group belonging.

Being connected with Ananda has been real joy. Communities like Ananda help break down societal barriers that we erect with our minds—be it from loneliness, lack of self-worth, or just all of the pain and suffering that people go through in their lives. So much of that can be transcended by living in community, because you realize that God is much stronger than any limitation. Through living in spiritual community other people become mirrors for the best that you are, and they become examples of overcoming limitations. When you are all seekers working for the same goal, the ties are closer than even that of most biological families. I think people in general in our society are very lonely. What I've learned living here is that through affirmation and increasing magnetism it becomes easier to focus on the positive, on the light. Once you choose positive qualities and goals, they become automatically drawn into your life. It's the simplest thing.

Ananta & Maria

Ananta

My parents were the ideal examples of living one's religion. They loved everyone, and they were forgiving and caring. My father was a scrupulously honest businessman, I saw him return money to customers who did not even realize they were owed it. We were Irish-Catholic and went to church every Sunday and every day during Lent. I was an altar boy and very much interested in the search for God. I knew I wanted to have the same ideals my parents did, but not within the trappings of Catholicism.

In the late sixties I began to feel that I would not have a religious experience within the context of the Catholic Church, and began to turn to Eastern religion. I visited all the swamis and East Tibetans who came to San Francisco during the sixties and seventies. I liked the fact that yoga addressed the body, mind and every aspect of our lives as a conscious venue for the search for God. My mother loved Yogananda's poetry, and my father respected Swami Satchidananda and other teachers I studied with and even learned to meditate. My parents were never sectarian in their outlook. Truth was their goal and they respected others' cosmology.

I was taking courses in levels of consciousness at Stanford University in 1971 when I first read Yogananda's autobiography. I had remembered seeing his photo on the album cover for *Sergeant Pepper's Lonely Hearts Club Band*. His picture was there along with those of Babaji, Lahiri, and Sri Yukteswar. I remember wanting to know who those people were. Later, after reading about Yogananda and seeing his picture I knew he would be my teacher.

I joined the SRF organization, bought Yogananda's books and studied the lessons. For a while I lived at Yogaville, Swami Satchidananda's ashram in Lakeville, California. I went there because of my interest in living in community with people working towards an ideal, in harmony with nature, building cooperatively and avoiding materialism. I had not heard of Ananda, but had always wanted to start a community myself based on Yogananda's teachings. I knew about Swami Kriyananda from his yoga postures book, and when I found out he had a community, I decided to visit.

The practice of the science of religion is the search for happiness in a very real way. I chose to live at Ananda because I knew people there were seriously seeking God, and that finding God would make them truly happy and fulfilled. I could see they meditated every day, and that they put into practice the higher principles of yoga. Everyone was doing yoga every day; it was not a put up job. I could also tell Kriyananda was a serious follower of Yogananda's work by watching the way he worked with people, with the community, and the explanations he gave. He never held out anything but the principles of right living. He showed us how to stick to our principles, even when it's difficult. And he never considered what was easiest, but what was the right thing to do.

My first job was in the garden, working for Haanel and Shivani. I understood that I was a disciple and that Shivani was my superior. For a boy with a Catholic upbringing this was no problem; I knew the drill. Eventually I became the senior gardener under Haanel, who was a master in his own right. Haanel had been an English teacher, so he corrected our English when we spoke. He taught us that to be great you had to learn discipline. At that time, most of us were not mature enough to understand the need for work and discipline, and the garden taught us that.

We met promptly each morning at 7:30 for our garden meetings; 7:31 was late. We had five acres and a four-person staff. There were 40 different crops of vegetables and berries and 60 different types of herbs and flowers; we grew about six tons of food each year. Haanel had created a biodynamic garden because he'd been a student of Dr. Ehrenfried Pfieffer, a biochemist who studied with Rudolph Steiner. The soil was horrible, and it was not the best climate for a garden, so it was a place that we could put the teachings to work against insurmountable odds.

Like the spiritual path, gardening takes an enormous amount of self-discipline and years of hard work. We were practicing Sister Gyanamata's aphorism and, through gardening, testing our religion in the cold hard light of day. With hard work the garden's organic material was increased and its production was more in line with a normal garden. The garden was a huge effort, and many of the apprentices couldn't stay with it. We kept expanding the garden, then added the dairy. Working at the dairy was hard as well, hand-milking the cows, hand shoveling manure, and picking up the hay by hand. We were basically using farming methods of the 1800s in the 1970s. All this hard work was analogous to the amount of effort required for the spiritual life. Most of the gardeners were in their twenties with little understanding of the spiritual path. The garden was a great environment to learn about obstacles, determination, humility and the effort required on a spiritual path.

Every night, Haanel would tell us that when we went home that night to meditate, we should give everything in the garden back to God. We had to learn *nishkam karma* — to not be attached to the fruits of our labors. It was wonderful to have this perspective from an older gentleman who had studied Yogananda's teachings for many years and was willing to mentor us in the garden to temper the enthusiasm of our youth. Ananda was a place where one always had to balance idealism with reality without losing the vision of living one's life for God. Since I was also living in the monastery I had to truly put this into practice; giving everything to God and not owning anything separate from God.

On one level, everything one does is for spiritual growth and the spiritual harmony of all sentient beings, yet Ananda wasn't going to take care of you, feed you, clothe you, or even provide you with housing. We all had to build our own homes, or bring in trailers or teepees. What Ananda did was give us the opportunity to serve God while still meeting all our worldly responsibilities. In the early days, Swami Kriyananda had to teach a lot of classes and find ways to raise money just so that Ananda could exist to give us the opportunity to serve God and grow spiritually. Kriyananda once gave a talk to the monks and told us that our responsibility in this community was to serve the householders. We were to be in charge of the children in the schools and Sunday school. Since we had no family responsibilities to fulfill, we were free to serve as educators or to run the garden that paid no salary because parents had to work to provide for their children. We could dedicate ourselves more completely to God by serving God and the families.

The goal of yoga and the goal of Ananda is to free the ego and to free the consciousness from identification with the little self. So to serve selflessly, to serve the larger family is to serve God through seeing God in all beings. When you serve in the garden you're not

Weeding and cultivating the comfrey patch in the early '80s.

doing it for profit, or for the produce, you're doing it for the ideal of being in harmony with organic gardening and to provide wholesome organic produce for the community. In whatever job we did, the goal was to serve God in serving one another. This was what Kriyananda taught us. He could have gone off by himself and written his books; he didn't need this community. He created Ananda because Yogananda had the ideal that families and community would set the tone for this age. Spiritual communities would be an opportunity for America to solve the isolation of the modern age and to cure the incredible dysfunction between materialism and spirituality. There is no dysfunction if you learn to harmonize spirituality and materialism.

Yogananda's vision for spiritual communities was to have job, home and church all in one place. There was no competition between people at Ananda because we all learned to see our work as service. It just so happened that Shivani, Maria and I were the best gardeners, Nakula was the best dairyman, and Jaya was the best planner. Later on we started switching things around. Swami would have us get together as a group and work in different areas of the community to help us learn that every part of the Village was important. This taught us to appreciate everyone and to be more flexible and willing to change.

Yogic theory says that our suffering and unhappiness comes from our identification with the ego, which blocks our knowledge of ourselves as the soul. In reality, we are all souls, spiritual beings. We unfortunately identify with our position in the world, how much money we make, our job description, our possessions and our status in life. By identifying so strongly with these worldly ideals, we limit the soul's level of joy to the level of status we have achieved. The idea behind living in an ashram is that the selfless service we give helps free us from worldly identifications.

When people would arrive at Ananda with preconceived ideas that they were the best publisher or the best manager and that they could "save Ananda" it was always like a bomb waiting to explode. Their ideas might be great in a worldly setting but were not accepted here because spiritual ideals were held in higher esteem. That was the great lesson of the garden—there was no profit, no success. The income of the garden one year was $2,400, which means that six people worked 40 hours a week, 50 weeks a year, and each person earned $33 per month. We were learning spiritual discipline, the principles of being free within oneself and non-attached. The garden was a great place for new members to work because it was a training process for selfless service. It taught us to disconnect from what we have, or what the world says we are, and to identify with our soul. Once we were strong in this concept, we could go back into the world and have material success yet not be attached to it or need it to be truly happy.

Everyone at Ananda was dedicated to learning to find our highest level of divine potential. We were all meditating and learning to practice non-attachment and inner joy. Ananda was a happy place, and we kidded ourselves about not having anything. The nuns were always giggling, yet they lived in trailers, with water that was akin to apple juice in its color and consistency because our well back then had so much mud in it. They were totally fulfilled and never felt lacking in anything because their inner work was to identify with spirit, to be loving and kind.

Sometimes people have unhealthy ideas about what being connected to a spiritual community or a guru is. There are stereotypes that society and others have created about living in a community, the main one being that we work in a hierarchical structure where someone always tells us what to do. No one tells you what to do on a daily basis. The only advice Kriyananda gave us when we started the

Sacramento community was "Talk to people from the heart, not from the head." He was asking us to be ourselves and talk from a point of love, and connect with people where they're at. My wife and I have run the Sacramento community for 13 years and we've never been told what to do or how to do it. I remember once an investigative reporter said that he had "gotten behind the scenes" and discovered that Kriyananda, Jyotish and Seva had written the bylaws in such a way that they could take all the money from Ananda and leave. I was asked about this, and I said, "What is there to take, the teepees or the outhouses or the 55 gallons of compost?" A worldly person looks for power rip-offs. I always remember the saying that when a pickpocket sees a saint, he only sees his pockets. The reality is that no one here is being abused or ripped off. The saints see only the good. Whenever people from Ananda visited Mother Teresa in Calcutta, she saw only beauty. Mother Teresa loved to hear the Ananda people sing.

Another misconception people have is not seeing the integration of material wealth and responsibility with the spiritual path. People tend to think it's "either/or." We constantly have to remind people that renunciation is an inner attitude. People think we have no furniture in our apartments, and that yogis don't integrate, we insulate. Or they think we're not interested in beauty. Other times it's hard for people to see the spiritual life as being integrated into a happy, fulfilled, prosperous, joyful existence. There's a Kali Yuga approach that says you have to totally renounce the world to seek God; if you're in the world you won't find God—but this is not what Yogananda taught. Ananda is one spiritual community that is proving that householders, families and single people can find God.

Ananda has taught me that true happiness comes from living in tune with God. Whatever your religion, your spiritual beliefs or your faith, if you live more for God and with God, everything else will work for you in this life. For me, God has manifested as love for all beings, as inner peace, respect, calmness, light, beauty, and truth. Even an atheist can live for higher ideals. Now that I have a strong inner relationship with God, I'm free to be who I am and share with others on a much deeper soul level. The more I'm on this path, the more I'm able to embrace all spiritual paths, which is one of the hallmarks of Yogananda's teachings.

Over time, the principles being affirmed and demonstrated here will be an example for others to emulate, but it will take time. There needs to be more unity among religions. I have no idea how long it will take before the inner aspects of religion, like selfless service, love for God and non-sectarian truth, are going to percolate out into society. The fact that this hasn't happened yet is not our concern. We have to work hard on ourselves and do our part, however small that may seem. Right now we're having fun, serving God and reinforcing those energies in society that promote harmony and unity.

Maria

My grandmother was a woman who was way ahead of her time. She was into health food, spiritual living and philosophical openness. I grew up in Pacific Palisades in southern California, and my family used to have Sunday brunch at what is now the Maharishi Center for Enlightenment, which is right next door to Yogananda's Lake Shrine on Sunset Boulevard. I remember afterwards feeding the swans at Lake Shrine, because in those days it wasn't all fenced in. The place felt very comforting and we loved being there. It wasn't until I visited Ananda and saw a picture of the Lake Shrine in *Autobiography of a Yogi* that I realized it was a shrine built by the great yoga master, and that his presence has so surrounded me as I was growing up

It was during my second year at Lewis & Clark College that I was introduced to vegetarianism and yoga. I met a fellow student, Garth

Gilchrist, who was also interested in meditation, and a small group of us would meditate together. When I expressed a desire to learn more about yoga and meditation, Garth suggested I join the apprentice program at Ananda. I understood I needed a support group for learning meditation.

The first weekend I visited Ananda, they were celebrating Kriyananda's birthday with a huge campfire and talent show, followed by a dinner of spaghetti with vegetarian meatballs. I was in awe of the sheer physical primitiveness of Ananda in the seventies. I was somewhat intrigued by the ideas I had heard and by people who were vegetarians, yoga practitioners or living in ashrams. It was all very new to me and yet familiar. After finishing college, I returned to Ananda to live, thinking I would stay for just one year. I worked with Shivani in the garden and lived in a tent in the "temple of trees." The women and men lived separately. We had satsangs in the temple, and I remember my first meditation being 20 minutes long—which back then seemed like an eternity!

The first year I worked in the garden at Ananda I didn't even get paid, so I worked in the incense factory at night to earn wages. I lived in a little yurt which I and my friends built, and worked in the garden each day. When the apprentices were at Ananda, there would be as many as 50 to 60 people working in the garden.

We often didn't have much to show for our hard work. Sometimes the plants would get diseased or flooded or frozen by a late frost. If you were the type of person who needed to see the results of your work, it just wasn't there. It was the ultimate lesson in non-attachment.

In retrospect, it was the way of life and looking for God that made me happy at Ananda. When I first came here I didn't even know what a guru was or even why I should be searching for God, but when I got here and found those things they all made sense. The second year

I was here, my mother sent me a package of things that had belonged to my grandmother. It contained books by Yogananda, Anandamoyi Ma and Gandhi. It was a touching sign that gave confirmation to the spiritual step I was taking and that these teachings and Ananda were my life.

When I first lived at Ananda, I stayed at Apprentice Village for a few months and then I wanted to move to the convent. I had met Ananta working in the garden my first summer at Ananda. He had long hair and a bandanna, and I wondered who was beneath that outward garb. He was living in the monastery at the time, and I admired him quite a bit. I thought if he could live the monastic lifestyle, so could I. Living in the monastery, we only saw each other in group settings. We worked in the garden for a year and a half before our friendship began to feel different. We both really loved being in the monastery and it was a difficult decision to be together, because we had such support to stay in the monastery. Not many people were pursuing a relationship then, and we caused quite a stir. We didn't want to minimize our spiritual commitment, but we did want to be together. It took some time for us to be attuned to what we were feeling and what was best spiritually for us both.

Ananta and I worked in the garden for 10 years before moving to Sacramento to co-direct the already existing center and to eventually start a community in the city. Living in an urban setting is different in an outer context only. We came here with the same idea of selfless service, so the principles we live are still the same. Our challenge is to serve God by teaching people the principles of selfless service, meditation, joyful living and the unity of all religions. With a group of about 50 people, we own an apartment complex where we can dine together, meditate together, and share the spiritual life and our love for God. We even have a little vegetable garden here. In the early days, working in the garden at Ananda was a *tapasya*, an impossible situation. We had to learn to trust in God that He would give us what was needed. Now, we have the opportunity to put into practice all the same yogic principles. The spirit is the same; only the form has changed.

Vidura

I first learned about Ananda after I had been divorced for a couple years and was raising my two children. Having gone through the trauma of having the normal middle class lifestyle fall apart on me, I was seeking a more fulfilling way to live. It was the early seventies and I was living in Berkeley, experimenting with yoga and meditation. I had read Swami Satchidananda's book on Integral Yoga Postures, which was a book that introduced many people to hatha yoga. I also got involved with Transcendental Meditation.

My love for the outdoors encouraged me to take a class in "Edible Plant Life and the Evolvement of Spring, from Death Valley into the Sierra Nevada Mountains." During this class I met Durga and we developed a friendship. At that time she was involved with a yoga group and was attending their meetings and retreats. We eventually started living together and pursuing our mutual interest in yoga.

In the early seventies we both attended a conference in San Francisco called The Meeting of the Ways. Kriyananda was sharing a speaking platform with Swami Satchidananda, whom I always respected, and Yogi Bhajan, who taught kundalini yoga. I was very impressed with Kriyananda, and his interest in cooperative communities. He talked about Yogananda's plain living and high thinking principles, which I felt very drawn to.

We eventually moved to Ananda in the summer of 1974 with our two children, Melissa and Dwayne. Our first home was a tent at Ananda's Seclusion Retreat. We lived on Sunset Boulevard, which was a fancy name for an old dirt road we all took to view the sunsets on Bald Mountain.

Since I had been a successful construction worker, I was able to get work outside of Ananda. I also had savings that allowed us to live the simpler Ananda lifestyle. The first nine years at Ananda I worked four to six months of each year away from the Village. At one time I even worked on the Alaskan pipeline. As a householder, this worked very well for my family. Unlike the city, there wasn't much economic structure here that could support families. My working outside the community allowed Durga to work or volunteer within the community and it offered my children a chance to grow up in a beautiful rural environment.

The development of children at Ananda differs from other places mainly because we use the *Education for Life* principles, based on Yogananda's teachings. We honor the uniqueness of each child and work to draw out his or her highest potential not by pushing, but by leading. Common sense values like kindness, love and honesty are instilled at a very young age so the children can learn to incorporate these values into their own way of being.

I first began working for the community when Kriyananda asked me to help build the Crystal Hermitage. He had received an inheritance from his father and wanted to build something that the community could also enjoy. Before Ananda, I had worked in the highly competitive environment of general contracting, which meant getting the job done at the lowest cost was the bottom line. Here at Ananda I entered a whole new environment where concepts like "People are more important than things," and "Instill everything you do with God remembrance" were being practiced. Ananda is a big experiment in how to achieve these principles and survive on a practical level. There has to be a balance between the spiritual and the practical, a balance that helps us draw the best from both.

Bringing these concepts into the workplace is achieved by first bringing them into your consciousness. We would begin each workday in a circle with prayers and dynamic affirmations. We would stop at noon and meditate for a half hour. We encouraged everyone to be high-minded on the work site. For instance, we would try to help someone who had the spirit but not the efficiency to do a job, and we would try to create a space for them to grow. We worked hard, but also had fun. This is a path of joy, so we were trying to stay loose while doing the best we could. These principles can change your whole outlook on life when put into practice.

Seeing one's work as service ultimately means not being attached to the fruits of your labors. The attitude with which a person performs his work allows him or her to serve God through that work. It's reflected in how he treats people he comes into contact with through his work, and even what he does with the fruits of his labors—like tithing. Bringing the proper attitudes of being positive, energetic and enthusiastic to whatever one does is one of the ways we work here. The old adage "Act enthusiastic and you'll be enthusiastic, feel enthusiastic and you'll be enthusiastic" contains many of the principles of yoga. Keeping the energy high, in the upper chakras, and being expansive and serviceful are other important attitudes we try to incorporate while working.

My favorite jobs at Ananda are projects that can be manifested on the physical plane. I suppose my background in construction finds fulfillment in concrete things! My strength lies in the ability to find people who can do what I cannot do, and then to support them, give them energy and empower them. I have been fortunate to work with a lot of people here I felt attunement with and trusted. Projects happen here through the magnetism, love, support and energy of a group of us working to serve a greater work, serving God.

In order to create magnetism you need to rely on a few basic principles: magnetism is produced by having energy, and you must have enthusiasm yourself to inspire it in others. As a good leader you must be willing to roll up your sleeves and dive right in with the rest of the workers. If they believe you're committed at this level, there are very few people who will not be magnetized as well. However, you cannot project on others your own style of magnetism. You can only help them perform to their highest level. First, you must magnetize yourself to your highest level. If you look at the great saints like Yogananda, they always used their spiritual practices to generate the magnetism they needed.

Ananda's success goes right to the heart of cooperative communities. Here, there are people who share common spiritual goals that enable us all to be in tune at the deepest spiritual level. This allows us to communicate on a soul level and accounts for harmony amongst people. Our spiritual connections give us a unique willingness to work together despite more superficial personality differences. Common spiritual goals have given us the strength to grow through many kinds of trials. We go to the temple and worship in the same way and we develop an attunement that allows us to work through difficulties without becoming unraveled at the surface.

I am always surprised at the fact that Ananda still exists. I have often wondered if we could make it this far. From a purely business perspective these principles probably seem surreal, but there has been a level of Divine Grace that has also helped us. I think the universe has responded to the sincerity and dharma of our position. We still have to work hard, which we do, but there is a divine spiritual connection that allows us to move forward as a family. I've also never felt that Ananda has reached its final form. We're adaptable. Our willingness to take a fresh look every day at the situation that confronts us allows us to be adaptable—even if this means changing preconceived ideas.

From a political standpoint, the core values of Ananda very much represent the early values that America was founded on—in God we trust. Kriyananda laid down the principle that the primary job of the spiritual director of Ananda is to guard the rights of the individual. He once said, "You do not exist for Ananda, Ananda exists for you." When you have many people enacting this principle, people look out for one another. For instance, the primary role of a minister here is to put the needs of others before his own.

One of the major turning points for me occurred when Kriyananda suggested things for me to do that he knew would help me grow and I balked at them. I remember I was driving the Joy Singers around the country and had said "No, thank you" to another tour. He asked me privately about going on another tour, and told me the work needed me to do it. This was a great turning point for me because, all of a sudden, it shifted me from thinking about doing something for myself to realizing that I had a way to serve a person from whom I had drawn so much inspiration. It was a major test for me. I had to sacrifice making a big income and do something I didn't really want to do. But everything worked out well. I retired from a lot of opportunity and income I could have taken advantage of, yet I have still had a life that's wonderful. I've traveled all over the world, and I was able to raise my children in a great environment. I don't have any money in the bank, but Divine Mother and God's grace has kept me in a fine style. No other way of living would allow me to have the time, freedom and the satisfaction of having done something meaningful with my life beyond just working and acquiring material possessions.

I do miss the days when Ananda was a much smaller, more intimate group of people. It seems that now we have the dharma to demonstrate the viability of this lifestyle to others. In order to do this, we've had to raise our living standards to a level that would be more middle class. This has put a lot of stress on us financially, and it has taken a lot of work. The earlier, simpler lifestyles here just wouldn't be suited to our current dharma.

I would hope that there is something that mainstream America could learn from communities such as Ananda. What really makes a community like this work is not a particular list of things. There are attitudes that exist here, ways of dealing with people and principles that make it work. The main attitudes are the basic tenets of our core belief system: service, attunement, guarding the rights of the individual, and people are more important than things. I don't believe that people can live this closely together for so long without a core belief system. Even the way we govern the community has been divided up with a spiritual director, a general manager, and an elected Village Council. All have influence, but ultimate decisions go to the spiritual director so that everything is viewed from a higher, spiritual level.

One of the most important lessons I've learned here is how to serve. The way to break the cycle of personal troubles or worries is to get out of yourself and to serve others. Then watch the transformation. The people here are the fruits of an effort to live the spiritual life to the best of their ability. There are not a lot of saints here, but there are many trying to live in God-remembrance. It is a great privilege to live amongst people with this level of fellowship, brotherhood and connectivity. I have 200-300 friends whom I could trust with my life. I know they would do anything within their ability for me. That is God's response to us, as God works through people around us. In the whole cosmology of yoga, people are the greatest instruments through which the Divine can flow.

Lakshmi

When I prepare food, I am very aware of chanting and meditating and the conscious flow of energy from my hands into the food. Cooking and nurturing are two inner things that offer me a way to share and give to others. One of the ways I made my living here was baking cookies. I would bless every tray that I put in the oven and say a prayer for the food. It was real interesting, because people who were allergic to sugar would say, "I can't eat sugar, but I can eat your cookies, and they don't affect me."

In the early days, and even now at the retreat kitchens, we chanted, prayed and meditated before we started cooking for the day. Throughout the cooking process, we'd play tapes of spiritual chants or music. The idea was to uplift our awareness and improve our state of consciousness so that the same energy could flow through us into the food we were preparing.

Before Ananda had more people living here, Kriyananda used to chant and sing a lot more. He's very sensitive musically, and we used to have these beautiful kirtans all the time. I've had spiritual miracles happen here that are very deep and personal. But my first real experience of God came during a kirtan that Swami led at the Whole Earth Festival in Davis. We were chanting to Rama, and I had an experience of God consciousness then, an actual expansion of aware-ness that came to me through chanting.

I came here in 1970, and until 1986, when I married Purushottama, my strongest spiritual practice was *japa*. Chanting, or repeating the name of God, helped me focus on God. Chanting opens up the devo-tion of the heart because you're singing songs of love to God, and that can be the most powerful thing. It helped me to get stronger in my realization that God is always present for me and that God is love. And it taught me that, through every test and trial, God is always pre-sent.

I started out as a single mother, so I naturally had the physical chal-lenge of needing to earn an adequate living. In the early seventies, I made $60 a month working at the retreat, and while money wasn't such a big issue back then, every dollar was! The hardest time for families was during the time of the monastery. If there was a satsang and Swami was be giving a talk, I would often need to leave with my two children. I remember once walking through the forest in tears, just needing to be with my kids alone. When you're a single mother, you always need to be with your children.

I have been a parent now for 25 years. I like all the paraphernalia of spirituality, and I certainly expose my children to it whenever pos-sible. But it's also important for parents to set good examples of right attitudes and to spend time with their kids. I've found that with chil-dren, they need to move outward. So in our family we talk a lot. I try to be present for their questions, and I try to instill attitudes that will lead them to a higher spiritual potential.

With my first two children, I really fought to maintain a daily sad-hana, and to some extent I think it was really hard on them, because I would always shoo them away and tell them that they had to be quiet; my meditation time was really sacrosanct. I felt a great deal of pressure to meditate, because Swami was urging people at that time

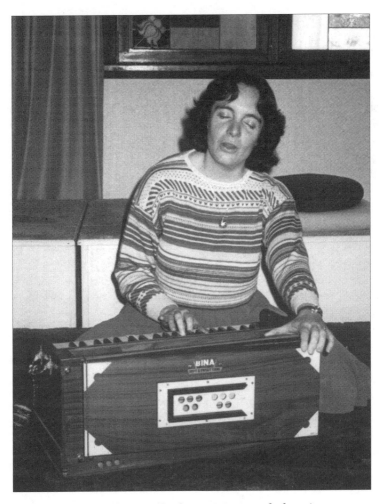

Lakshmi playing the harmonium and chanting.

to meditate three hours a day. Because I had so much emotional turmoil, I used to spend a lot of my meditation time in tears just sort of offering the dysfunction of my life up to God.

But over time, I thought, "Well, I just give everything to God, my ability and my inability." I thought that if I could just hang on to the desire to even *want* to meditate, then that intention is as important as actually meditating. What most people don't realize is that there is much more to yoga, meditation and the spiritual path than just doing the spiritual practices.

There was a man who lived here once who probably meditated more than anyone. But meditation can also be completely egotistical if done with the wrong attitude. If you think, "I want God-realization for myself, and I don't give a damn about anybody else, because it's all just a dream, and other people aren't important anyway," then it's a trap. Since he left Ananda, he's spoken against us in the most malicious ways possible. So I don't see what hours and hours of meditation does for anyone if they're not also learning service, compassion, love, and non-judgment.

Yogananda said shortly before he died, "*When I am gone, only love can take my place.*" He was saying that only love can teach us what we need to know. What he meant was that no person, no scripture, no word can give us our truth, because truth isn't something that you can say with words. Truth is an intuitive understanding within your own self, and you can only reach that when you're in a state of love. *Love is the ultimate teacher.* To love unconditionally is the highest thing you can possibly do, and all the yoga, meditation and spiritual practices are merely tools. Meditation is simply a tool to internalize one's consciousness and free one from attachment to the world.

When we first started the Village Council, there was a small group of people who basically ran everything. We would have meetings and the phrase, "What's trying to happen here?" was ever-present. Before each meeting, we would pray and meditate, and afterwards we would all say what we thought, and try to reach a higher level. We didn't argue to get our individual points across, but we would always try to work cooperatively to do what was best. That's one of the important goals of living in a spiritual community. To try to put into practice, in a very conscious way, the principles of love and truth.

Bharat

When I was a young boy, I spent most of my free time in nature. I started reading Thoreau when I was sixteen, and soon became a vegetarian, and began to spend a lot of time on my own, trying to figure things out. Many times I could feel a deep stillness in nature that was quite joyful for me. I remember Thoreau said that all wisdom is the direct result of either conscious or unconscious discipline. When I was about 18, I knew I needed to meditate; so that's what eventually brought me to Ananda.

I grew up living right near the Feather River bottoms and would get up every morning at the crack of dawn to go running there. On my runs sometimes I would go right through the marshes and continue on. I felt an expansive, exuberant joy in nature. Migrating swans, ducks and geese by the thousands would be flying overhead and the whole sky would be moving. Once I was riding my bicycle at the Gray Lodge bird reserve when a flock of 250,000 snow geese erupted all at once and filled the entire sky with their bodies. It was an incredible roar; I think there is more life energy in a marsh than anywhere else on earth. These experiences were so dramatic for me that, to this day, I have always felt a deep connection with nature's energy.

John Muir said that Nature, God and Beauty are all synonymous. In the late-'60s I was spending a lot of time in the wilderness feeling the stillness of nature, and I wanted those same feelings inside of myself. I'd been interested in sharing nature with various groups: the Boy Scouts, the National Audubon Society, school districts and outdoor education camps. This was a very big part of my life, yet at the same time, I wanted to go deeper.

I joined a Zen monastery at Mt. Shasta in 1972. I really liked it there; the monks had a strong sadhana and they often meditated 10 hours a day. I remember walking through the snow with a young resident monk my age named Eko. It was the middle of winter and quite cold, with the wind coming off the mountain. Eko and I were feeding the goats when I noticed him glancing at his watch. I thought, "Aha, maybe it's meditation time, and we can get out of the cold." So I asked him what time it was, and he turned to me and said with a smile, "Just because I made a mistake, I'm not going to let you make one." And then he turned around and just continued walking on through the snow.

Whenever the postulants would go into town (we'd go one afternoon every two weeks), the senior monks would just walk along very focused, and then they'd go into a store to buy things like boots, etc. Meanwhile, many of the new postulants would hit the ice cream store and eat as much ice cream as they could! I remember one postulant coming through the monastery gates trying to finish three ice cream cones at once before he entered the monastery grounds. I also remember digging for weeks through snowdrifts and frozen ground searching for an underground pipe. We never did find the pipe but the work was very good for learning not to be attached to the fruits of our actions! There was a wonderful quality there of trying to go beyond likes and dislikes. The monks didn't talk about devotion, but by getting rid of the likes and dislikes, they were establishing purity of heart.

I enjoyed the Zen monastery and gained a lot there but knew it wasn't my ultimate path. I had visited Ananda briefly and liked the people there. One day while I was in the High Sierra mountains, I was sitting on the ground overlooking a lake being very, very still, and feeling a very deep peace. The thought came to me, "I am going to go to Ananda." I acted on my intuition and hitchhiked to Ananda.

I was standing on Route 49 in the rain, outside of Nevada City, and waited three hours trying to get a ride to the Ananda community. Finally, a little green Volkswagen pulled up alongside me, driven by a man in his late forties. I got in the car, and he seemed like a long lost friend. We talked. He asked me about my life, and I felt I could tell him everything. He was like nobody I'd ever met before; I remember feeling extremely joyful in his presence. Then as we turned onto Tyler Foote Road and started getting closer to Ananda, I looked at him. He was wearing a beret. I asked him, "Are you Swami Kriyananda?" And he was. He said, "I normally don't pick up hitchhikers, but I thought you were going to Ananda." A sweet part of this story is that the car we were riding in had been given to Kriyananda by my future wife, Anandi.

When I came to Ananda I lived at the Seclusion Retreat and for several months did various jobs to stay on. There was a grain mill factory in Kali Lodge, where we would assemble home grain grinders. I was not very mechanically minded; that's why I have said I became a ⋆naturalist! But I did what was available to earn a small income. The men lived at Kali Lodge, which at that time didn't have glass in the windows. At night the wind would roar through there; that's why we named it Kali Lodge, because it was so terrifying at night. There was a beautiful simplicity to Ananda in the early years, and material things just weren't important. I was really enjoying meditation, and I wanted to be in a place where that was prized above everything else.

I had to wait to become a member before I could join the monastery at Ananda. The monks had a little teepee temple and we would have five-hour meditations every Saturday. The most memorable part of the monastery was the strong camaraderie of energy we all shared. Once we decided to have a retreat called "48 Hours in Eternity." We stayed awake for 48 hours, meditating and doing *sadhana*. By the second night we had to energize three times in a row to stay awake! It was the middle of winter, yet the energy came to such an incredible climax that after 48 hours a group of us went running through the manzanita to swim in a nearby pond.

One of the monks had a cave with a cabin built around it. So Nitai, Agni and I decided to dig pits in the ground that we called caves, and covered them over with logs and dirt. The caves were insulated from the restless vibrations that regularly pass through the open air and so were very conducive to deep meditations. I remember having a 12-hour meditation in my little dirt cave. It was so easy to meditate there.

Joining the monastery was a wonderful way to come to Ananda, because we were developing our own relationship with Divine Mother and Master first, and finding joy inside ourselves. With marriage, what can so often happen is that you look to your spouse for your happiness. At the monastery, our focus was renunciation and getting rid of likes and dislikes, which was wonderful training for the marriages that did happen.

I remember giving a Village tour for a young man when Anandi and Parvati walked by (they were nuns at the time); he waved to them but Anandi and Parvati didn't respond at all, and just kind of scooted along. My male visitor asked, "Aren't we supposed to talk to the nuns?" I explained that to keep your focus as a renunciant you had to be impersonal and reserved when interacting with the opposite sex. Eventually, the community became more open and out-wardly expressive of our love to others, because we were trying to do something different from traditional monasteries. The change to a householder renunciate community allowed us to be freer in express-ing our energy to one another.

The most important thing at Ananda is one's relationship with God. You have to develop that whether you are married or a monk. Often the problem with relationships is that people become attached to having things be a certain way. Once we approached marriage from a spiritual perspective, there was nothing more important than our love for each other and our friendship. We just weren't that attached to having things a certain way. I really saw that in Anandi; things just didn't matter, and she could change her energy immediately because harmony was more important. That came from her training in the monastery. So when Anandi and I ran the program for new members we always told people to first develop their spiritual relationship with God, Divine Mother, with Ananda, and with inner peace. Then, when you get into a new relationship or some situation in your life, you'll have something tangible to compare it with. And you'll know if it is bringing you closer to God or just fulfilling a desire.

When I first joined the monastery in 1976, I asked a friend if he would write a book about the method of nature education I had been using, since I thought a monk shouldn't be authoring books. He, however, didn't have the time to do it. I felt very strongly that the book should be written, because I had seen how children and adults responded so favorably to the games and activities I had been using. While writing *Sharing Nature with Children*, I thought of it as my last gift to the world. When I started, I didn't really know much about writing. What was so beautiful about living in a cooperative commu-nity was that I had lots of help! I like to think that my first book was really a community project. I worked on it for over two years. I found

Bharat playing nature games with Ananda school children.

an old board in the forest and nailed it into my little trailer. There, with pencil and paper, I wrote *Sharing Nature with Children*.

During this project I was meditating a lot, and I remembered Swami saying that if you tune into *Aum*, you will tune into the source of all creativity. I was writing 10 to 14 hours a day, and kept myself fresh by putting my elbows on the table and doing the Aum technique for 20 minutes at a time. I didn't have a publisher, but fortunately money came in as a loan, so in 1979 we printed the book. At this time, the United States was just becoming receptive to experiential education with nature. My book showed that learning about nature could be fun and joyous. It also emphasized learning with one's intuition and heart.

Yogananda said that intuition is soul knowledge; we never can really understand anything unless it's through our intuition. He said that science describes, but with intuition you perceive. Science can only see things through the senses. But everything is united in spirit, so that to know nature you have to know it through spirit. You do this through intuition. *Sharing Nature with Children* got people in touch with these concepts. It used multi-sensory activities, and what I found later was that this stopped the thinking process. When the thinking process stops, then, in the stillness and calmness, people aren't focused on themselves, but are open to the world around them. This makes people more expansive. As you do this, you feel more love. So the book helped people get in touch with nature in a much deeper way.

In the early '80s I started my *Sharing Nature* work, and now I travel throughout the world lecturing and giving outdoor programs. Our goal is to help people experience a sense of unity and harmony with all Life through joyful nature activities. We feel this is essential because when one's consciousness is uplifted, one's perception changes. And when their perception changes, their behavior changes.

It's been a challenge balancing my work and my spiritual life at Ananda. I remember when Swami asked Anandi and me to go to Palo Alto to be the ministers in the early '80s. I was just getting ready to write my second book when he said, "Your work is wonderful and it's a wonderful business for Ananda. But you've come to Ananda to find God and I have to honor that." I've found that the best way to support my outer work has been to be in tune with the flow of the community, and to feel that my career is really about growing closer to God.

For example, when I went down to Palo Alto, I taught the meditation classes. Out of this experience came a very important book, *Listening to Nature*. Taking advantage of the opportunity God offered helped me deepen my own meditations as well as deepen my approach to sharing nature with people. Over time, I've learned to do my work with a sense of freedom, a sense that God is doing this through me. Working in this way takes away the sense of personal tension and attachment in trying to build this work, and so it's a lot more enjoyable.

I've found that God will use other channels too, and that's how Sharing Nature Worldwide has happened. In fact, the man in Japan who has organized our work there has devoted his life to helping spread this work. Divine Mother wants this world to be beautiful, so by keeping Her first, She will then provide other avenues for people to help. More and more I trust that. And more and more I've really seen the beautiful results of living for God first.

The greatest benefit of living in a spiritual community is of course satsang, being around like-minded people. I have so much enthusiasm for *Sharing Nature* that it's important for me to be in this environment to go deep spiritually. It's also important for me to be around people who share my highest aspirations. And through this experience I've been able to carry it into my work and my books.

Worldly activity exists mostly on the conscious level, and that's the level of the mind, and the mind is always separating and distinguishing. There's no sense of underlying unity when one thinks this way. By having a more spiritual, more unitive view of life, you see how things come together in a harmonious whole. And so I've found that by tuning in spiritually, by using one's intuition, we're able to understand things in a much higher, clearer way.

One thing that we've done at the Village is to put all our houses in clusters, so our impact on the land is much less. I find that everybody here loves nature because meditation expands our personal boundaries beyond ourselves. When people first came to Ananda, they all built homes far away from each other, because they were used to living in the city. Then we found that our "neighbors" were actually very nice people and it was fun to share our lives with each other.

All the years I spent at the Seclusion Retreat have given me a special bond with the land. Living there puts you away from everything; there are no businesses, no traffic, and the vibrations there are totally still and serene. It's a small retreat where people are living very simply in little cabins. It's very wild and the deer, the birds and all the animals live right along with you.

We've built this community with a sense of self-offering to God, and with a sense of responsibility, but not that WE are the people to do this for the world. Swami has told us to not take what we are doing too self-importantly because God will ask somebody else to do it if we decline the task! Yogananda wanted to have world brotherhood colonies where people of all walks of life could find God. At Ananda we've tried to bring to manifestation a way of life that will inspire people out in the world and let them take their inspiration and express it in their own way. When Yogananda came to America from India, he brought the essence of yoga, and he left all the cultural trappings behind. He called his work Self-realization, which means to inwardly experience of God. The techniques of Self-realization can be used by people in any spiritual tradition, which removes the barriers that religion often creates.

In a traditional monastery you try to give up your will, in order to get rid of your ego. But what Swami Kriyananda has done for Ananda is to teach us to use our will, but in expressing God and letting God be the doer. We're taught not to be afraid of self-expression, but to tune in to the source of infinite power and allow that to come through us. So I've always prayed to Divine Mother before I started a project.

When people begin to really tap into spiritual energy, they start to become more creative, their magnetism increases, and all of a sudden opportunities can come to them. And there's a strong temptation that often comes to the *devotee* to think, "Gee, I could go out and do all these things." Nothing, of course, is good or bad in and of itself; only if it expands one's consciousness and takes you toward God or not. By being in a more protected setting of a monastery, worldly opportunities don't come as much. So the trick at Ananda has always been to keep your clarity and purpose in mind. You can have discrimination if you keep your goal always before you. And by being able to be around other people who see that goal very clearly, and feeling their joy, their love for God, then you want that, too. You have to do more to keep your focus, but because you have to do more, your strength is greater.

It doesn't work when people come to Ananda and are only interested in certain aspects of Ananda, like our schools or community. If they aren't interested in the inner spirit, they will eventually leave. As a small community, Ananda can't compete with the world—with the latest technology or the latest salaries. When people aren't honest with their spiritual life and they haven't had a chance to process what they believe or what kind of person they are, it's often hard for them to maintain a strong momentum here. For example, I've seen a couple of cases where young men were seemingly doing everything right spiritually, but in their minds they were actually trying to please others, rather than please God. You can only do this for so long. More and more what each of us are trying to do is to develop that deep sincerity of relating to God directly.

I found out very early on that Kriyananda's view of me was a lot more exalted than was my own view of myself. I realized that he knew me better than I knew myself. The beautiful thing about the way Kriyananda works with people is that he helps you to become strong yourself. As he says, the greatest yoga posture is the one that helps you stand on your own two feet.

I remember when Roshi Suzuki died in the early '70s. There was a funeral in San Francisco, and all the Zen teachers were there. Zen Buddhists center their energy on the third *chakra*, the will center, and they're very, very strong. They were coming into the funeral room in lines, marching in like warriors—the energy was so strong. And one of the Ananda monks looked, out of the corner of his eye to the side, where a person came walking in with energy like a little child. It was such a contrast. He looked again, and it was Swami Kriyananda. The energy was so different because our path's focus is on the heart, and his energy was so sweet and childlike. At Ananda, we focus more on love than the will center; and we try to purify that love and bring it to the spiritual eye, the point between the eyebrows.

I've seen people visit Ananda with an attitude of "Well, I may not be perfect, but I'd feel a lot better if my teacher was perfect." This attitude says, "I don't have any personal responsibility or power." I've learned to trust my experience of Kriyananda, rather than putting him in kind of a mold, because he is much greater than that. I've always looked at my relationship with Kriyananda as one of divine friendship, because friendship is more unconditional. Otherwise your

Bharat leading one of his famous nature treks.

relationship becomes one of doing business, and not of learning to express the divine qualities that your teacher can inspire in you.

Often a person wants to be special and feel he's above the next person, or thinks his religion is better than others. Along with this thinking comes the tendency to think that you don't need to make the personal effort, if your teacher or your religion has status. The important thing is not to dwell on whom you're affiliated with, but to bring those qualities into yourself. And you do that through unconditional love, respect, and divine friendship with somebody. And then your friendship is genuine, and you have gratitude for the teacher as he is and not for his role. And because you are concentrating more on giving than getting, you receive more.

Yogananda wouldn't tell people things; he would have people *do* things. And in the doing, people would put out the right kind of energy that would change their consciousness. So at Ananda we all have things that we do for our self-offering; that self-offering purifies us and changes us. And then we have spiritual practices that we do. In the beginning, Kriyananda, being much more experienced, had to do everything; but he now has stepped into the background more and more. And now we're running the community ourselves, and so he has enabled us to grow strong ourselves.

Kriyananda has taught us, through his example, that it is better to be a good disciple rather than a teacher. This has inspired the whole community to be better disciples. And discipleship means ultimately to be open to life and to a greater Reality, which is an attitude that keeps one pure and expansive. Yogananda never took personal credit for the Divine Power he felt. Once when one woman was denigrating him by saying he had lost all his powers, Yogananda looked perplexed and said, "I never knew I had any power!"

I remember when I was first learning to meditate. I was in college and I had one roommate who was very cynical. As I was meditating, he walked by and said, "What are you trying to do, become a saint?" And the way he said it made me first think, "Well, no, not me!" But then I realized, "Well darn it, I *am* trying to become a saint." And I realized the importance of being around other people who encourage our highest aspirations. I think it would help people greatly to create a situation where their higher aspirations get nurtured and where they can grow further into them.

Uma

As I walked into the meditation temple, I could hear the sound of Aum permeating the room, yet it was totally quiet and not one person was talking. I remember creeping in very reverently and sitting near the back. During my first moments at Ananda, in the silence of the Seclusion Retreat temple, I knew that I was home.

After the meditation and service a vegetarian lunch was served to everyone in the Common Dome. There was a table in the middle of the room and a group of women all dressed in yellow ate there. I asked who they were and someone told me they were nuns. Another deep sense of being home touched me. After I had been at Ananda for a couple of months I went to Seva, who was head of the convent, and asked if I could join. I ended up being in the monastery for about six years. I lived (as did most of us) in a tiny 15-foot trailer with no electricity or running water, but what a wonderful sense of freedom and simplicity. What a blissful time. We meditated and energized together daily. The nuns did practically everything as a group and those years hold a very special place in my heart.

My first year and a half at Ananda, I lived at the Seclusion Retreat and worked in the kitchen as a cook. My first home was a tent in the woods. When winter came I moved into Gayatri House, which was a woman's dorm with about three or four little cots, very simple and ·

rustic, but I loved it all. My third home was a little six-sided cabin in a meadow. I remember building a porch for that cabin because the rain would just blow in the minute you opened the door. I had helpers, but I drew a plan, took measurements, got wood from the Sages sawmill, cut it myself, built the porch, put the roof on, the works! Now, guests who take seclusion at the old retreat use that same little Lahiri cabin.

After my time at the Seclusion Retreat, I moved to Ayodhya, the name for the land that housed the monastery. I now had a new job working in the school. I was the "house mother" for the girl's ashram. I had about eight girls ages ten to twelve. I boarded with them during the week, and they would spend weekends with their families. Our ashram was located in what is now the Village Office. It had a big kitchen, a few rooms and a larger room that I converted into a dormitory with bunk beds for the girls. My bedroom was a little corner of the living room. The idea of the girls' and boys' ashrams was to give them an experience of the spiritual life at Ananda. The children in the ashram knew what the purpose was and wanted to be there.

My whole experience working with the girls' ashram reinforced the idea that you need to help children sit up and pay attention to life, and that limits and boundaries are important. Having been born and raised in England, I felt that in my bones, so I created a structured environment from the very beginning. The girls didn't have a second that they weren't scheduled. In the morning, they got up, attended sadhana, had breakfast, and got ready for school. After school, we had sadhana together, did homework, made dinner together, and cleaned up. I very consciously kept things tight before I would loosen up on the rules.

I tried to find ways to get the girls excited about meditation. I remember trying out an idea where they would sit cross-legged, facing each other with their eyes closed. They would sit very quiet and still. Then one of them would think of an image or a number, and the other would try to guess what it was. It was a great little experiment, because they really concentrated and listened inwardly. It worked. When they weren't still and focused it didn't work. And during the process they were meditative for about ten minutes or so.

We had lots of extracurricular activities for the girls. There were horses in the village barn that we could ride, and sometimes we'd take these long walks all over Ananda. Bharat, who'd written *Sharing Nature with Children*, had lots of nature activities for us to do. And once a month I would take the girls to town, which was a big deal in those days. We'd have pizza or ice cream or go to a movie.

Once the entire group was being really naughty, as if they had planned it somehow. Over and over again I kept warning them, and finally said, "We're not going to town." Our monthly sojourn was coming up in two weeks. So I said, "If you don't stop, that's what I will take away." And they didn't stop, so I said, "OK. We're not going." Time passed and they began asking when we were going to town. And I said, "We're not going." They all went wild. They did everything they could, hoping I'd change my mind, but I kept my word. The next time they were misbehaving, all I had to do was *mention* not going to town and *instantly* their behavior changed!

I remember one winter there was a day when I had a terrible time getting them up for school. They were all grumpy and uncooperative. I called up Nitai, who was the school principal, told him what their behavior was like and said I was keeping them all home from school. I let them remain in their nighties then made toast and cocoa, and we sat around and talked and played games.

One of the principles Yogananda taught was to be very impersonal, yet still come from the heart, from love. I really did let the girls know I cared about them. I tried to impress on them the importance of the spiritual life. Just sharing spirituality with them in a very gentle way, and being concerned for their little souls, brought us all very close. They asked me, "Did you ever have a boyfriend? Were you always a nun?" And I said, "Of course not, I have only been a nun for a short period of time." Being with me in a natural context allowed them to see me as a normal person who happened to have a spiritual life. Before long, they were leading Energization Exercises and leading chants without me having to constantly prod them.

The girls learned to care for me, as well. I once stepped off the stairs and twisted my ankle. All of them came to help me up. I thought my ankle was broken. In the middle of the night, I called Kalyani, and she took me to the hospital. The girls really did have to help me because I was laid up and on painkillers for quite a while. They were so sweet and helpful, I was so proud of them. Today from time to time, I still run into about three of my former alumni. They're all lovely young women, in some cases with families of their own. They fondly remember their ashram experience in amazing detail.

After running the girl's ashram, I worked for Kriyananda for about five years. I helped him with projects—music, slide shows, photography, I cooked meals and took care of his home. Working for him was a great blessing. I learned so much, on so many levels. I could always feel him giving so much energy to me, to others, and to building this community. He was gracious, courteous and kind. He was also very disciplined, concentrated and crystal clear. His personality is very cultured and refined, he has a pure heart, an impish sense of humor and is always a loving and sincere friend and guide.

I remember noting, and being deeply impressed, that Kriyananda never missed Energization Exercises, which Yogananda recommends practicing twice daily. I would often work near him from early morning until late at night, and sometimes I'd walk in and he'd ask, "Did you energize yet today?" and if my answer was no, we'd energize together. It was a rare opportunity to observe this great soul at close quarters and in such every day conditions.

Watching him and understanding him on inner and outer levels was, and continues to be, a source of true guidance in my life. There were so many valuable lessons learned and insights gained. I would often jot down something he would say, and always wished I had a tape recorder, even though it wouldn't have been appropriate most of the time.

Ananda and Kriyananda have taught me to think of others, and not just myself. We are a *cooperative* spiritual community. We try to think of others as much as, if not more than, ourselves. We may not have a perfect relationship with a neighbor or co-worker, but our teachings encourage individuals to try and work things out harmoniously and respectfully. Individual responsibility is a very significant part of cooperative living. Refusal to live in harmony with the spiritual goals of our community disappoints people who come here expecting to live as they have in the past. If we don't at least try, with good grace, to see God coming to us in the circumstances and events of our life, people become resentful, and want to blame everyone else for what is wrong. If we don't work on ourselves, it can become too difficult to be here.

In some ways, Ananda is not much different from any other community. We go through all the same ups and downs of humanity — birth, death, marriage, divorce, upsets and estrangements between friends. But we deal with them differently because of our spiritual focus. We try to live Yogananda's principles of yoga, simple living, high thinking, self-control and cooperative obedience. We live in relation to, and not just independent of, each other. I think of the Amish, who also live cooperatively. They help each other. They don't need any insurance, because if a house burns down, your neighbor comes and helps you rebuild. That's Ananda. It's a very wholesome and holy way to live.

The spiritual life is all about developing faith and trust in God. Meditation helps us in this because we begin to understand that our inner life—feeling God's presence, knowing His love and joy—is what gives life meaning and depth. When you can look at yourself as the cause of what ever goes on in your world it makes you humble, which opens your heart. I love the line from Kriyananda's song, *Shawl of Gold*, where he writes, "...it's kindness that softens the human heart." Giving to people, selflessness, self-control—these qualities strengthen us and open our hearts. When our heart is open we meet all the circumstances of life with love. Of course this doesn't happen overnight, but even wanting to live this way changes our life.

Over the years, I've watched friends here go through all the challenges of life. People faced with death, disease, betrayal, "all the woe that flesh is heir to," but they face it with nobility, faith and integrity, not with blame or resentment. Their trust in God remains strong, even when the thing they hold most dear is being attacked. You can't pretend faith and integrity, it shines out. These things speak to the heart and soul and have continuous power to encourage and inspire.

Ganesha

I remember one night visiting a far-out anthropology professor in Sacramento in the late sixties. He played a recording by Alan Watts called *Aum, the Sound of Hinduism*. When I heard Alan Watts talk about Hinduism he made it all sound so cosmic—he was talking about these vast ranges of time and space. And I thought, "Really, people believe that and work with that as a spiritual teaching. My! My!" This was my first introduction to Eastern thought.

In the fall of 1970, I began a yoga class series offered by Swami Kriyananda at the YWCA. Toward the end of the class series I visited Ananda's retreat which Kriyananda had started in the foothills about two hours northeast of Sacramento. I remember thinking, "These people really know how to live." I was really impressed by the quality of the people I met. There was a lack of pretense and an openness and honesty which I found refreshing.

I began to have an increasing desire to live at Ananda and be in a spiritually supportive environment. It was the best way to live that I could imagine. At this time I was also feeling a pull from my job and friends that was taking me in another direction. I had learned to meditate yet didn't have enough time to meditate. I wasn't keeping the kind of company that Yogananda had stressed was necessary to support one's spiritual life. There was drug use among my friends. I thought, "If I blow it and fail to get out of this situation, in ten or 20 years I'll kick myself for not having made the move I knew I should have made."

I did move to Ananda, just before Christmas of 1973. Ananda had recently purchased an additional 326 acres and was applying for a use permit from the county, which had reevaluated our status as a "church camp." They decided we were a "planned development" which required a master plan and an environmental impact report. My first job was to help Sam Dardick and others produce these documents. I studied pit privies, compost privies and methane digesters because it would be far too expensive to develop the necessary infrastructure for flush toilets.

The county said we needed more water, septic tanks, and a whole lot of things we didn't have. We were used to having outhouses and simple dwellings. I remember going to the county planning department to talk to them about how we wanted to develop Ananda. I don't think I was very successful in persuading them that we could live without septic systems. We eventually made the switch from outhouses to septic systems. This whole experience taught me a lot about how to build our community, but it wasn't my real purpose for being here. I wasn't here to develop compost privies or to concentrate on alternative energy solutions. I was here to meditate, to learn to serve selflessly and to grow spiritually, and the rest was just a byproduct of trying to live a simple life.

By their very nature, spiritual communities seem to foster experiences that help us grow spiritually. When Saraswati and I were first married, I had this habit of reading a newspaper quite a bit, and she had mentioned that she had a problem with this. Once, we were working in the recording studio next to Kriyananda's home, and I had the opportunity to go upstairs and talk to him. I thought, "This is a wonderful opportunity to talk to Swami." When I got upstairs he was reading a newspaper. I'd say something and he'd just give a one-word response or something and continue reading. It was obvious that any of my plans for a conversation would be an intrusion. I thought, "Gosh, this must be what Saraswati must feel like." And I looked at him, and I thought, "Is he doing that on purpose? How could he know?" I reasoned later that he was in some kind of flow where he could reflect back to me a lesson without even being conscious of what he was doing, because he was so conscious of being with God.

One of the most comforting things I've learned here is that all people are children of a benevolent God who truly does love each of us individually. Yes there are events in life, even mass events, that may look bad. But it's not a roll of the dice, it's not just who's in line to get slapped, or who's in line to get rewarded. I believe there is a conscious plan that's special for each one of us that is administered by a benevolent consciousness; a loving, helping consciousness. If we have to go through hard times, we do, but knowing that God is loving us and not delighting in torturing us helps us to see events in another light. Fear and anxiety are cancerous. I've learned not to worry, and this is very freeing. There was a time many years ago when we were running the Sacramento ashram and the events in my life were horrible. I remember thinking, "This is great. How much worse can it get?" Because my spiritual life was strong, I wasn't as worried about the outcome of events. I think society promulgates too much worry. Could there be a nuclear war? Could we have a pole shift? Could we have sunspots? Could we have earthquakes, volcanoes, aliens? Whatever it is, it *could* be true. Spiritual teachings show this could be true; reality is very broad. Whatever it is, it's managed by a God or consciousness that's all-powerful and that loves us.

One of the ways I've always enjoyed serving here is in the dramatic arts. The culture at Ananda is unique because it's been created by our own residents, not society at large. Popular culture can be such junk. It's here to a degree, but we also have so much other culture going on that is available to us. We have our own plays that we create and perform, we have different types of dance, and we have our own music. We try to create cultural activities that are healthy for the mind and the soul. We try to emphasize activities that are uplifting and elevate the mind or give more challenge to thinking rather than pulling one down into sensuality and lower enjoyments. That doesn't mean we don't have humor. There's *lots* of humor here, but we're not getting it from television programs that are crude and uninspiring. Many of the shows on commercial television aren't very uplifting, and I think that's why people here are discouraged from watching it. If it wasn't for the lifestyle that's available here, I would probably be very much into popular culture!

An enjoyable chapter in Ananda's performing arts began for me after seeing Happy Winingham and her players present a P.G. Wodehouse story one Christmas many years ago. Happy was a professional actress who lived here and directed much of our theatre. (She recently died after a ten-year battle with AIDS.) I told Happy how much I enjoyed the play and the next time she did a P.G. Wodehouse production, she called me up and had a little part for me. It was perfect because I work all day as an engineer at Beale Air Force Base and I was grateful to have this little project that connected me with other Ananda residents. This got me out of the house and communicating with others. The fun of performing a play with friends was so enjoyable.

These simple, wholesome activities of people sharing and connecting can set the stage for the deeper bonds that humans need and crave. What we have here constitutes a common sense approach to life. The problems of loneliness or feeling separate are big issues in our society. At Ananda you have two hundred friends, many who truly care about you and your spiritual growth.

When I look back over 24 years of living here, there's so much that I can now take delight in seeing. Just driving up a paved road and thinking, "This used to be a peanut butter road in winter for so many years and we finally got together and paved this thing." There's the sense that *together* we created this road, or we created this building, we created this community, isn't it beautiful? Come Fourth of July, people are down at the Village square celebrating, and there's not one person who's drunk or being obnoxious or contentious. What a relief it is to have a lighthearted, innocent celebration of unselfconscious patriotism. Or, to have a group of people gathered together to meditate—a roomful of people who are absolutely quiet and giving all their energy to helping themselves and each other with the spiritual pursuit.

Hridayavasi

I received my spiritual name from Swami Kriyananda when I got married. In Sanskrit, Hridayavasi means "the Lord dwelling in the heart." I had an immediate attunement with it, yet it's taken me years to fully understand why he gave me this particular name. He usually gives a name when you have similar qualities to it, but also when there's something that you need to learn from it. I've seen the meaning as something I'm aspiring towards, pointing out lessons I need to learn.

Every so often someone will ask me what Hridayavasi means, and that always makes me contemplate deeper. I begin to want to meditate on it and discover what it means for me *now* as I interact in my daily life. I come back to the thought of learning to expand the love in my heart from a personal love into a vast love for others, and then finally into a love for God. My name has always been a reminder of a beautiful quality to aspire to.

I had a strong spiritual upbringing. My grandfather was a Congregational minister and we went to church every Sunday. It was a big part of my life, but the only time I felt connected in church was during communion or singing certain hymns. I could sense there was always something more I wanted from religion, but I wasn't sure what that was. My answers came in nature. I discovered I could feel Divine Mother's presence not in church, but in the beauty of nature.

I grew up in Illinois and my mother's family were farmers. We had a farm that had been in the family for over 100 years. That farm was what kept me going when I was a kid. I felt unhappy a lot, I felt displaced, I felt—what was I doing in this world? But I could feel uplifted just by being by myself in the woods or in the cornfield. I could feel a Divine presence there that was so peaceful and fulfilling.

When I came to San Francisco in the early '70s, it was just past the Flower Child days and there were a lot of stores where you could find metaphysical books. I was interested in yoga, meditation and astrology. During this time, I read *Autobiography of a Yogi* and I found Kriyananda's book, *Your Sun Sign as a Spiritual Guide.* I read about Ananda from the back of the book and decided to visit.

The quiet and peaceful vibrations of Ananda struck me right away. I came up for short visits several times over a period of a year and a half. When I first moved here I didn't come specifically for the spiritual teachings. I was more interested in community life. After I had been here for two months, I met Govinda, who helped me focus even more on Yogananda's teachings. We'd read his writings together and we'd meditate together. Without that it would have been very easy for me to slip away during those first months. Eventually, I began to realize that there was a lot more to Ananda than just a community of like-minded people. I began to meditate more and to learn how these teachings could apply to each moment of the day.

A couple of years after we were married, we left Ananda for six months because Govinda was feeling like he needed another environment, a smaller place. We wanted to look for land to start a small community. We happened to be staying in Santa Barbara during the time Ananda's Joy Tours came through. I loved everyone from Ananda and I felt so sad inside because I thought I had made this huge mistake in leaving and that everybody was going to judge me. But my heart just drew me to see all my friends again and I attended their music program.

To my surprise, everyone was open, loving and accepting of us. The judgment I was expecting was my own projection; it never happened. When I saw Kriyananda he asked, "What are you planning to do?" I said, "Oh, we want to buy land and start a little community." He said, "Well, that sounds good." He had total acceptance of us. After the evening's program everyone from the tours left. They were all staying at the Sunburst Community, which was run by Norman Paulsen, who had also lived with Yogananda.

Somehow, Kriyananda's keys got locked in his car and everyone else had already left. It was about 11:00 at night and the only thing we could do was ask him to come home with us. I was very nervous, but Kriyananda was just totally flowing with what needed to happen, like a child. Here he had no change of clothes, no toothbrush, and he was coming to my in-laws' house with us, where we hoped there was an empty bed for him. It turned out that Govinda's 12 year-old sister was gone and she had a room with a canopy bed. At the time, I was pregnant with my first son, Ramiah. Kriyananda helped me put the sheets on her bed then he said, "Does your father-in-law have some pajamas that I could wear?" There were no pajamas from my father-in-law but I remembered that Govinda's grandmother had made me pajamas for my pregnancy that were huge and had big roses all over them. I said, "Swami, I might have something for you." He thanked me and then returned shortly modeling my pajamas. "What do you think?" he said jovially. There was so much joy and depth in his eyes, I barely know how to describe it. There was more total acceptance and love flowing from his eyes than I'd ever seen before from anyone.

From that point on I didn't feel bad about being away from Ananda because I felt his love no matter where I was. The next morning he came out in my big rose pajamas again and did Energization Exercises while the whole family was there. He was as natural as could be. That experience was a turning point for me because I began to see who he was on a deeper level, beyond his outward personality. And after six months of traveling around looking for smaller communities, we returned to Ananda.

Before we left Ananda, and before I was pregnant, I worked in the garden. I started as an apprentice and loved it. The garden was huge back in those days. Residents in the community could pre-order their produce. On harvest days, which were twice a week, we would make little boxes up for everybody. When I first arrived, Parvati had just started the market. I think she started it by buying a huge box of oranges. It was an important addition to our community and over time she added bulk items, produce, and a variety of things.

In March we planted the lettuce and spinach and all the early crops. The area where the swimming pool is now was the tomato garden. Along the side was the herb garden. All the apprentices worked in the garden, because we needed all that labor to keep it going. People worked in the garden all year long, with summer having the largest staff.

For the winter we'd raise potatoes, squash, carrots and beets and then store them in root cellars. We also sold produce to places in town, and sometimes we'd take produce into the farmer's market on Saturdays. Financially, we always made it somehow. In the early days, we had next to nothing. We didn't have credit cards. We just lived from little paycheck to little paycheck. There were no car payments to be made because people shared cars. I used to hitchhike to town to do laundry. It was a much simpler lifestyle.

The first winter I was here I went to Oregon with a group of Ananda members to plant trees. We had high expectations of being able to make money for our individual membership fees as well as

Preparing the garden for planting.

make money for Ananda. And of course, it just turned into a "learning experience" where many of us did not make much money at all. I went up as a cook for six weeks. We stayed in these big army tents and it rained and snowed all the time and at one point a nearby creek even flooded our tents.

In retrospect, that whole episode was all about knocking off our rough edges and teaching us non-attachment and action without desire. Our struggles and tests bring us closer to God. If we take our tests in the wrong way and become bitter, we can't learn from them. But if we see it as Divine Mother just trying to chip away at the rough edges to show us where our *real* security lies, then we began to understand how God teaches us.

Anyone *can* find God, but that is easier said than done. In one sense it should be effortless, but in another sense, it isn't; it is a struggle. As we go through all the different tests life gives us, and we go through them with the right attitude, we get stronger. Do I choose to live in anger and bitterness? Or do I choose love, acceptance, non-judgment and understanding. There's a beautiful sense of freedom that comes when you let go of your expectations and attachments and trust in love.

Living here has given my two sons a really strong background for being able to bounce out into the world. They are now both teenagers, so I think that's what they're doing—bouncing out into the world; they need to. One of my sons once told me about a friend of his. He said, "Gosh, his dad doesn't understand him and he says things to him in the wrong way. My friend gets real mad and they're always fighting. His dad doesn't understand that he shouldn't talk to him in that way." So we talk about being able to appreciate what we have in comparison to the situation that his friend has. And we talk about how *we* treat our friends, so that my son understands compassion for others, as well.

I have always been interested in children and I'm currently the school principal. In the early days of the school, Nitai, the original teacher and administrator, developed curriculum and methods to foster spirituality and help build positive values in the children. He worked on ways to help them be loving, balanced, centered, and to understand other people's realities, so they learned compassion and selflessness, besides learning academics.

Many great teachers and administrators have added their talents and love to the school over the years to make it what it is today. The priority of our school is to help raise balanced and happy children who can become spiritually as well as academically successful. Classes are limited to only twelve kids, and with each one of those kids you've got to be aware of them on the deepest level.

What has been the greatest benefit of living in a spiritual community? Living for God. I just feel happy and complete inside. Money, power, recognition, and material comforts are things that do not affect my happiness. The work that I've done over the years in my meditations, even if it's sometimes just slugging it out, has gradually changed me. Through meditation I've learned how to go inside for my answers, my guidance and, ultimately, my happiness.

Agni

One of my first childhood memories of God and religion is of a minister ranting and raving that all the people who didn't follow Jesus were going to Hell. And he was citing different people from around the world, the Chinese, the Africans, the people who aren't into Jesus are going to Hell. I was frightened. I was about six years old and I was standing out on the street afterwards with my mother, who was holding my hand. And I just had this strong thought that God wouldn't be like that. He couldn't be like that.

The day I first arrived at Ananda, it was raining, and I had driven up to the mountains in my little Volkswagen. I remember getting out of the car and smelling the kitkidizzi, feeling the moisture in the air. I was instantly aware of the stillness of nature and the trees. And there was a feeling in my heart like I had arrived back home—a real warm feeling in my heart. The first thing I heard was Kriyananda chanting Yogananda's *O God Beautiful*. We were in the little dome temple, and I was struck by all the people singing. It was like angels singing. It was such a *beautiful* thing. It was one of the strongest memories that I have from the early years.

I knew from the beginning that I wanted to be a monk. I moved to Ananda and asked for an interview with Kriyananda. He was writing *The Path* at the time. I asked him for Kriya initiation in that interview, and I asked to be a monk. He said yes to both requests. I wanted to move to the monastery immediately, but he reminded me afterwards that I also needed to go through the process of membership. When I came, there wasn't any kind of apprentice program. So I lived for six months at the Seclusion Retreat. It was one of the best times of my life.

I stayed in what looked like a hobbit's place called Shanti cabin. It had a little platform for a bed, a little desk, and a kerosene lamp—no electricity, no plumbing. It was very simple. It was quiet there, and so very restful. I immediately shifted from all my past worldy concerns to just having the time to read the lessons, *The Path*—which was being written—and to read *Autobiography of a Yogi* again. It was a time to absorb myself into spirituality.

After six months, I moved to the monastery. The men I met there were all such wonderful people. They had integrity, energy, and they were so selfless. I think that was the thing that struck me the most. The magnetism they had created by living together enabled me to join into that energy and benefit from it. All we wanted to do was to serve God and build something for other people.

One of my favorite stories from the monastery was about Dinanath's house. He had built a teepee platform, and on the platform he decided to build a house. So he went to a lumberyard and bought some green lumber, which weighed a ton, and were very short pieces. He built this cabin that had eighteen-foot walls. It was jury-rigged, the whole way it was built. He didn't have the money to buy roofing boards and plywood, so he decided to put all these 2 by 4's sideways to create a roof. Well, it weighed an enormous amount. It was on the side of a hill, on a teepee platform, with 18-foot walls and a giant ceiling that was extremely heavy. It was quite a structure!

It was also the biggest place we had. So we would have our monks' meetings there. One evening, about 25 monks were in his house, so there was that much more weight on the platform. In those days, a lot of us didn't know about building codes for structures. Dinanath had built his teepee platform out of pine logs put directly into the ground with no treatment. By this time they'd been rotting out, and by natural law, the house should have fallen over! Well, the next morning, when everyone was out of the house, and he had just left for work, the whole thing just fell down the hill! It just completely destroyed everything that was in the house. We were all sure that someone was watching over us because, with all the extra weight in there, it should have fallen down the hill that night.

One of the other monks built a house that was so little, all you could do was just kind of sit in there. You'd sit up, and you'd have this place where you could meditate, and you'd have to crawl around in this little space. It was the tiniest thing I'd ever seen; it was like a mole's house!

The fellowship of other monks was really the most meaningful for me in those days. And being around Kriyananda was always a learning experience. He showed me how one could be so deep in the teachings yet so practical about being in the present, by doing what was in front of him with no pretense. Once I was in the dome with him, and he was cooking; he was boiling a potato for himself. In those days there were cracks and crannies in the building, and little critters got into the houses more easily. It seemed a frog had crawled into the cupboards and he and I were trying to find it, because every once in a while it started croaking. Then, Swami looked right into the pot on the stove and said, "Oh, my gosh, what is that?" And in the pot next to the potato, actually it was bigger than the potato, was a huge green ball of slime. It had come down through the pipes from the spring box (a hole with wood around it) and was in the pot. He turned to me and said, "You have to do something about this."

So I talked with Nitai and Haridas, and we decided to have a monks' work day. All the monks went up and we pulled the top off the spring box, and it was filled with green slime—it's actually a moss. But floating around in the water we found a dead mouse, and we didn't know how long it had been in there! That was the water supply for all of us! We never told the nuns. We just threw it out. We cleaned the spring box and I think it was about a year later that we finally put in the correct equipment to hold and seal our water.

The other things that really touched me were the times when Swami did ceremonies. He did a blessing for all the monks; he gave people vows. We talked him into it and Nitai had been asking him to give us vows. And Swami wouldn't. He wanted our commitment to be more in the heart, and not just an outward statement. So we finally got him to say he'd give us vows. He said, "I don't want to give life-time vows. That's a tremendous commitment. And I don't feel that people are ready to do that." And it's interesting, because it was about five years later that people started to marry. I always wondered how he had the insight to know that, in time, the direction would change for all of us.

Several years later, after the monastery began to evolve to a householder order, I noticed that the committed monastics who were getting married all seemed to be really dynamic couples. In turn, this set an example for the community and has drawn to the community people who are dynamic individuals wanting to live as householder monastics. When you create an energy like that, it attracts people who have the same kind of energy.

What does it take to really find God, to find enlightenment? The conclusion I came to was that it doesn't matter if you were a monastic or if you were a householder; what matters is that you follow what God wants you to do. If you feel guided inside to marry, then that's what you need to do. And if you don't follow that, it would be more detrimental to you. And if you were supposed to be a monk, and didn't follow your guidance, it would be the same. The first step is to be honest with yourself.

Swami used to set examples for us in how to trust our inner guidance, being very clear and using our intuition. He would say to us, *"Take a step and see how it feels. Take a step and understand for yourself. Feel if you're more in tune, and then move in that direction."*

Once, Kriyananda spoke to me about how it was for him to write music. He said, "The process I use is easy for me, but I want you to know that it's all my years of meditation, all my years of attunement that allows me to write. And it's also from hard work, of taking the process and developing it."

And then he said, "Every note that I've written, in every song that I've ever written, has come from meditation." And another time he said to me, "I hold the notes up and see if they're right; and if the direction is not right — it doesn't feel correct in my heart — then I'll go in another direction." He's always taught me that creating music is not personal, that it's not what *you* want, it's not about expressing your ego. The idea is to learn how to be in tune and to express something that's from a higher part of ourselves.

Music rightly applied, in terms of the divine, is a doorway into spheres of higher consciousness. My whole emphasis has been to help people to experience God through music and to share that with other people. When we create music or perform music, we try to learn how to experience it from the *inside* first. If we approach musical interpretation too much from the standpoint of what we think it should be, then it's us expressing the song. The music that we're expressing has to have some depth to begin with. If it does, you can learn how to express what's in it. And if it's divinely inspired, you express that too.

People often ask me why I only perform Kriyananda's music, and why I don't do other things. It's because I feel that what he has done is profound and that his music is divinely inspired. He is *bringing* something new into music, not *creating* something new. Through meditation and living a life connected to God, his music has taken me to places that I couldn't get to on my own.

When we produced the *Life Mantra (Chant of the Angels)*, I found that when the choir would sing the song in the right way we touched into the Divine. When I was conducting the choir to sing this song, *"God is love, God is joy…"*, it was as if angels were singing, and it was so inspiring to me that I was in tears. With music that is divine, if you go deeper and deeper in it, it can take you into a place that's beyond yourself, into a higher state of consciousness.

That particular piece was so moving to me yet it received such poor reviews from music critics because people are generally so geared toward movement—motion and activity. It's difficult to understand *Life Mantra* because the song is all about the feeling of living your life totally for God. Much of Kriyananda's music is the same way. And it finally occurred to me that for people to understand this music, they have to do something *beforehand* that helps them become quiet.

The restlessness of our society, the anger and frustration, has created certain kinds of music. People don't realize that when they listen to that music, it encourages those same vibrations in them. And so one is encouraging the other. It's like commercials on television; everything encourages peoples' restlessness and has made it impossible for most people to sit still to experience something. Isn't it true that the music enjoyed most by our society represents the state of consciousness of our society?

When I was living in our European community in Italy, I became acutely aware that the Renaissance period was created by a handful of people. They all knew each other and shared ideas. You could just imagine what their lives must have been like: one would go over to the other and say, "Hey, look at this." And that would give the other person an idea. The magnetism created by a group of talented artists living in close proximity must have been extremely stimulating.

You can apply these same principles to a spiritual community, and it could be for any kind of religion, not necessarily our tradition. The same magnetism could apply to Zen Buddhists or Christians living together and having the company of other people going in the same direction you are. In community, you're more aware of what other people are going through. Things like caring about each other when someone's sick, and praying for each other are common. Apart from a religious standpoint, I think the same idea of communities could be applied to artists and musicians. It can be applied to any group, because one of the things we do here is we spark each other's energy and interest and ideas by all living together. It's a tremendous solution to some of our problems right now, because many people feel so disconnected and alone in the world.

Anandi

I was visiting an old friend on Quadra Island in British Columbia when I began my spiritual search. It was 1970 and I was on summer vacation. There were only eight people in my friend's community and they all practiced Zen meditation. I learned their practice and participated with them. Just as when I learned Transcendental Mediation a few months before, I felt I was on the right track but hadn't yet reached my goal. After a month or so there, I met a young man who said to me: "You're looking for something, and I can't help you, but I think I know someone who can." He described to me a friend of his from law school. She had dropped out, hitchhiked across the country, and ended up at a place called Ananda. When he said he'd received a postcard from her that said, "I'm so close now, I can almost touch it," I felt: I have to meet her. Her words told me that she had been on a similar quest and had found some real answers.

I left the next day and hitchhiked to Ananda from Canada. I had no idea what to expect, knew absolutely nothing about yoga. When I arrived and asked for Shivani, I was told she was "in silence." She appeared and silently listened as I tried to explain who I was, what I was seeking, and how I came to be there (somewhat awkwardly since I'd never tried to speak to someone "in silence" before). At the end of my speech, she broke her silence and welcomed me like a long lost sister. As she showed me around the Village, she began talking to me about deep aspects of the yogic path, and later taught me some yoga postures. I spent my time at Ananda picking blackberries, working with Shivani in the garden, meeting people, and talking philosophy. I could only stay four days because I needed to return to Berkeley for graduate school. In that short time I became a vegetarian, a hatha yoga lover, and most importantly I had found a place inside myself that I had been seeking.

That Thanksgiving I came back to visit. Ananda was a new and unfamiliar world to me. I remember bringing Shivani a gift of a tiny bag of Calmira figs. This time on my arrival, someone said, "Oh, Shivani is in seclusion, but she just started, and I'm sure she'd want to see you." Nervously I approached, uncertain about the etiquette involved in this unknown situation. Just as I walked up to her teepee, the door was blown open by the wind, and she emerged to pull it closed. She exclaimed, "Oh, I was wondering how I could find you again!" We spent the afternoon talking about many things, including my uncertainty about whether to drop out of graduate school. Her simple statement, "Don't worry, it will all become clear to you," helped me to relax and be open inwardly.

I moved to Ananda on my 24th birthday in 1971 and began helping with the health food candy business Shivani and a couple of other women had started. We would volunteer in the garden in the morning, leaving for work at 7:30 a.m., then return home to our "paying" job in the afternoon. It was many months before we made any money, and the highest salary we ever earned was about $90 a month. I had one of the few cars at Ananda, and my little Volkswagen served as our pickup truck for the business.

One of the dearest people to me in those days was Haanel Cassidy, who started the garden. He was 68 when I arrived at Ananda. At our first meeting, I remember climbing into his pickup truck and seeing a copy of the *New Yorker*, where he had been a photographer for the Conde Nast magazines. There he was known as "Cassidy, the Waltz King." He also had a magnificent bass voice and loved to sing Negro spirituals. He was an excellent cook. Everything about him was orderly and sophisticated.

Haanel Cassidy was a striking contrast to the early days of Ananda. We were mostly young people, just out of college, exalting in a sense of freedom from meaningless rules. We were seeking Order on the highest level, but down here on earth things were quite casual. Haanel faced endless frustrations working with us. But we were his friends, and he loved us.

Haanel had become a disciple of Yogananda right after Master died in 1952. He was very loyal to these teachings and to meditation, waking each morning about 2 a.m. to meditate for three hours or so. Swami Kriyananda met him in the late '60s and invited him to retire at Ananda and just meditate. But Haanel was an extremely serviceful person and felt that a community should have a garden, and it was up to him to start it. He sometimes wondered if he had sacrificed his own spiritual progress to do this. Haanel was also a loyal friend to us all. I'd go to his little cabin and sit down and have a cup of Pero, prepared to perfection. He invited a group of us to meditate with him every Sunday night, just to help our meditations. He also gave lessons in singing, elocution, or calligraphy to anyone who asked him. He could be the grouchiest person or the dearest.

My mother came to visit me after I'd been here about two months. I was then living at the Seclusion Retreat in a decrepit, green armored truck. My mother was in shock her first two days here. At that point there were almost no buildings at Ananda, and no outward signs to indicate any stability. She spent a lot of her time here wondering where she'd gone wrong as a parent. Perhaps I had enjoyed Girl Scouts too much, or perhaps she'd failed to answer my questions in the right way. She plied me with questions about Ananda. Her main fears were about my financial security and my seeming isolation from the world.

On her second day here we went to the Village area so I could work in the garden. While I worked, she wandered off and began talking to some of the Ananda members. She had a long talk with Jaya about his background in anthropology and how he felt about the work he was doing now. She talked with several others as well, and by noon, when I came to find her, she was buoyant. She referred to my armored truck lightheartedly as "The Grasshopper," and suggested that we paint it. We bought some paint in the nearby small town and painted the insides, a room 4' high, 7' long and about 6' wide. (Luckily, I lived here only through that summer, and moved into a trailer in the Fall!)

On her last day here Swami gave a traditional Indian fire ceremony, during which he talked about seeing each day as a new beginning. Then he gave the Sunday service, which she attended. She was thrilled by these experiences and bought some of Swami's books to take with her. A few days later I received a letter from her from San Francisco, where she was visiting my sister. She wrote, "I feel like I'm walking along in a column of light, looking at people without any criticism or judgment." I was amazed at the change in her. Unfortunately, when she returned home and talked with my father, she began to doubt her experience here, and all her original doubts about Ananda surfaced again.

In August of 1971 Swami started the monastery here. On some level the monastic life called to me, but it also frightened me. I had just come onto the spiritual path and didn't feel ready for another leap at that point. It took a year or two for me to sort out my feelings. Early in 1973 I asked Swami if I could join, and he seemed pleased. As we chatted about other things, I said, "Don't you want to tell me anything about what I should do as a monastic?" He said, "No...you know what to do." It was true. Once I opened my mind to it, monastic life was perfectly natural to me. I think I have spent many past lives as a monastic.

In the early days of the monastery, because of the feeling of family here, the monks and nuns felt close to each other like brothers and sisters. Swami called us to his house one evening and said that if we wanted to be monastics, we should not be fraternizing with the opposite sex, even in seemingly innocent ways. We should not look into each other's eyes, because of the magnetism that comes through the eyes. That meeting was thrilling, and a great aid to our clarity. As we left the room, everyone was being so careful to avoid eye contact with the opposite sex that we were kind of bumping into each other clumsily as we put on our shoes to leave.

After that we said goodbye to any friendships with the opposite sex. We wouldn't get into any conversations that were personal. We might talk about business but learned not to talk in a way that drew attention to ourselves. It helped me to become more giving in my energy, less asking for attention from someone else. I moved to a trailer in the Ayodhya monastery that was quite cozy inside, with a wood stove. Every morning the nuns would wake at 5:15 a.m., energize under the large oak tree, and meditate in our teepee temple. Then we'd head off to work, many of us working in the Publications business together.

In 1980 Seva asked if I would move to the Seclusion Retreat to be David Praver's assistant. Our guest program was located there at the time. (In 1983 it moved to its present location and became called The Expanding Light.) I moved to the Seclusion Retreat still a nun. Seva even sent a sister nun, Catherine, to the Retreat as a support for me. But my monasticism was beginning to feel contractive. Up to that point, my years in the monastery had been tremendously strengthening to me. Committing my life to God alone had helped me to become more focused and centered, stronger in my spiritual life. Yet as I examined my heart, I felt that now I needed to be more inclusive of other people's realities, more loving and accepting of everyone.

Thanksgiving of 1981 I had dinner with Bharat at the Seclusion Retreat. I consciously relaxed my impersonal approach, and we had a warm and interesting conversation. As we talked I felt as if I knew him very well. Inside, I felt a voice saying, "This is your next step in renunciation." This was a shock to me, but it felt like inner guidance.

On the one hand, I have always felt extremely blessed by that experience and by my marriage to Bharat. And at the same time I've found marriage to demand a much deeper level of renunciation in me. When I was a nun, my will power was supreme. Suddenly I found myself with someone who wasn't following my orders. And, in addition, he had a will of his own. What a shock this was to me in the first years of our marriage! Now my desire to live according to what I think God wants has to be blended with what my husband thinks God wants! It keeps me on my toes, helps me renounce likes and dislikes on a deeper level of my being. It is a great blessing to be with someone who is trying to do the same thing. For each of us God is our first love, and that is what brings joy and harmony to the marriage.

One of the things I noticed about Ananda my first days here was the respect with which people treated each other. Each person is given the space to develop naturally from the inside out. People give each other the space to make their own decisions and let their own integrity guide them. Moving here, I remember feeling almost a tangible sense of increased personal space around me. People don't give you unsolicited advice, nor do they require deep interpersonal, emotional sharing. I was impressed with a feeling of interpersonal cleanness and freedom.

People here are reluctant to give spiritual advice to others because we realize that people are all different, and what works for me will not necessarily work for another. In this Swami has been the great model. He has watched many people do many stupid things. He lets us make mistakes because he knows it's the only way people learn, and he trusts that our good intentions and intelligence will bring us around to the truth eventually. If you've ever tried to give anyone unasked for advice (and who hasn't?), you know it simply doesn't work.

One of the great blessings of living at Ananda has been the opportunity to be with Swami Kriyananda. In my early years I used to be somewhat suspicious of him, always watching him and wondering, "Is he coming from ego?" I had a very doubting nature. At one point he said to me, "Doubt paralyzes you." That helped me break the doubting habit.

Watching Swami work with people opened my mind to what true friendship is; to love and accept a person completely brings the truest understanding of their nature. I have watched him guide people in such a sensitive and insightful way. Rather than explaining to people what their spiritual blocks were, he would put them in a work situation that would force them to develop the opposite spiritual strength. If a person was dealing with spiritual pride, he might encourage them to take a job that was especially humble, or to work beside someone who expressed true humility.

A few times I asked Swami for guidance about a new direction in my life. He would invariably throw the question back in my lap: "Meditate on this. Ask God what He wants you to do." He wants us to develop our own intuition, to learn to get our answers from within.

I have heard people complain that Swami is not perfect and that this is some kind of an obstacle. *Our biggest obstacle on the spiritual path is ourselves, our own attachment to our limitations and desires*. If we can find someone who knows more than we do, who is going to help provide challenges and opportunities for us to grow, I think we should tune into them as deeply as possible. Swami does not see himself as the guru, and has been very clear about this to us. That doesn't mean that it isn't helpful to tune into his wisdom, since it is greater than mine.

In my early years here Swami hired me to work for his publications business doing promotions. He suggested a certain direction, and I disagreed with it quite strongly. It's not as if I were basing my opinion on any experience in the publications business. I was about 26 and hadn't had much business experience at all. Asha asked me about the situation, and I explained Swami's idea versus mine, and how, being a writer, he had an egotistical attachment to his own idea. Asha's next statement was one of the strongest single statements anyone has ever made to me. She said, "Who do you think has more ego? You or Swami?" The implications of this statement exploded in my mind. Swami's ego was not the key factor here. The big problem I faced was *my* ego.

I try to tune into Swami's soul as much as I can in my heart. I try to be open to the flow of God through him. For me it has been a doorway to expanding my consciousness. I also try to do this with other devotees whom I respect spiritually. This doesn't interfere with the fact that Yogananda is my guru. I try to open myself to Yogananda's influence to the core of my being. And I feel that the people in my life are sent to me by him: some to test me and to help me grow stronger in non-attachment; others to be spiritual examples.

The guru is very alive in my life, in terms of inner communication. I try to ask inwardly which direction I should take, what I should say to a person who needs help. If I feel a contractive or nervous energy in my heart, that is the wrong direction to go. If my heart feels calm and happy, that is the right direction to go, or the right thing to say. The guru helps us grow toward our own highest potential.

People sometimes ask, "How has Ananda changed since the early years?" On the one hand there is much more physical development and much more organizational structure. But on the human level there is not much change. The people who came in the early years were sincere, humble, devotional, and enthusiastic about serving God. The people who come today are the same. The community has just grown deeper in all of these qualities.

One of the things that strikes me about Ananda is the superconscious approach to life. By this I mean that people, while aware of problems, don't give too much weight to problems. Instead, we are always seeking solutions, and always assuming solutions exist. In the early days, as I've said, there was practically no money. And yet it never occurred to most of us that the place could fail. We've always held a positive attitude that we will find the solutions to whatever obstacles face us.

Ananda has its own vibration. Certain people are drawn to live here, others aren't. When people come to Ananda, their soul is leading them. Otherwise it's not worth the risk of giving up a high-paying job for an uncertain future in the country. People come with high spiritual aspirations, as well as outer images of community life: lots of friends, a comfortable life in the country. Sometimes when they face loneliness or tremendous obstacles on the physical plane, they feel Ananda has failed them. Their disappointment about not living up to their spiritual aspirations makes them want to blame someone other than themselves.

I've found that if people can accept the challenges in their lives and the challenges here, there is an atmosphere that is tremendously helpful to the spiritual life. Spiritual growth is not handed to you on a platter. Most people feel enthusiastic to face challenges on the path, but then when the tests come, we feel, "Not this test. I was thinking of a different test. This one is too hard!"

Anandi at her desk in the early '70s.

A friend of mine was sent off to head up one of our city centers. It was torture for her. Her personality didn't mix well with the people in the center, and she hated the particular city she was in. At one point, she said to Swami, "I don't think I'm the right person for this center. They need someone more lively and outgoing." My friend is a very deep, inward person. Swami's reply was, "I didn't send you here for them, I sent you here for you. I thought it would help you develop as a person."

This is the kind of life tests Ananda gives. You think that you are needed to build the work. Then you see the work is here to build you. The more we realize we're the ones who need to change and grow to adjust to the circumstances of life, then we're seeing things in the right way.

I feel Ananda is an ocean of sanity, where people respond to life, for the most part, in a healthy fashion. We try to live simply and find joy within. We treat all people with respect and honor the goodness in other people. This environment helps one express the best qualities within oneself: the natural love of the heart, as well as openness, kindness, and trust. In such a nurturing environment people develop deeper faith in themselves and develop their inner strength. I see this in community members, and I see it in guests who come to visit The Expanding Light even for a few days.

True humility is self-forgetfulness, not thinking about your smallness, not thinking about yourself at all. Humility is very personal because it has to do with your relationship with yourself. Are you obsessed with your own thoughts and feelings, or are you trying to discover what God wants? My partnership with God is not a matter of philosophy. It's a moment by moment experience. Sometimes it takes me aback to feel how close He is, how much He is paying attention to my thoughts and actions. Yogananda used to say, *"God is the nearest of the near, the dearest of the dear. Do not keep Him away."*

Kalyani

A spiritual community is a place where God is the center of your life. Living here is like being in a deeply peaceful valley—on a track being pulled toward God.

Before coming to Ananda I was seeking truth. I knew there was more to life than I had been shown, and I loved to learn. As a 4th-grader living in Oregon, I remember walking with my dad under the stars one night. I asked him, "Dad, what is a wise man?" After a thoughtful pause, he replied humbly, "I don't know." Something happened deep within my being at that moment: I began my search for a wise man.

From 1964-1969 I attended UC Berkeley. A year-long marriage and the birth of a son in 1967 interrupted my studies. To secure a means of livelihood, in 1970 I took a graduate year of study for a California teaching credential. During finals I ran into a college friend I hadn't seen in several years. She said I looked like I needed a break. "Get a baby-sitter for your son and come with me to a place I know of in the forest. We'll sleep out under the stars," she said.

That week I also contracted for a job teaching 8th-grade English and drama in Modesto, CA. With a job and a newly rented 3-bedroom house, I felt ready for a break. Friday we drove under a beautiful night sky, winding up Highway 49 into the foothills of the Sierra

Nevada Mountains. We stopped once to observe in awe the appearance of what seemed like two shooting stars headed straight toward us, hovering not far away. What could they be, we wondered.

I was surprised when my friend led me to the domed Ananda office around midnight. I wasn't expecting any buildings. Satya, a long-time mariner and yoga practitioner rose from his cot and pleasantly greeted us. He turned up a kerosene lamp. When he said there would be a small charge to stay, I told him I didn't have any money. As I was about to leave he gently offered that it would be all right to pay later, whenever I could. I was impressed—and we stayed. I've often thought that without Satya's kindness, I would surely have left then and perhaps never have known Ananda. I happily paid the money out of my first paycheck.

The next morning Satya strolled throughout campsite playing a two-sided Indian drum slung around his neck, rousting with sweet chanting all the forest-floor slug-a-beds. At the temple dome he led us in my very first experience of yoga postures and meditation. I found meditation both intriguing and pleasant. We spent Saturday in silence, walking in nature, and experiencing the peace as we sketched a grove of trees.

Arriving at a third dome-shaped building for Sunday breakfast, I found people very animated. After a day of silence they were talking eagerly about certain mystical and phenomenal events that they had observed during the weekend. I enjoyed the electric atmosphere, but nothing compared to my experiences later that day when I met Swami Kriyananda. Here was the wise man I had been seeking. I felt such Truth in him! I wanted to give up my job and move to Ananda immediately. He suggested I wait to move until I had completed my teaching job in Modesto.

On an auspicious Tuesday in June 1971 I moved into a tiny, freshly painted chicken coop sitting on the front lawn of what is now

Master's Market in downtown Ananda. It may have been a humble beginning, but I saw only a future bright with hope and beauty. We lived there through the summer, until a bigger chicken coop opened up behind the farmhouse. This is where my son Prem grew up and where, with several remodelings, I lived for the next 25 years. Raising my son at Ananda in the 1970s wasn't easy. There were few children, few organized activities for kids, and friends came and went.

My first job at Ananda was as receptionist. Day after day, week after week visitors came, some intent on setting up shop. Many were spiritual, others were heavily into drugs or other self-deluding practices. Most had erroneously heard that there was free land up in the hills and had come with all their relatives, kids, animals and belongings, arriving in a colorful array of painted and creatively rebuilt homes on wheels. Some of them did not want to hear that Ananda was a spiritual community for those seeking a life of dedication and discipline, not a place to retire!

Just before Prem and I arrived, the members had voted on three rules for Ananda that we have maintained all these years: no drugs, no alcohol, and no dogs. There had been much discussion as to whether dogs fit in at Ananda or not. We were told reasons for not having dogs: 1) Dogs chased and killed wild animals, which offended people who loved the wild creatures, and also offended against a basic yoga practice, *ahimsa*, or non-violence. Dogs didn't kill for food, but for sport, yet no one was willing to permanently restrain their dogs. 2) The dogs would run through and dig in the community garden, ruining many hours of work. 3) Dogs frequently challenged visitors and frightened small children. 4) Dogs would bark at night, sometimes ALL night, disturbing sleepers and meditators alike.

We had to find a home for our beloved black Labrador. Ananda's no-dog policy has always been hard to explain, and harder still for some people to accept.

Kalyani greeting guests visiting Ananda.

What was it like in the beginning? Rustic! People hauled water, propane tanks, and wood to their homes over deeply rutted, often muddy roads. For years I had the only Ananda house with electricity and phone, because I lived next to the farmhouse. None of us had television. The first year a friend helped me plumb my place for water, and on the coldest nights we sat in front of a small electric heater. By the third year a friend installed a tiny wood stove for me; someone else built a woodshed onto our house; another delivered a load of wood.

Prem and I had to go up the hill across the street to the outhouse and showerhouse, which used unfiltered pond water. It was a very lively place: California newts and tree frogs climbed out of the walls, and occasionally slime would ooze from the pipe—I hated the smell of the water. One time we couldn't take our showers until we removed a large black widow spider and her countless newborn babies hovering above the doorway. In keeping with the practice of ahimsa, I carried them all safely away.

It has been a fascinating process learning how to infuse our spiritual principles into education, business, and social interactions. Our families have truly been pioneers in this arena. Only a few of the children from the early years have embraced this path as their own. My son Prem has continued in this lifestyle, marrying a devotee of Yogananda and living for many years in our Sacramento Community.

Raising my second child, a graceful girl named Mirabai, was much easier in the 1980s. By this time there was a support group of families with clarity of vision as both yogis and parents. Now there were 100 children, activities for families, dance classes, a pony club, a swimming pool, sports, and a thriving school dedicated to Yogananda's ideals of spiritual education. Ananda has a beautiful lifestyle for children, and it serves their parents too. Caring for a child can be the best spiritual training we'll ever have, because it teaches us selflessness, an absolute pre-requisite to Self-realization.

Prakash

I discovered yoga in the early seventies, when I was teaching English at a small college in North Carolina. I had been having problems with my health, and began taking kundalini yoga classes, which is Yogi Bhajan's method. It was the perfect kind of yoga for me at the time because it was very physical, with lots of breathing techniques, so it was a good cleansing yoga. The yoga had helped me a great deal, so I moved to Yogi Bhajan's place in New Mexico and stayed there for about a year and a half. It was a community, but more like an ashram. Yogi Bhajan's teaching was very regulatory. He had programs and *asanas* and *kriyas* and dietary methods for every moment of your life. It was very detailed—perfect for someone who wanted a total makeover.

After I left that ashram I went into a dark time. I think this must happen often to people who taste the spiritual life and then, for whatever reason, are out of it. You can't go back and you can't go forward; you're just kind of stuck. I ended up going back to Kentucky, and my father gave me a job remodeling a little cabin there.

I remembered hearing about *Autobiography of a Yogi* and decided to read it. I located it in a library and read it in about two days. It encouraged me to practice meditation, so I experimented. I made my first effort in front of a picture of an ancestor whose name was

Henry—he'd been a slave-owner in south central Kentucky, and he looked just like I did at that time, except of course dressed in the frock coat and hairstyle of his own time. The story I was told was that great-great-great grandfather Henry was whipping a slave named Jim for disobedience. Jim broke free and killed Henry with a knife he had hidden in the hay. I could feel Henry's presence as I meditated; he was an unhappy ghost. Being able to feel the presence of another soul was something I had never even thought about until I read Yogananda's book. So that was when I said my first prayer, which was for poor old Henry—still hanging around, and in a lot of pain. I could feel something lift, a change in the energy. The portrait was just a portrait after that.

My experience with Yogananda's book excited me and I wrote a very enthusiastic letter to SRF, wanting to come out to California immediately and devote my life to this wonderful thing. I spent the next three months checking the mailbox about four times a day, and getting more and more depressed. Finally a very formal letter came, telling me that they didn't think it would be a good idea for me to take the lessons. They felt I was still too connected to Yogi Bhajan's ashram to begin Yogananda's path—and that would be a conflict. It was a crushing blow, though I understood somehow that Yogananda was behind it all, because for whatever reason SRF was not going to be the path I would follow.

I returned to North Carolina for a visit, and while I was there I found *The Road Ahead*, which was Kriyananda's little book about Master's prophecies. I read the words "Yogananda" and "community" on the back cover. I was deeply thrilled. Fearful of receiving another letter like the one from SRF, I decided not to write first but simply to go. As quickly as I could tie up loose ends, I headed west, hitchhiking. Part way across country a blinding headache settled over me. By the time I reached Boulder, Colorado, I could barely distinguish light and dark. I lay under a bush in a public park.

I think I must have been in that state overnight because of changes in the light that I could see. Then I felt kind hands picking me up, and gentle voices. A young couple carried me to their home and laid me down on their couch. The woman put her hands on my forehead. The pain lessened and my vision started to return. I asked her, "Where did you learn to do that?" And she said, "Yogananda." I knew I was going to make it.

When I got near Lake Tahoe, I could feel the energy shift and there was a sense that I was coming home out of this blighted landscape. It was at that point that a lady in a Mercedes stopped for me and actually took me directly to the Seclusion Retreat at Ananda. She herself was coming to Ananda for the first time.

When I first came to Ananda, I did work-exchange. My first task was shingling the roof of the Common Dome at the Seclusion Retreat. It was there that I first saw Swami Kriyananda. He walked by and looked up and smiled. I felt a wonderful energy pouring into me from him — it was as though his smile rushed up my spine. I could not keep my balance on the ladder, and I sagged against the roof of the building. Unsuspected dimensions even doing mundane tasks in a spiritual community!

One of my significant memories of the early days was attending my first community meeting at Kriyananda's dome. People were asking questions that seemed inappropriate to me — about housing and who owned what. I don't ask questions generally, but I stuck my hand up and I asked him if he'd known right away that he was Yogananda's disciple. As he spoke in response I realized that somehow he was enabling me to experience what he had experienced when he realized that he was Yogananda's disciple.

I came to Ananda because I wanted to be Yogananda's disciple and to be able to serve something larger than myself. There was very little organization of any sort when I first came to Ananda, very little external direction. Swami himself encouraged us to look inside for guidance. Service I learned by simply showing up and doing whatever was asked of me. Discipleship came through being around Swami, and those who had been with him, learning to meditate, studying the lessons, both Kriyananda's *14 Steps* and the SRF lessons. As much as I could I stayed alone on Bald Mountain, at the Seclusion Retreat, to study and meditate. It was wonderful discipline, because it created a constant interplay and feedback between inner listening and study of the lessons.

I joined the monastery and began meditating more and more, until I was meditating 8 hours a day during the week and 14 hours a day on the weekends. Fasting became a secondary passion, especially when I found that fasting more allowed me to meditate more. But finally I became so thin that Swami had to step in and nudge me back in the other direction. Less meditation, more service, and more respect for the needs of the physical vehicle.

One of the special treats for the monks was the opportunity to ride with Kriyananda in "Air Force One"—an aging former Air Force Chevrolet he'd bought for $75. We used to spend hours struggling to keep it working and to keep the dust out. Once in a while I'd hear someone speak about how Swami drove around in a luxury sedan when others had to get by in cheap cars. For all of us who bumped up and down the pothole roads of early Ananda in that old car, I think we did feel that we were experiencing a spiritual wealth that we would not have dreamed of trading for any worldly luxury. A deeper truth in the midst of a superficial misunderstanding.

Gradually there got to be a little bit of structure in the monastery. Nitai became the head monk, and worked hard to give us the structure we wanted—though once we had some structure, we weren't always so cooperative. The old anarchy was what we were used to. The monks started having workdays and group meditations, and more monks came. Even our housing began to improve. One monk built a shack with not one but two rooms, and, even more amazing, both a wood stove and a gas heater! My response was to go through the winter without heat of any sort, and with as little sleep as possible. Two hours a night was my goal, though I quickly found that I could only remain awake when actually moving. The moment I stopped moving, I fell asleep.

Looking back on the whole first period of Ananda's history, I think Swami was giving us the latitude we needed to work through the tendencies we had brought with us from previous lives—tendencies about how to proceed on the spiritual path, ideas about what it means to be a devotee or a monk or a yogi or a minister. The community and our approach to the spiritual life was more eastern than western. Swami wore his ochre robes. The monks and nuns wore the traditional yellow. Many of us had Sanskrit names. Swami's talks were Vedic discourses. Speaking for myself, I was working through some rather extreme ideas about the spiritual path as renunciation—self-denial in food, sleep, shelter. The special blessing of Ananda was that Swami allowed me to find out for myself that none of these directions would take me to the goal, and did so with complete respect and love.

Kriyananda does not impose his will on us. He's come, of course, to help spread Yogananda's teachings. But the central teaching is Self-realization. Our directions come from a kind of inner listening—some quiet feeling that comes and stays, and keeps on feeling quietly right. And the community—like a larger self—is there to support, expand and refine the individual directions of each one, and to help him find a way to harmonize his own directions with those of others and of the community as a whole.

I would say that if you want to live in a spiritual community, go there to learn and to be of help. And spend a long time just listening and trying to understand what's there and trying to release whatever ideas you've brought with you, because they all just get in the way.

I remember Shivani saying, "You need to have a bottom line in your spiritual life." With all the great teachings and programs Ananda offers, you can get discouraged if you don't have some kind of realistic goal that you can maintain. For myself, my bottom line has been—whatever I have to go through—to do it at Ananda, in the vibration of my spiritual family.

About ten years ago I felt an inner shift trying to take place, from teaching and writing to working on the land. I wasn't sure that such a radical shift would sit well with the community. But this community is rooted in compassion and respect, each member for the other, whatever personality issues may be at stake. And so the shift was able to take place, and the spiritual journey to continue, only in a new field of learning.

I remember when I first came to Ananda, feeling Yogananda very strongly when I was walking through the forest at the Seclusion Retreat. I could see him, though not in the way of a vision. But he was there. His energy was clearly expressed in the forest. I knew he was there and that he blessed the land and that he was with us. I still feel that just as strongly today.

I understand what Ananda is when I go away to work in Colorado and then come back. It's really lonely, spiritually, out there. I'm with my family, and they're very supportive and nice, but there's no Ananda. When I return, I go through the same feelings I had when I first came over the mountains near Lake Tahoe and started down the other side. The energy shifts at a certain point, and I know that I am coming home.

Parvati

True Yoga is a whole way of life, a philosophy blended with attitudes, hard work and meditation. In the early years at Ananda, one of the spiritual practices most emphasized was meditation—deep meditations, in the morning, at noon and in the evenings. On the weekends there were always longer three-hour meditations. Through all this we were developing our inner life so that we could carry peace and calmness out into everything we were doing—which was quite a lot! Ananda has always been a place of daily spiritual living and not just intellectual theorizing. Because of this emphasis on meditation we could experience the interchange between a deep, inner, spiritual life and going about our daily activities of working at our jobs and interacting with people. It was a wonderful way to test the teachings and see if we were really getting it.

As one of Yogananda's close disciples said, you must test your spiritual life in the cold light of day. There were plenty of opportunities for doing that in pioneering a spiritual community. Swami Kriyananda kept us going in the right direction by offering Yogananda's teachings at Sunday services, classes, and at weekly teas at his house where he would talk and people could ask questions. When Kriyananda would talk about his life with Yogananda, the whole spiritual path became so alive and real.

I have always felt I have many strong *samskars* of living a monastic life. When I first moved to Ananda, I knew that I would eventually live as a monastic. It so happened that I was living with someone at the time I moved here, yet I felt that the spiritual path was about being alone—it was a solo journey. What made perfect sense to me, and inspired me deeply, was being a renunciate. Since my heart was so strongly set in this direction, this move eventually happened.

I lived as a monastic for ten years. It was a time that was deeply inspiring, fulfilling, and spiritually challenging—a great adventure! The word monastery can conjure up images of stone walls, bells and small cells. The monastery at Ananda was much more Indian in feeling and even looked like a simple hermitage in India. For the nuns, our daily routine was to ring the bell at 5:30 each morning and meditate in our teepee temple for at least half an hour. Then we would either continue meditating in the teepee or return to our trailers to finish meditating. We generally meditated anywhere from 45 minutes to two hours in the morning, but nothing was required. Since we each had our own living spaces, only each individual and God knew what was going on. Suggestions about the spiritual life were given, but it was up to the individual as to how she would live it. This was true for the monastery as well as the rest of the community. Ananda has never been a rule-oriented community.

Life was simpler then but our daily routines were much more rigorous. We had to walk from Ayodhya over the hill and down to the farm just to take a shower, which was about a 20-minute walk. (It was considered a luxury when a shower was finally built at the monastery. Before then, people took bucket baths, or rinsed off with a hose.) Often the nuns would walk together to work. We used to laugh about the fact that all the other spiritual groups had robes and we didn't. Trudging back and forth over the hill and through the mud didn't allow for this kind of clothing. However, on special occasions we sometimes wore yellow saris, the traditional custom in India for *brahmacharis*, or novices. When Swami Satchidananda came to visit Ananda, he saw us wearing our yellow saris. He told us that the spiritual path is like being fried in oil: in the beginning you're just yellow, and by the time you're a swami, you're well done and turn to orange!

During the 1970s Ananda had a strong monastic vibration, and I remember a number of people remarking to me how impersonal it felt. There were families living here as well, but it was not easy for them. But Ananda has always had pioneering energy, and after many years, the idea of a renunciate householder community seemed to be where we were going. And, though Swami sometimes talked about the concept, nobody really knew what it was. He encouraged people who had families because he knew that was the whole purpose of creating a spiritual community.

Creating a spiritual community that also included families was a huge undertaking. In *Autobiography of a Yogi* Yogananda wrote about Lahiri Mahasaya's desire to give *Kriya Yoga* initiation to all sincere seekers, not just monastics. To take on the creation of a householder monastic community required Swami's depth and breadth of vision. I've always felt as though he took all of us who wanted to go along with him on this spiritual adventure, and he worked with us. He introduced us to the basics of the spiritual path and taught us about energy, yoga philosophy and consciousness. And he did this by example. His own life he shared with us in every possible way. That is why his life is so meaningful to people here.

I remember around 1980 Swami Kriyananda told some of us that he felt a change was coming in his life. He had done the main things he felt he was supposed to do in starting a community and completing the writing of his autobiography, *The Path*. Then, in January of 1981, he met a young woman on the island of Kauai who he fell deeply in love with. For those of us in the monastery these were very interesting times. In one way, I think many of us felt that something expansive and wonderful was about to happen, if we could just go deep enough to understand it. For me personally, it was definitely a test, but a good test spiritually—one that I will always be grateful for. It made me look beyone the mere form of things that I cared deeply about and see the consciousness underlying them.

I think my main question during this time was, "Although Swami has changed his lifestyle radically by taking on this relationship, has his *consciousness* changed?" And over the ensuing months as he took all of us through this newly-forming relationship and way of life with him—through informal satsangs, classes, events, and just simple heart-to-heart talks—my question was more than adequately answered. He was the same. The same person I had trusted and followed as my spiritual teacher for almost 10 years. It was beautiful to see this evolving friendship as Swami felt his way, completely open and natural about it all—his doubts and hesitancies, his joy, his love, the deep soul connection he felt with this woman—all was very tangibly there for everyone to see. The two of them gave a number of satsangs together before the whole community, and it was sweet to see the energy between them. Swami talked a lot to us about relationships and how you deal with having a deep spiritual life while being with someone.

This was all thrilling to see, even though it signaled to me that this probably meant the end of the monastery. I felt that Swami was trying to open our consciousness up and show us that renunciation didn't mean simply living as a monastic. During that period of time he had also given a talk in which he said that there is no "householder path" to God as such. The only path to God is one of inner renunciation, then whatever lifestyle you choose after being a renunciate inwardly—be it married, single or monastic—depends on what your dharma is in this particular lifetime. I think Swami always knew that sooner or later he would have to attempt to provide an example for the community in this arena. The community probably wouldn't have happened otherwise. For me, as a nun, this was a very expansive time; as if someone had come along and opened up my mind and asked, "Have you thought to look at it like this?"

During this time, I had the great spiritual adventure of going from living in a bus in a monastery out in the woods (no running water, no electricity) to living in a 45-room mansion at our San Francisco ashram. My life, needless to say, was changing drastically at this time! I still felt to be a nun, and yet I found myself living in the middle of the very worldly city of San Francisco. Naturally, I felt the pull of this energy and began to feel that if there wasn't going to be a monastery, I probably would end up leaving this lifestyle. And I also felt that to grow spiritually, I could probably benefit from going in what felt to be an expansive direction.

Over time I felt more pulled in the householder direction. I met my husband, Bent, in the San Francisco ashram, where we worked together for about a year. We had also known each other at Ananda Village for several years before that. I think I would agree with what Swami has said in the past; it certainly is a lot easier being a monk or nun on the path because you don't have the householder "pulls" on your energy. But it is also said in the Indian scriptures that the higher path (because it's more difficult) is the householder path. And it seems that this is what many of us are being asked to take on in this lifetime.

Yogananda had a wonderful phrase that relates to this. He said, "Be in the world, but not of it." This is our test at Ananda right now, and we are still in the process of exploring it. I believe we are the pioneers of renunciate householder communities. In many ways, this is part of the shift from the time of *Kali Yuga*, which sees form as the only reality, to *Dwapara Yuga*, which is the age of energy. In Kali

Yuga, if you wanted to find God, you couldn't be married and have children, and you couldn't be "in the world." You *had* to shut yourself away and be a monk or nun, and not have a lot of contact with the world. This way your life could be concentrated only on God. But now, as we enter Dwapara Yuga, there is more awareness of form as energy, and it is possible to feel the energy behind the outward forms. This new awareness will help many people to understand how they can live a deeply spiritual life while at the same time fulfilling their outward responsibilities.

I think it would be very helpful for people, as they go through a lifetime, to spend time in a monastic setting—especially having this experience for a year or two at the beginning of one's spiritual life. It's vital to our progress on the spiritual path that we know ourselves. To do this we really need time alone with God. Living as a monastic and developing our spiritual practices can set the stage, so to speak, for everything else that follows in life.

Ananda has provided an example of spiritual community that I think can be very meaningful to people. Yogananda spoke of communities based on "plain living and high thinking." This, of course, will manifest a little differently for each person. What some people call plain living may look luxurious to others. But actually plain living is living with what you need, not what you want. High thinking comes from having a spiritual path that helps you to expand your consciousness and your sympathies. I think that plain living and high thinking are what most spiritual paths are all about, regardless of the outer form. In this way, Ananda is just an example—like a little seed.

Nirmala

"Who am I? How was the universe born? Who is the Maker? What is its material cause? The intellect has no answer for these questions; hence the rishis evolved yoga as the technique of spiritual inquiry."

In *Autobiography of a Yogi*, Paramhansa Yogananda was mirroring the long-pondered questions of my youth, and handing me the key to their answers. At last I learned about karma and reincarnation, Kriya Yoga, and the ancient path of self-mastery. I caught a glimpse of a far greater reality than I had ever dreamed of, and its ancient wisdom soothed me. At last I had the tools: now I would spend the rest of my life—and I hope not many more lives—mastering their artistry.

A friend once mentioned Yogananda's *Autobiography* to me, but it wasn't until I came to Ananda that I read it, and realized what a treasure it is. I joined the Apprentice Program when I first arrived, and worked in the garden the rest of the summer and fall. It was a wonderful experience to finally be able to give completely without any reservation. That, for me, was the beauty of those first years of Ananda: There weren't very many people, and countless things needed to be done! It was thrilling to be needed, and have my energy utilized fully without restriction.

When the apprentice program ended that fall, Parvati hired me to work at Master's Market where I had been volunteering. She was my first boss, a mentor to me, and a wonderful friend. I remember her showing me how to do *Maha Mudra* on the market counter! After a year or so, she got another job, and I took over running the Market. Even though I was young and new, I was given responsibility. It's a blessing to have that kind of opportunity to grow. Ananda has always asked things of me that I didn't know how to do: making stained glass windows, doing publicity, being a salesperson, teaching classes, public singing, the list goes on and on. That's the challenge and the joy of living in a small community—*everyone has to do everything.*

People often think that in those days Ananda was a cozy little family, but to my view it has always been impersonal. There are deep friendships here, and they are a gift from God given to us to help us grow. But that's what Ananda is about: growing spiritually. It's not about getting cozy, or creating a utopian community. It's about helping people grow spiritually. For me, those first years were rich in a sense of shared blessing, and also a time of being alone a lot and working hard—at my job and on myself. I was lonely sometimes, and certainly cold—my first winter at Ananda was the coldest winter in the history of the world! Still, I wouldn't trade those years for anything.

I never minded the hardships of a very simple life—of course I was a lot younger then! No car or electricity; no indoor plumbing; carrying water and groceries home; doing laundry in town when you could get there; walking everywhere, and if you forgot your flashlight, groping your way home. There was no sense of deprivation: it was all part of the joy of life. Plus, it was how everyone lived—householders, monastics, and single people—we were all on the same economic level: broke! The material simplicity brought a camaraderie of shared experience; life consisted of serving, meditating, and keeping the basics together. And laughter. Always lots and lots of laughter. I must admit that camping out has very little appeal to me these days, having been virtually camping all that time. And now, of course, the big question is: Without the Franciscan lifestyle, can we remember God while owning a dishwasher, a washing machine and two cars?

We've always had elements of the populace here that were a little offbeat, a little out of step with other rhythms. That's a part of Ananda's beauty, the rich tapestry of humanity. Diversity united by devotion to God. For a while in the beginning, for example, I was the only single woman at Ananda. Everyone else was either married or a nun—actually, I did join the convent—for 24 hours! I had expressed some interest in joining, and I remember being invited to Kriyananda's house with the other nuns, and being accepted in such a kind and gracious way—it was an idyllic moment. Leaving the gathering, one of the nuns and I walked up the hill arm in arm— sweet friendship. She mentioned a couple of things that are helpful about the monastic life such as not looking directly into the eyes of members of the opposite sex. Her well-meaning comments brought on a torrential flood of memories from my years in parochial schools: Rules! Vows that might be broken! Scandal! Death! At the time, unfortunately, all I could verbalize was my resignation!

Instead of going in that direction, I characteristically threw myself into my work. I especially loved community workdays; the energy was wild and beautiful, like a garden in springtime. I loved giving all my energy to a greater reality, to something larger than my little life.

I lived in many interesting "houses" through the years, but my favorite was one built by one of the monks for $12. A few years after he abandoned it, I moved in. He had built it just tall enough that he could lift his arms to energize, just wide enough to stretch out to sleep, and just long enough to do yoga postures. That would have been fine for me except for one thing—he was quite a bit shorter than I am! In the morning when I got up I had to watch where I put my feet: my roommates were black beetles. At night I slept with ear plugs so I wouldn't hear the mice in the walls. I was working for Swami at the time, though, and my "house" was so close to his dome—as the crow flies—that if he wanted to ask me something, he could just stand on his deck and call out to me. We didn't have telephones, and we didn't need them.

As soon as I arrived at Ananda, I started playing the harmonium and learning chants. Prakash, the leader of the Apprentice Program, had me play chants for him when he gave classes, so I helped out in that way from the beginning. A couple of years later there was a need for people who could sing on pitch, and that's how I got into the *Ghandarvas* singing group. In 1978 I went on a nationwide tour with Swami, the singers, and a few other people, visiting 18 cities in the U.S. and Canada. I remember how deeply people were touched by the music: it went straight to their hearts. Kriyananda sometimes calls his music "painless philosophy" and "sermons in song" because it bypasses the walls of the intellect and touches the soul. Yogananda said that "music is a divine art to be used not for pleasure but as a path to God-realization." Music has tremendous power to uplift and transform! Master also tells us that of the eight ways to experience God, sound is the easiest: we are vibrational creatures, and music affects us on a vibrational level, changing our consciousness.

My life at Ananda has revolved around art and music—back in the days of "cut and paste" I put many a poster and newsletter together while sitting on the floor with the pieces on my lap! The arts are fundamentally different at Ananda (sometimes outwardly as well as inwardly!). Doing art work, writing books, singing, theatre—everything comes from a sense of giving, of serving others through what you're doing. It's a very different mind-set from the world's preoccupation with self-expression, fame, and monetary gain. Here, we're trying to utilize artistic creativity for spiritual growth, so that everything we do is an offering to God, and a partnership with God. With that conscious intention, all the arts—and every act of life—becomes a joyful experiment in trying to become more and more "in tune" with God, the source of all creativity. This is what we strive for in all our singing groups: to blend to become as one voice, and to feel that oneness with Spirit.

The first step toward that experience is loosening the grip on the ego, and turning the flow of energy out in blessing to the world. It's not just the key to good singing; it's the cure for unhappiness! The beauty of Ananda is that people here are not fixated on themselves and their own little lives, but are learning to broaden their sympathies to include a greater reality. In that sense, a workday at Ananda is the same as the choir singing together: it's many voices united as one voice, many hands united to serve together.

I tell beginning singers what I've learned from Swami Kriyananda: to make yourself a channel for God's vibration to others; to sing from the upper chakras incorporating traditional voice placement exercises; to expand your aura to fill the whole room and everyone you're singing for; to "live" the words you sing in order to convey their depth; to sing with a pure, clear tone; to sing with devotion instead of emotion; to sing as a service rather than as an ego accomplishment; to forget about yourself, and focus on what you can give as a channel for God.

If you're overly concerned with yourself, nothing is ever good enough. A young woman came here to join the monastic training program after living in one of our urban communities. She didn't observe the rule that suggests people wait a year after coming to Ananda before getting involved in a relationship, the consequences escalated, and she eventually filed a lawsuit against Ananda saying we brainwashed her! The lawsuit brought out all the negativity and criticism disaffected people have had about Ananda from years past: housing isn't good enough, jobs aren't good enough, and failed relationships

The Ghandarvas singing group,
joined by Kriyananda in the back row.

are Ananda's fault! The unselfishness of the Ananda way of life can either inspire people, or make them feel the burden of their own self-ishness. If they don't want to face their own high potential, it's easy to "chop off the heads of others to appear taller yourself," as Sri Yuk-teswar said. To expect perfection in the outer world is to create "a nest of troubles," but when you give your life to God, life becomes a "nest of fun," as Master put it. The trick is to put your trust in God, not in any institution. People and all outward forms are designed to disappoint you, but God will never disappoint you. And if He appears to do so, it's because He has a higher good in mind for you, and He *will* reveal it to you eventually.

When you offer your life to God, you are in effect admitting at last that you don't know everything after all, that God knows better than you do, that you want to trust God, and give Him a chance to help you in your life. God is infinite in possibilities. God is without limit. God is not understandable by your little conscious mind. Why bother to have expectations when God is so far beyond them? The best way to live the spiritual life is with your heart open, your mind open, your hands open to serve. Then you have the Lord of the universe as your best friend.

All we went through with this lawsuit has led me to re-examine my own life and my initial decisions about Ananda. I came as a young person, and I dove in. I didn't hesitate, I didn't deliberate; I gave my heart instantly, and I've never regretted it. I've been here 23 years, I gave Ananda my youth and energy—did I make the right decision? The answer is an overwhelming "yes," because I've lived my life for something greater than my own little ego, and I would do that again a thousand times.

As I look back on my life before living in a spiritual community, I am increasingly grateful that God led me here. My religious school-ing helped me to see at close range the vocational struggle between the love for God and the need for human contact; and also how spiritual inspiration can become shackled by rules and regulations. After high school, I quickly saw many ways I could spend my life: I studied art and photography at the university and learned that art that comes from the ego is like the emperor's new clothes—no substance. I worked at a crisis intervention center and saw fear, addiction, and despair up close. I worked in a state job and marveled that anything ever happens in a sea of red tape! I landed a job in a huge aircraft company and realized how easy it is to get hypnotized by a paycheck. I worked as a member of a church council and found out that "religion" can be totally worldly. And I traveled enough to learn the truth in the adage, "No matter where you go, there you are."

To me, Ananda is the closest thing to heaven on earth; the ancient teachings of yoga as expressed through Paramhansa Yogananda, and the example of discipleship, dedication, and devotion that Kriyananda exemplifies have been blessings in my life too profound for words. Living here compels us to develop qualities within ourselves that will draw us closer to God—unselfishness, unconditional love and a non-judgmental attitude. Yogananda's phrase: "Living for God is martyrdom" is one of my favorites because it sums up the spiritual life—not in a heavy sense at all, in fact I'm smiling as I say it—because it's martyrdom of the ego, martyrdom of the dross within the soul. It's a joyful purification process—hard to take sometimes, but ultimately blissful.

Kirtani

I was divorced, living in Berkeley, and teaching German and Spanish in a middle school in nearby Lafayette when I began to attend a yoga class in San Francisco. I had an experience of energy and interiorization that led me to begin my conscious spiritual search. It wasn't long before I realized I was ready for some changes, both inner and outer.

I took a year off from teaching to travel in Europe, and just before leaving California I made my first contact with *Autobiography of a Yogi*. My best friend from childhood read aloud to me from the chapter "An Experience in Cosmic Consciousness." I remember thinking, "I have to read this book!"

Christmas of that year found me in Greece. I had written to my family to send books as presents, asking for one on meditation, and specifically mentioning *Autobiography of a Yogi*. On Christmas Eve I met someone at the pensione where I was staying who was a member of SRF and had a copy of the book. I read it straight through and knew I had found what I was seeking. When I returned to the U.S. I taught for another year, joined the SRF organization and went to the services at their Richmond temple. While I felt no magnetism from the organization, the techniques were powerful and I practiced them regularly. I met another yoga teacher, who had been to Ananda. It was interesting to know a community existed where all were devotees of Yogananda, but it wasn't until I met Swami and other members of Ananda that I was magnetized to visit.

I remember seeing a poster for Swami Kriyananda speaking in San Francisco. I wanted to hear this man talk. Hearing and seeing him for the first time was like finding a direct line to Yogananda. I could feel Yogananda's love and sweetness coming through him. In the following days there was another lecture where I remember looking all around for Swami and not finding him until it came time for his talk. In contrast to the orange robe and long hair of the previous talk, this time he had his hair pulled back under a beret and was wearing a suit! It was the first of many times that Swami Kriyananda refused to be put into a box of my making!

My soul was flying from the inspiration of Swami's words and of the music sung by some of the Ananda members I met that night. I knew I had to visit Ananda. It took me all of two weeks of being at Ananda to know that I would stay. I felt I had come home. It was June of 1975 and I was 28 years old.

Four years after I had been living at Ananda, Swami decided to do a tour of Europe. Friends in Europe had been frequently asking about the possibility of starting an Ananda community in Europe. I was invited to go along on this tour. Little did I know what it would lead to for me personally. We visited England, Holland, Germany, Austria and Italy. Swami gave inspiring talks and daily examples of the ideals behind Ananda: "Energy and joy go hand in hand" and "People are more important than things." Always, in the back of his mind was the question: "If Ananda in Europe…where?" When we got to Italy, the question seemed to be answered. Italy was the country where the heart's devotion was most evident, where Yogananda's teachings would most easily find fertile soil in which to germinate and grow.

The seeds were sown and a few deeply sincere devotees made it possible in 1984 for Ram and Dianna and Jyotish and Devi to come to Como, Italy to launch the first Ananda community in Europe. Alessandra Rombolotti provided the villa that served as Ananda Europa's first retreat location. One of the things we had to learn to deal with was the different tastes for food among the European guests coming to our retreat. I remember Swami helping us out of the dilemma of what kind of food to serve our guests. "Give them food for their souls, and they'll feel so satisfied they won't worry about the food."

Within 18 months of living in Como, we had outgrown the villa. We began to look for a place in Umbria, near Assisi, Italy. I must say that the old adage "ignorance is bliss" has certainly applied to the development of Ananda Europa. Had we known in advance all of the obstacles and pitfalls, we would very likely have made our way back across the Atlantic! It wasn't until we had a larger number of Italian residents in our community that we could get the help we needed. The Italian residents were capable of understanding and helping us move through the obstacles of the Italian bureaucratic web that one can so easily get stuck in.

While the outward aspect of developing Ananda Europa is always with us, the most important part of its development, the part that Swami has said is so vital to a successful spiritual community, is the people. Slowly and steadily, throughout the years of Ananda Europa's existence, the people have grown stronger spiritually. We started as a group of four people, then grew to eight...then to twelve. The inspiration of a strong core of devotees living Yogananda's teachings as Swami so patiently and lovingly inspired us to do, eventually brought more and more Europeans to Ananda Europa in Assisi. Today, we are a community of 50 residents from Italy, the U.S., Germany, Switzerland, England, Ireland and Croatia. Our Temple of

Light, dedicated to all religions, is a symbol for the ray of God's light that flows into the hearts and minds of all souls who come seeking it and who take it away with them into their daily lives.

Savitri

I was born and raised in Memphis, Tennessee and attended the second largest Southern Baptist church in the world. I went to Baylor, which is a Baptist college in Texas, and when I graduated I moved to Houston and got a job working for an airline. I never felt in tune with what was being taught to me by the Baptists. I didn't want to hurt my parents so I told myself I'd do what they want up to a certain point and then I'm on my own. They figured I'd marry a nice Baptist boy and settle down. I was the only one of all my college girl friends who graduated single.

I was already searching for answers about spirituality. I read Edgar Cayce's books, and books written about Tibet and living in Tibetan Monasteries. Reading these books was like coming home, it all seemed so familiar. When I read *Autobiography of a Yogi* I was thrilled. It answered all my questions about the search for God. I tried to learn to meditate on my own, but wasn't very successful. It never occurred to me that there might be other devotees with whom I could share my spiritual search.

About this time I was becoming interested in living in community. I've always had an interest in communes and communities and enjoyed reading books about utopias. In about 1971 I found a copy of the Spiritual Communities Guide that the Sufis used to publish. I found a small paragraph that described Ananda as a cooperative spiritual community in Northern California, founded by Swami Kriyananda, where everyone follows the teachings of Paramhansa Yogananda. I instantly wanted to visit. Back in Tennessee, my mother used to say that California is the land of fruits and nuts, so you don't go there. Stay away from it. There's pagans, cults and God-knows what! Not that I believed that, but I grew up in the South—in Tennessee and Texas, which was considered the Bible belt and very conservative.

I discovered a community called the Peaceable Kingdom that was in central Texas, not too far from Austin and Houston. The people who lived there were dedicated to arts and crafts and organic gardening. That's where I got my interest in herbs. I first visited there for an herb society meeting and ended up living there for about five years. While I was there I was studying the SRF lessons. I still remember the first letter I wrote to Ananda, asking them to send me information on their community. I got a personal letter back from Kalyani inviting me for a visit.

Shortly afterwards, I found a little ad in *Communities Magazine* that said "Apprenticeship Program at Ananda Village, $55 a month." That was in my budget. So I arrived here in the summer of 1975. Parvati picked me up from the Greyhound bus station in a little Volkswagen that the nuns owned together. She was mostly in silence and seemed very centered and austere. I had never met anyone like her. I was so excited to be coming to Ananda that I was bubbling over with hundreds of questions. I wanted to know all about the community. I'm probably getting my karma back now by working at *The Expanding Light* because people come here the same way I came, just wanting to know everything.

I was used to the country, but when I arrived at Ananda it was so rustic that it reminded me of a pioneer scene. It was Kirtani's first summer here too. I asked her all about Swami Kriyananda, and she answered my questions. She was my first friend here, and we've always stayed close even though she lives in our Assisi colony now. We worked in the garden together. I loved working in the garden. I had a strong connection with plants before I came here, but working with Haanel and Shivani taught me how to garden with consciousness and how to tune into the nature spirits. It was a wonderful experience.

I pitched my tent in Apprentice Village which is where *The Expanding Light* is now located. There was a men's section, a women's section and a couples section in this area. I hadn't been at Ananda more than 24 hours before I realized how alive Yogananda's teachings were. People here were living it. The first *sadhana* I attended everybody was doing Yogananda's Energization Exercises. I had been doing them on my own through reading the SRF lessons, but I wasn't doing them right. All the things I had read in theory were being put into real life at Ananda. It was a revelation for me.

The monastery was practically all there was when I came here. I never became a part of it because I was married before I came here. I had a first marriage that was crumbling at that point and so it wasn't appropriate for me. I never really wanted to be a nun, and even when I divorced and could have been a nun, I didn't feel it was my destiny. I was kind of out of sync with everyone else here. I wasn't really single, I wasn't married, I wasn't a monastic and I wasn't a householder.

Shivani married Arjuna shortly before I first visited Ananda in 1975. She said something to me like, "I'm trying to learn how to be a householder." I didn't know what she was talking about. She said, "Well, I've been a monastic for years. I don't know how to cook, I don't know how to take care of someone, I don't know anything. But it's okay, I'll learn. Arjuna and I are having a monastic marriage." I

A view of "downtown Ananda" from one of the
many ponds throughout the community.

was too polite to ask her what that meant. I thought that meant they were going to be celibate. In fact, for a whole year I thought that. After a while I realized that wasn't what she was talking about. So later I asked her, "How would you define a monastic marriage?" She said, "It's really quite simple, you just put God first. Your marriage is for each of you to support each other, but your spiritual search is first." According to the *Bhagavad Gita*, that's the highest definition of monasticism anyway. Monasticism doesn't have anything to do with your marital status or celibacy. It was a new concept to me that made a lot of sense. Swami has always developed that theme, so when I married Sudarshan I felt very comfortable with that concept too.

I met my husband Sudarshan here. He was on the staff at the Seclusion Retreat. He was the maintenance man and I was the cook. We had an interesting courtship because people in those years didn't have courtships. The theme at Ananda in the early years was very monastic. Many of the householders here complained about feeling like second class citizens because there was such an emphasis on the monastery. If the householders felt de-rated, imagine what it was like to just try and explore whether you wanted to get married or not. I always felt like I was sneaking around. It was funny because many of us came from the "hippie free-love" generation and all of a sudden we were living in this monastic community. It was certainly a contrast.

Sudarshan and I talked a lot about relationships. At that time, Swami was giving a class on How to Spiritualize Your Marriage. At the end of the class he asked for questions, and Sudarshan and I were sitting together. It was one of the first times we had sat together in public and when you did, of course you knew everybody knew something was going on. He raised his hand and said, "Swami, you always talk about spiritualizing marriage. Could you talk about spiritualizing the dating process?" I just about crawled under my chair. Swami just looked at him and smiled. And he said, "You know I don't have any experience so I just can't speak to that at all." Then he stopped for a minute and said, "Well, it's just like everything else, you put God first."

We talked it over and realized Swami didn't have any ideas so we had to invent a way to spiritualize the dating process ourselves. One of the things we decided that we should do was to meditate together. Every Sunday morning we got together and meditated for a couple of hours before Sunday service. At that time, Sudarshan was in charge of the Ananda Press and I was managing the office at the Seclusion Retreat. We were both real busy as usual, so even seeing each other or taking a hike together was rare. We were married by Swamiji on August 17, 1980.

In our marriage we're very supportive of each other. When one of us is down, the other tries to pick him or her up. Sudarshan is a very strong meditator, but I have my ups and downs. He has always been very sweet about not chastising me for not meditating enough, but always encourages me. And so encouraging each other is what makes such a big difference spiritually. Having someone to talk things over with makes a big difference. Often we'll listen to talks by Swami in which he brings forth new ideas. It has been wonderful to have someone to bounce ideas off of while knowing that they are as completely loyal and dedicated as you are. Not that we question Swami, but often we are trying to more fully understand some of the new (to us) concepts he is presenting.

I really cherish our marriage. If you want to have a spiritual marriage, I would recommend both partners having a real strong relationship with God first. Try to be sure that the person you're going to marry is as strong or stronger than you are on *exactly* the same spiritual path. After my first marriage, I wasn't about to get married to somebody who wasn't absolutely committed to this particular path. Being in a spiritual community is helpful. There were already good examples here of strong married couples living a spiritual life, so we weren't the first to explore marriage. Two or three times when we did have some problems, as all couples do, we could go and talk to other couples who were ministers.

Service is a major component of living the spiritual life here. At Ananda, as with many religious traditions, your religion is not just practiced on Sundays. It's not just something you do occasionally. You need to have an outlet for it. It's hard for me to conceive of two people who were strongly dedicated meditators, and all they did was meditate together. Anyone on a serious spiritual path needs to have a way of giving, of serving.

Service keeps the flow of love going and keeps you from getting stagnant. I think Yogananda set it up so that if you're going to be on this path and be successful in your spiritual life, you have to serve. Service is like water. God pours the water of grace and love into you and you have to give it back out again. Swami uses the image of a spring—if you don't keep the weeds cleared and the outward flow going, then it just doesn't work.

Most people think of a job as a 9 to 5 experience where you go home and have your own life after the clock stops. At Ananda, it's set up so there's many ways to serve. You can help lead a study group in the evenings or participate in workdays. Every department and every business here always needs more volunteers. When there's something important that needs to be done in the community, like a workday, I've learned to put aside my own desires and needs and concentrate on the project at hand. This is often the way we're able to pull off big events here. I know this thought came to me when I first came here: "I have a college degree. What am I doing here washing dishes?" But it's what was needed in order to make the whole thing happen.

The magnetism builds when you can feel your oneness as devotees doing something together. It's a thrilling feeling. That's what happens at our annual Rajarsi Day. Hundreds of people come together here to help build walkways, paint buildings, or do landscaping, for one entire day in May. People just love it. There's a magnetism that grows when people put their energies selflessly in a certain direction. It's called *karma yoga* — seeing God in your work and not being attached to the fruits of your labors. Work should be done without thinking about what you're getting from it. You set your desires aside and let the joy of God's energy flow through you without worrying about whether anybody is helped or if anything is happening.

When I first came here I didn't know who Swami Kriyananda was, so I asked Kirtani, "Is he the Guru here?" She said, "Oh no. He's a disciple of Yogananda. He lived with Yogananda before Yogananda died." She told me the story. That helped me because I was kind of fearful that I would come here and there would be this guy up on the throne who would say, "Bow to me, give me all your worldly goods, because if you want to check in here that's what you've got to do. You have to do everything I say, too." I wouldn't have stayed if that was the case because I'm too independent. The first time I saw Swami Kriyananda was a week after I got here. He was giving a class at the Seclusion Retreat. I was absolutely thrilled to my toes, because he was so eloquent and funny, open and natural.

Before I came here, I knew enough about communities to know that the community is the reflection of the leaders. The people I met here were such high quality people. I could actually see the light in their eyes and their faces. I figured it was Yogananda's blessings, but I also figured they were getting the right guidance because I'd lived in communities before and had seen what happens.

One of the first things I heard Kriyananda say in that first talk I heard him give, because I suspect he was actually tuning into my question, was, "I'm not the guru. I'm a follower of Paramhansa Yogananda and a disciple. However, I have had years of experience on this path and I'm happy to share that with you. So if you are interested in that, then I'm happy to be that to you." So for awhile I thought of him as a brother disciple on this path. As I got to know him better, I was in awe of his spiritual stature. I still hold him in great awe and wonder because of his spirituality and all the things he does. His leadership capabilities are beyond belief. Besides meditation, a significant part of my *sadhana* is listening to tapes of Kriyananda's talks. I have hundreds of them and I listen to them constantly. I do that for two reasons. One, because I teach all the time, so it helps me be a better teacher. The other is just to attune myself to him so, to Master and to this ray of energy represented through Ananda.

Attunement is like a musical term — like when you're trying to tune a guitar. You try to harmonize your vibration, to get on the same wavelength, so to speak. If you want to be a good airline pilot, you hang around the best airline pilot there is because there's more to it than just learning from books. What you learn from someone is quite often not something that comes through words, it's done by the exchange of energy and electro-magnetic energy and magnetism. When you're in the proximity of someone who you suspect is a person of high spiritual stature, be it a saint or be it a spiritual teacher, you benefit by putting down your own barriers and opening yourself in some way to receive, not just their words, but their energy and their vibrations. And that's what I've always tried to do with Swami Kriyananda.

I'm a person who loves nature. The physical setting of Ananda is totally inspiring to me so I spend a lot of time in nature. I love taking walks, talking to friends, and sitting around the dinner table. I live in a housing cluster where we have a large common dining room and we eat dinner together every night. We all take turns cooking so it's a great time-saving device.

I enjoy the simple pleasure of community living—like the talks after dinner with friends. It's very important because it's satsang on a human level. During these times, all sorts of things come out, funny stories, lots of laughter. I think one of the most wonderful things about Ananda is the laughter and joy we're able to keep through all our trials. There's a level of humor here that is quite healing—you see it in our plays, the music and the way we interact. I think a lot of people take themselves way too seriously. And of course, Swami has lead the way in that. He laughs at himself, he laughs at P.G. Wodehouse, he laughs at many things.

There have been hundreds of utopia-type communities in this country, some which still exist. We're not the only intentional community, but we are unique. I believe Ananda has succeeded where many others haven't because of Swami Kriyananda's leadership, because of Yogananda's blessings, and because the first thing we did was to open a retreat where other people could visit and we could serve them. I think it's important for communities to serve the greater world in some way. I think Ananda is successful because we have always thought in terms of what we can do to serve others and not just try to create a happy little life for ourselves and our families.

Guests come here and their consciousness is uplifted without them even knowing what has happened. They're vibrating at one level when they get here and they're vibrating at a different level when they leave. That's due to a lot of different things. Mainly it's the laws of satsang, of magnetism, and there's a "joy zone" here that people get just by physically walking into it. The delivery men that come here comment on it. Sudarshan says that the guys who deliver to our job sites tell him they just like coming here, they don't know why. It's peaceful here. People come here and think we have some of the most beautiful gardens they've ever seen. And I realize that what they're responding to is something else—it's not really the gardens, it's the love and the energy that's expressed here.

When a large number of people are focusing their energy in the same direction, they create a magnetism—through meditation, through service, through their love for mankind and nature. The grace that people feel here is the blessings from our guru, Yogananda. I've looked at this place all these years and thought, "How could it keep going, how could it survive?" It has to be the grace of God, because it just doesn't work on paper. There have been so many miracles here that I cannot explain.

There was once a lady who came to our Elderhostel program—she was a large woman, in her seventies, athletically built, but she walked kind of slowly. She had some health problems and she was discouraged about her life. We taught her Energization Exercises and the simple stretches that we do for Elderhostel guests. At the end of her five days here, she came to me with tears in her eyes. She said, "You know I was ready to die and had given up on my life. I had nothing to live for. I couldn't use my body in the way I used to. I was always active and athletic. You have given me back my life." Swami has always told us that the greatest thing we can do is to give people our love and energy—that's the main thing they'll remember and benefit from the most.

What we do at Ananda is to try to live spiritual principles to the best of our ability by walking our talk and not making spirituality some kind of philosophy that you read in a book. A lot of it has to do with meditation. Years ago I remember just reading and reading and reading. And one day I just threw whatever book I was reading across the room—it might have been *Autobiography of a Yogi*—because I'd read it so many times. I thought, I can't read it anymore, I have to do it, I have to experience it. Ananda is that for me—a living laboratory for spiritual theories.

Everyday is a lesson for me in learning how to trust God more. How to trust that everything is going to be okay; no matter if it doesn't look like it's going to be okay, it's *still* going to be okay. There have been a lot of small things where I personally haven't had enough money to get my teeth fixed or something, and somehow it always comes to me.

One interesting story was when I was first driving out here to Ananda. I was in West Texas and became sick and couldn't go any further. I had some kind of stomach flu so I couldn't drive and didn't have enough money for a motel. I was stuck in the desert. I began really praying to God to help me. I kept clearly getting the message, well just try going a little further. When I arrived in Las Cruses, New Mexico, I again prayed to figure out what to do. I saw these two girls standing over on the side of the road hitchhiking in the middle of the desert. One had a guitar case. Yogananda had always said, "Don't pick up hitchhikers." I thought, well, no, wait a minute, this may be God answering me somehow.

I drove over to where the girls were and asked them if they were trying to get a ride somewhere. They said, yes, they were looking for a ride to Sacramento, California. I said, "Can either of you drive, because I'm not feeling well." One said, "I have a chauffeur's license. That's what I do for a business." So they hopped in and drove me all the way out here. This to me was like an angel story. And the interesting thing was that they had been praying that somebody would come along and pick them up! That's a wonderful answered prayer story. When I told everybody here about my story they said, "Oh, stuff happens here all the time." It's the land of miracles.

Prayer and trust in God helps you have faith in God. You can't learn faith any other way than by having the experiences come along. I've seen things like this happen too many times not to know that it's God's grace. My faith gets stronger when I come up against something and begin thinking I'm just not going to make it this time. Then I remember back on all the miracles and all the things that shouldn't have worked out but did. The grace of God and the blessings of Yogananda definitely take up the slack.

Ram & Dianna

Ram—I was a defensive linebacker for UC Berkeley when I first met Dianna, although we didn't become friends until much later. My last year at Berkeley, I was selected to be a part of an all star football game in Japan. While I was staying in Japan, I read *The Teachings of Buddha*, which had been placed in my hotel room, just like many American hotels sometimes have the Bible. I was quite drawn to these teachings.

I was the head of the black athletes' association at UC Berkeley, and there were some coaches who didn't like us and made it difficult for us. So I would use what I knew of Buddhism and the words of the 23rd Psalm to guide me "...*thou preparest a table before me in the presence of my enemies...surely goodness and mercy shall follow me all the days of my life.*" And, as the psalm says, I was protected the whole way. I passed my exams and graduated.

I tried out with the San Francisco 49ers at the end of my college career, and was with them for several months before I moved to Los Angeles, which is where my parents lived. Yogananda's *Autobiography of a Yogi* was in my family home, so I began to read it and I realized Yogananda had temples right here in Los Angeles. I wanted to visit them.

Dianna—The way I heard about Ananda was through *Autobiography of a Yogi*, which I discovered through studying another spiritual path. I remember having lunch in a park in Los Angeles, and I was reading a book on Transcendental Meditation (TM). I saw a man meditating nearby and it turned out he was a TM teacher. I attended his class and he taught me how to meditate. He also gave me a copy of Yogananda's *Autobiography of a Yogi*. I didn't know anything about Kriya Yoga, meditation, or the gurus, but it just felt right. For quite some time, I had been praying to meet a friend. I had been attending SRF services and one day I visited Lake Shrine.

Ram—I had gone to the SRF Lake Shrine the same day, and that's where I met Dianna. It was love at first sight.

Dianna—We had known each other from college, and when I met him at the Lake Shrine, I knew that Yogananda had brought us together.

Ram—That summer I met a person who gave me Kriyananda's *Yoga Postures for Higher Awareness* book. Dianna and I had both heard about Ananda from SRF; people said it's a place up in the mountains, where Yogananda's teachings are being lived in a community. So I began visiting Ananda whenever I could. Then, once I moved up here, Dianna came.

Dianna—When I came to this spiritual community as an apprentice, it was very different for me, because I'm from the city. I was coming to the country, after having never gone camping my entire life. I wasn't really comfortable here, because it was so different from what I was used to. And I didn't know anybody but Ram, and by this time, he was planning to go into the monastery. We had been dating before, and when we came here he decided he wanted to become a monk. It was a big hardship for me. He was my only friend and I was losing him to the monastery.

I lived at the Seclusion Retreat. The first night I slept in a little pup tent, and a family of raccoons came to the tent in the middle of the night. There was a scratching on the screen of the tent and it just scared me to death. I moved to a cabin after that. It was just too *rustic* for me.

When Ram moved into the monastery, there wasn't a lot of discussion, so I was sort of left in the wings. I didn't have any friends and I didn't know anybody, so I soon left Ananda and went home to Los Angeles. I thought maybe I'd come back sooner, but I didn't come back for three years. They were three terrible years. It was the worst time of my entire life.

After these three years I came back to Ananda, and within about two months, I decided to move into the Atherton ashram in the Bay Area. After that, my life just took off again. Ram was still in the monastery and the type of letters I'd get from him were all about "I love God and Guru." I had been through so much in four years; I was ready to be a nun. So after a few months of correspondence, I wrote Ram and told him that I was going to be a nun. And he wrote me back immediately, saying, "No! Wait! I'm coming out of the monastery!" That was around the time many of the monks were leaving the monastery.

Ram — A few years earlier, while I was still in the monastery I had a reading from a well-known psychic who reads the *akashic records*. She had said I would be married in this lifetime, and my wife's name would start with a D. After the monastery began to disband, I moved to the ashram in the Bay Area, and we eventually got married.

Dianna — We both lived in the ashram and worked for a high technology company in Menlo Park.

Ram — Ananda had a big ashram in San Francisco and Kriyananda asked us to help head up the activities there and train with Jyotish and Devi, who had been living there and were returning to Ananda Village.

Dianna—Shortly after we moved to San Francisco, Swami Kriyananda came back from giving talks in Italy, and everybody at the San Francisco ashram had a dinner with him. We were all seated around a big dining room table and we were all so happy to see him. At one point in the middle of the conversation about Italy, Swami just turned to me and said, "And Dianna, I'm thinking about going back there in March, and I'm thinking about taking Ram and you with me." And that was it; everyone's jaw dropped! I had no idea this was coming. I'd never traveled *anywhere*. He continued talking about Italy, and his comment to me was, "I hope you like to travel." I was shocked. And people were a bit afraid for us. So when Ram got home, I told him about the dinner with Swami, and he talked to Swami, wanting to know why he thought we should go. Our friends were wondering about black people going to Italy, that we may not be well-received. But Kriyananda was optimistic. He thought the Italians would like us.

Ram—We had no money, so I immediately started giving concerts to raise the funds to pay for our travel. I sang spirituals and some of Kriyananda's songs.

Dianna—Kriyananda had been giving lectures throughout Europe for many years, so he had various friends everywhere. We were going to Europe with a few other Ananda members, and Kriyananda said to us, "We'll go there, and if it doesn't work out, you can just see it as a nice vacation." So he didn't pressure us. We didn't know how long we'd be gone, and Ram had only raised enough money for three months.

Kriyananda had gone with us for part of the time, and before he returned to the U.S. he said we should meditate and attune to God and Yogananda, to find out what we were to do in Italy. So I had to use a lot of sadhana and prayer. He never gave us an outline or told us how to start our center. He just said, "You should feel what's trying to happen there. I don't know if it's supposed to be a retreat or a community. You need to find out."

We planned to give year-round yoga retreats at a summer villa on Lake Como in northern Italy. There was no central heating in the house because the people who owned the house would only go there in the summertime. I remember the first winter. Coming from LA I had never even really seen snow before. We were all alone, a small group of us in this cold, cold villa on Lake Como and it began to snow every day. There were very few Europeans who came for retreats because of the weather conditions. So it was a time for all of us to work on our inner strength and clarity of mind.

Ram — There were about eight of us, including Jyotish and Devi. It was a good group, and despite the weather and the lack of money, our attitude was such that we were able to approach it as an adventure, like a nice vacation. We had to be very creative. It was simple living.

Dianna — Many times we wanted to go home. But then we'd think about the people in Europe and there were some who wanted us to stay so they could learn yoga more intensely. We just had to stick it out.

Ram — The first business we created was hosting pilgrimages. Tours would come from America to Italy and we'd visit the holy sites of Saint Francis and the other Catholic saints.

Dianna — The best part was the close friendships we made from living in a spiritual retreat center together. When you all go through hard times together you develop real close bonds of friendship. Living in our European retreat was where I really grew spiritually; that's where I matured the most.

Guests would come and I had to *constantly* put out positive energy, and creative thoughts to keep things going. And that's where I began to really feel Yogananda's presence, more than any other time. It was the beginning of Ananda's European community. There was nobody there, nobody to call. People didn't really write and Christmas was meager. The first Christmas we spent in Italy, we didn't have what we were used to having for Christmas. We didn't have money to buy many presents. We didn't have all the festive things. Yet we were there to make it Christmas for the guests staying at our retreat.

I remember on Christmas Day Anandi called up from California and Devi and I were both crying on the phone. It was hard. After that I realized I was not in Italy to think of myself, which was a big turning point for me. I was there to think of other people. And when that lesson really sunk in, then everything turned around. The first nine months in Italy were the hardest, but after that my attitude changed and things flowed much better.

Ram — I would never change any of it, and I have no regrets. It was wonderful in Italy because it gave me the opportunity to serve others in a selfless way. It was challenging because we had to learn the language. But it was also a great blessing. I learned how to play the guitar in Italy, as a way to share the songs and chants we did. It was a very creative time. We developed a music group that toured around Italy and Europe.

I remember our first performance was near Como, Italy in a little town called San Fidele. We got paid about $200, which wasn't much. An organization paid us to sing at a fund-raising for blood donations. The emcee came out on the stage, and he said, "Well, we have a very interesting group here today. They don't eat meat, they don't smoke, they don't drink wine. But, they got a lot of joy. They're the Joy Singers!"

After we moved to Assisi, we sang at the Basilica of St Francis, and while we were there, one of the priests said, "Well, why don't you sing for the pope?" We were allowed to sing for the pope, and at the performance we had to warm up, so we sang before the pope came out. We did Yogananda's chant, *Door of My Heart* in four-part harmony, in Italian. The Italian people immediately felt the vibration and the words, and they began to sing too, so there were 10,000 people singing along with us. It was beautiful.

Dianna — Learning to serve in Europe together was very strengthening for our marriage. Our relationship has always been one of shared service to God. I've always felt that Ram and I are together for this reason. We've been married now 17 years. We always meditate and pray together. But if we didn't have a way to serve, I don't know why we would be together. Just to sit at home by ourselves and eat nice meals and have a nice house and go on vacations isn't what gives us joy. In our hearts and souls, I've always known that's not the life we're supposed to be living.

Ram — The purpose of our marriage has always been to be spiritual partners.

Dianna — I have learned that living a spiritual life means not just reading about it or hearing it from somebody else. Firsthand experience of living the teachings of yoga is what I've received at Ananda. And also having the support of other people living this way. And the third thing I've received is having the possibility of living at least some of the time in the community with a direct disciple of Yogananda, who is our teacher.

Ram — I thank God that I have the ability to serve in any little way. When I serve, when I'm with others, I always try to remember, "It's God sharing with God." Ananda has helped me to see the God in others and everywhere.

Dianna—For me, the opportunity to serve my guru's work directly, and to feel his blessing flowing through me, through my desire and willingness and openness to serve others, has been my greatest joy.

Ram—Every day there are miracles here. I've learned to be open to seeing them manifested in everything—like the feeling of His presence when my thoughts go to rest, when I'm at a point of perfect stillness, and I ask, "Are You there?" and I feel the response, the smile in my heart. More than anything, it's the recognition that God is that smile.

Saraswati

In our culture, there's a tendency to put a lot of emphasis on being successful and having money. I've never understood the "go out and get yours" consciousness that many in our society so blindly embrace. When I was in Junior High School I remember feeling so alone and very different—so unconnected with the goals and desires of those around me.

I remember reading the book, *Walk Across America*, about a man and his dog on a walk across the United States. One time in a big city, I think he ran into some trouble and *almost* got attacked. Every other story in the book was about all the people who helped him, took him in, fed him, gave him jobs and showed him such kindness in this world. But that's not what the media is telling us. That's not the message that we're getting about this world. We are shown all the sensational, irrational, ego-centered behavior of some people and asked to believe that the whole world is like that. It's no wonder that people become cynical and look for the worst in each other.

It wasn't until I came to Ananda Village that I found—"Ah these are my brothers and sisters. These are people who have spiritual goals and ideals and who want to help and support each other." So, if I'm doing something for myself, why not put out just a little more energy and do it for the good of a few other people, too? Ananda is a place where you can honestly help and serve people and do something to benefit others—beyond the end of your own little nose, and greater than just your own little world. I feel as if I've stepped into a whole new world!

It was inspiring for me to observe my husband, Ganesha, and to watch his spiritual life evolving. He has always been very slow to move into new things—carefully considering all the details, very reasonable and rational. Before we were married, I watched him quit his job as an engineer making lots of money, take up meditation and move up to this community in the hills. I had to stop and take notice, because this was not something he just rushed into without any thought. He had done a lot of soul-searching to make such a drastic change in his life and life-style.

Ananda is a place where you can raise children and feel that they are loved and supported, because there are so many friends, like "aunts" and "uncles" to help care for all the children. Our children can safely walk to school, probably knowing every person who drives by on their way to school. It's such a positive, nurturing environment for children here. I've taught in the school here at Ananda, off and on, since the mid-seventies. We try to really nurture and bring out the highest in each child. We show them how to claim their own inner strength and wisdom, helping them to stay centered throughout the challenges and changes of adolescence. We honor the fact that children are individuals and have their own unique ways of maturing and developing.

Before coming to Ananda, I was involved with a meditation group that got together once a week and meditated a bit, then discussed lessons and theories—all in a very cerebral way. Here, at Ananda, I've found the missing *heart* quality, so necessary to be able to expand beyond the theory of it all. Life at Ananda puts you on the spot to live the teachings of yoga every minute of every day. That means that you're going to be falling down a bit and dusting yourself off sometimes. Ananda is a living workshop to practice the art of truly living the teachings of brotherhood, service, compassion and unconditional love.

We try to take time to reflect on our actions and thoughts and to understand what is the right thing to do for the highest good of everyone. Do I feel more love, more expansion in my heart? If I see someone having a hard time, am I able to reach out and help them? In this way we are constantly unfolding and expanding. Yogananda's teachings can become just an intellectual ideal, if you're not testing them, minute by minute, in the cold light of day.

At Ananda our lives overlap to the point where we go to church together, we raise children together, we work together and go on Lake Tahoe vacations together. Sometimes one needs to take a break from community life, to get a little better perspective. The reality of living in a laboratory where you're constantly trying to be open to inner guidance to direct your choices in expansive, creative ways can get a bit intense at times.

The nice thing is that here we have other devotees to talk things over with, so that we don't need to feel alone in our struggle to deepen our understanding of the lessons that life brings to us. We don't need to be self-conscious about asking a friend, "What is the truth of this situation? What's trying to happen here? Is my ego getting in the way?" We support each other to find in ourselves the even-minded and cheerful attitude to not only accept, but to embrace joyfully what comes to us, because it is personally designed for us to make us stronger and wiser. This is the path of yoga.

I think at some point, when you are really sincere on the spiritual path, you are given guidance and blessings in your life—openings in areas of your life that were closed before then. One such opening for me, personally, was when Swamiji gave me my spiritual name. In the past, Swamiji would meditate on a person and come up with a spiritual name that would be a quality to aspire toward, or a spiritual goal.

I wrote to Swamiji and asked for a spiritual name. Before meeting with him, I was looking through the SRF *Cosmic Chants* book and I was immediately drawn to the picture and the name of the goddess Saraswati. I remember thinking what a beautiful name it was. Then I read that it meant, "Divine Mother in the aspect of wisdom, learning and music." I thought, "Sure, it's a beautiful name. It's a name for Divine Mother! I need a name like, 'Hang in there, baby!' or 'You can do it, you can do it!' not a name for Divine Mother."

I had felt really drawn to the name Saraswati but also felt very humbled about what name would be the right name for me. So I want to see Swamiji, and he said, "I have a name for you." I waited breathlessly. "It's Saraswati," he said. I remember feeling rather dazed and numb for a moment, then thinking, "How amazing."

Then Swamiji blessed me at the point between the eyebrows. I had to step away from the blessing, because I felt it was too much for me to take in, all at one time. Then, for three days afterwards, I felt in an uplifted, joyful state of consciousness that I had never felt before. It was like I was a bubble that had risen up to the surface and was shining and glistening with sunlight all of a sudden. I felt incredibly free and lighter than ever before in my life.

Shortly after I got my spiritual name, Ananda sent out *Joy Tours* around the country to lecture on organic gardening, meditation, and our school's philosophy. Since I was then teaching kindergarten in the Ananda School, I was asked to go out with Nitai and give talks about our school. I was so incredibly shy that I knew I couldn't do it. I remember the first talk we gave, there were about one hundred people in the audience. As I stood up at the podium, I looked at Nitai, and I was thinking, "If I burst into tears and run out of here, Nitai

Saraswati with Ananda school children.

won't ask me to do this any more. I could be done. Wouldn't that be great?"

At the same time, I felt Divine Mother watching over me, waiting to see what I would do. I felt Divine Mother say, "It's you and Nitai. Who else is going to do this for me? Can you come up with what it takes to do this?" I knew this was it—my chance to do what *God* wanted, in spite of what I wanted, or didn't want to do.

I remember reaching inside myself and saying, "Yes, I can. I don't have to be a shy person, incapable of doing anything. I can rise to the occasion and do what needs to be done. And I'm the one who has to do it, so I'll do it." I took a deep breath and I just relaxed and started talking about what I enjoyed, about working to bring out the best in children. Somehow, after the blessing of getting my spiritual name, I was able to let fall away that part of me that was so painfully shy. Since then, I have been able to do what is asked of me with a calmness and a deep willingness to serve God's will in all things.

I think it was Socrates who said, "An unexamined life is not worth living." This community has given me the opportunity to learn to introspect, to look closely at the patterns of my life. If I don't like what I see, I know that I have the power, with God's grace, to change. The big secret for me to discover was to learn to get my little self, my ego, out of the way. Something is trying to flow through me, to unfold like the petals on a flower, and I finally realized that I don't have to pull the petals off one at a time with my own hands. I just have to remember to let myself be a part of that effortless flow of grace, like the river that runs back to the sea. All I need is the courage to let go— and to let God's grace guide me.

Peter & Catherine

Peter — I was working as a researcher in a pulmonary function laboratory at UC Irvine while I was attending college in the early seventies. It so happened that some of the very earliest research on meditation was being done at our lab. Some of the well-known meditation researchers were part of a team to study the effects of meditation on the human body. Dr. Howard Benson was at a different institution, but was part of this collaborative effort along with Dr. Archie Wilson — who was also well known. We were studying blood oxygenation and what happens to different hormones and blood sugar when people meditate. Back then, some researchers thought meditation was really just sleep. We were actually doing brain wave studies, hooking up people to EEGs and studying the brain waves of those who were meditating. We were running out of meditation subjects that we could use, so they taught me how to do the TM technique. I went in and sat down and promptly fell asleep and slept for a full 35 minutes of the study! It turned out that I was one of two people out of the 50 tested who actually fell asleep. We did show meditation and sleep were different, however.

I was impressed with the people who were meditators in our studies because they were clearly different in positive ways and it was obvious through our research that something significant was actually happening during meditation. It aroused my scientific curiosity. Meditation was the first thing that I had ever found that improved one in more than just a psychological way. Meditation actually worked with your body and brain chemistry, and had some very positive long-term effects.

The summer before I went to medical school, I spent a month at a TM ashram and retreat center in Switzerland and meditated four hours a day. It changed my life. Even there, however no one talked about God and meditation, they'd only discuss meditation and expanded states of consciousness. I was beginning to get an idea that there was something more to meditation. Aside from becoming a TM instructor, there wasn't a way you could really immerse yourself in meditation. I wanted something more.

The next summer, I was in my first year of medical school, and was traveling through this dusty little Mexican village called Oaxaca. I was in the market area and just about to jump on a bus to go to Guatemala. I walked by a man sitting on a park bench, and he just seemed to be very magnetic for some reason. I was going to get on the bus and instead I went over and started talking to him. I very quickly learned that he was a meditator too. I was talking about some of the experiences I had, and he said, "Oh, you need to go to Ananda. It's in Nevada City." We talked so long I missed my bus to go to Guatemala, but there was something that happened in that interaction. I never did see this gentleman again and found out years later that his health had become so bad he never came up to Ananda again. He was a mathematics professor at UC Davis.

The following summer I was considering attending one of the Buddhist meditation centers in San Francisco for a long retreat, when I saw this little purple mimeographed flier from the Seclusion Retreat at Ananda. I remembered what the man in Mexico had said about "Ananda." I came up for a visit and loved it.

Catherine—I'd been living in Japan teaching English and studying traditional Kimono weaving. I had read *Autobiography of a Yogi* in Japan in the mid-seventies and the book completely changed my life. Like many others, I remember sitting up all night and reading and weeping and immediately trying to memorize the poem, *Samadhi*. I instantly realized that what Yogananda was saying was the truth. As it so happened, two American friends who were interested in the spiritual path had been to India, trekked in Tibet, and were staying again in Japan. They were also very interested in living in a spiritual community. They left Japan to move to Ananda and some months later I decided to visit them as part of a longer return trip to the U.S. Unbeknownst to me Ananda was a community dedicated to Paramhansa Yogananda. When I walked into the temple and saw Yogananda's picture on the altar, I felt immediately at home.

At the time, I really didn't like the idea of group living. My underlying fear was that community was like an encounter group, and I had already experienced the pitfalls of such groups. So I had a real dilemma. I so much wanted to learn Yogananda's teachings, and I knew that I needed help with my meditation practice. I went back to Japan and the following fall I returned to Ananda and met Prakash, who was running the training program then. He taught me Energization Exercises and the Hong Sau meditation technique. I began to notice that Ananda wasn't an "encounter group," and that people lived very privately. What touched me most was the sincerity of the people I met, their innate goodness, and the fact that meditation was obviously working in their lives—they all seemed calm and centered. While a sweet friendship was offered, people were working out their psychological "quirks" in meditation.

After my apprenticeship I lived in the monastery. I ended up serving my apprenticeship mainly in the Publications building because of my abilities—I could write, type, and I was game to learn the crude typesetting machine we had then. Being around the nuns who worked in Ananda Publications helped me mature spiritually. They were spiritual models for me, they were my big sisters, and I was inwardly drawn to a monastic life. I did not feel male-female relationships were the answer.

The dissolution of the monastery and Peter and I coming together occurred around the same time. For me, the spiritual path was fairly black and white at that point. I was in the mode of renunciation and cutting away, rather than in the mode of seeing God in everything. So it was actually quite painful to watch the monastery disappear. The head nun was Seva, and her approach to what was happening was actually brilliantly intuitive. She saw that there were renunicate couples who had a spiritual dynamism and were true monastics in their hearts. So she had one such couple, Ananta and Maria, move into a little cabin down near the nuns' area of Ayhodha. In this way she tried to keep a dynamic renunciate spirit going.

Peter—I should tell how we got together. I was in the monastery from the late seventies until 1981, when the men's monastery was starting to disband. There really weren't many of us left and I felt that it was Divine Mother's wish for me to be a householder. I knew that although I was going to be a householder my life would be one of service, and I would need to be with someone with whom I could serve. So I had that thought in my mind, and I wanted to start a relationship consciously rather than have it be impulsive.

When I was in the monastery I always felt that the householders were a "breed apart." There were the single people, the monastics, and the householders. No one really knew what the householder path to God clearly meant or could look like. So it was an enigma at that point. No other American yoga community had ever had a large householder order that I was aware of.

Catherine—The model of being a monastic householder existed, but I had little contact with those who were living that life. I didn't know Jyotish and Devi for many years, and had no contact with Jaya and Sadhana Devi, who were other community leaders and householders. I was aware, however, that there were very senior, well-respected householders in the community.

Peter—I realized that Catherine would be someone worth exploring the householder monastic path with. I had seen her in the group meditations, and had served with her on some small projects. After I'd meditated on it, I actually went up to her one day and said, "I think we should date. I think it would be a good thing."

Catherine—I said, "Well, the most important thing is my life is God and following this spiritual path. I would have to feel that same level of dedication in you or I'm not interested." It probably sounded so cold at the time, but that's how I felt. I thought, "Well, we might as well get this on the right footing immediately."

Peter—It was the right thing to say.

Catherine—We'd both been here about six years before we started dating.

Peter—We were here to serve this work rather than try to create a perfect little relationship where we catered to each other's needs. We both felt to do something that was bigger than both of us or our own egos; we wanted to serve others.

Catherine—In my early years here, the nuns were always serving the larger community. Our "private lives" were in our meditation rooms. When Peter and I first got together, I made a lot of mistakes. My thought was that marriage was an extension of my private life. It seemed to me that paying attention to the marriage and its needs was just a form of self-involvement. I thought Peter and I should just be serving all the time at the guest retreat or elsewhere in the community instead of giving any energy to our marriage. Peter was patient while I slowly came to understand that my concept of service had to expand. I had to be less theoretical about what a spiritual house-holder relationship was and a lot more practical. For instance, you don't respond to your spouse by saying, "Gee I'm sorry you're feeling a little ignored but you shouldn't feel that way, you should feel more detached. So, I'll see you later." That's a horrible exaggeration, of course. We needed to be realistic about the fact that neither one of us was rooted in *nirbikalpa samadhi* yet. As householder monastics, we are helping each other toward the goal of God-realization, but we have to acknowledge and work with our human realities as well. That's the challenge.

Peter—There are lots of ways we help each other grow toward God. In my wife, Catherine, I have a spiritual friend and a counselor I live with. In my work as a medical doctor, I'm often in work situations that are challenging on a personal level for me. Many of the people I see are in terrible crises. Living with someone like Catherine, who has a clear mind and really understands the spiritual path as well, is a real benefit for me. Many times she'll save me from staying mad at someone, or even doing the wrong things, because I'm able to talk things through with her and get a spiritual perspective to my problems.

It was unrelenting financial, physical and psychological stress to found our rural medical clinic, particularly in its early days. I'm sure that it was no fun for Catherine to be around me sometimes, I was so stressed out. In the beginning I had to do everything. Out here in the country, it's "people intensive" medical care and you have to work with people where they're at in their thinking. There's zero medical support from other doctors. Its not like you can sit down in the lunch room and ask a radiologist about a complicated x-ray.

The San Juan Ridge was a lot different back then, it was a much poorer area in the '80s. Now we have retired federal judges, and retired professionals living here as well as many people in their for-ties and fifties who do computer work, or are animators or program-mers, working from their homes. In the early '80s, there were still a lot of gold miners and back-to-the-land hippies living here. Back then, it was not that unusual to have someone ride up to the clinic on a horse! Every year for two solid days in the spring there was a cattle drive right down Tyler Foote Road blocking it! The first year we opened the clinic we had to put up a sign that said, "If you want to be seen by the doctor, you must leave your gun or your knife at the desk." I'd end up being in these little examination rooms with loggers and gold miners wearing a revolver on their belt and a big bowie knife strapped to their thigh and I'd think, "If I do something wrong here, this guy will kill me."

In my first months I was swamped with patients, I didn't have any take home pay to live on and I didn't know how long I could go on like that. Luckily, another doctor, David Kessler, came to live in the Ananda community. He said, "I'd be willing to work part time for whatever you'd be willing to pay me, and I can go work out in other jobs to make money." So gradually we were able to build the practice. He was with the practice for about 13 years. We added three nurse practitioners, and all three still work with us. The practice grew and developed until it reflected the kind of care we wanted to offer. Even-tually we made the clinic a tax-exempt non-profit corporation and donated it to the people of California. Our board of directors is rep-resentative of everybody in the San Juan Ridge area.

The way I relate to my patients is with a very impersonal love. It's a feeling of kindness and love, not a " I love you because you're my friend" kind of love. I love my patients because they're all children of God, and I want them to be well and healthy because that's God's desire for all of us. I'm not working at this clinic because it is intel-lectually interesting, because it's a great professional thing for my resume, or because I'm in it for money. I'm doing it because it's a service and it's what God wants me to do. When I feel myself serving in this way, I feel it's God's power serving through me and I can feel joy from that.

Catherine—The greatest thing I've learned from living in a spiritual community is that happiness *never* lies in thinking about yourself. Happiness lies in service. Through meditation, we come to realize that all our answers *are* inside, but genuine intuition can take years to develop. What happens is that sometimes we don't know whether what we're feeling is of God or born of subconscious desires or *samskars*. If I'm in a situation like this, I often will check out what I'm feeling with those whose wisdom I respect here in the community.

Peter—In the world of medicine and academia I was working because I found it interesting, or because I could make money. What I've had at Ananda is a chance us to serve God in others. This doesn't mean just service to other people, *but serving God in those people*. I've learned there's a tremendous joy and freedom in overcoming my likes and dislikes. In our culture it's easy to get hypnotized into thinking that if you're using the right talent or have the right job then you'll be happy. I've learned that happiness is an attitude that comes from my own inner peace, not from something that's outside of me.

When I first started meditating I just wanted to be a better person. After about 10 years, I realized it was possible to have an actual relationship with God—it wasn't something intellectual, it was an interior experience that I had actually grown into. Meditation and devotional practices have helped me grow tremendously. I now have a very dynamic *inner* life. If things are happening in my life that are challenging, I talk to God. I don't need to go outside of myself for answers or need someone to tell me what to do as much as I used to. Instead I talk with God about it, which is very different. There's a joy, a calmness, a peace that comes with knowing I have that inner connection with God. Here at Ananda, we have a powerful technique in Kriya Yoga, which is an advanced meditation technique that actually helps one develop a deeper inner life.

Catherine—Peter's work as a doctor demands that he be with people a lot. So, we're probably different than other couples here, in that we don't meditate together. He needs to have his own space when he's meditating, and I respect that. One of the best things that we do for each other is help each other to make *dharmic* choices from moment to moment. We try to support each other. In doing what's right rather than coming from our own personal emotions, and "likes" and "dislikes." We also seek to help one another feel encouraged about how we're doing spiritually. I'll listen to Peter handle a phone call about a sticky issue. When he gets off the phone I'll say, "I think you handled that very well. What you said was very important and encouraging to her." Obviously, we try not to do things that will *discourage* the other.

Peter—One of the real strengths in our marriage is that we work with each other in a magnetic way rather than telling each other what we should or shouldn't do. If I see her struggling with something, rather than say, "Catherine, you should do this," I'll wait. Then, when she does the right thing, I'll say, "It's great you did that." In this way we're not trying constantly to counsel each other. Through all the spiritual practices here, we've learned how to be intuitive with each other and to help each other do the right thing.

Catherine—Living here as a householder monastic all these years, I now understand what Yogananda meant when he said *environment is stronger than will power*. Our greatest ally is to be surrounded by others who are doing the same thing we are. It's not impossible to do what we're doing without a community, but the sheer magnetism of a group can be very helpful, very supportive in trying to live connected to God.

Durga

I had always wanted to be part of a work or consciousness that was meaningful and would somehow express the peace that is so lacking in the world. When Vidura and I first came to Ananda, I remember driving down the dirt road across Malakoff Diggins out towards the Seclusion Retreat. The day we arrived there was a Kriya initiation and everyone was in silence: meditating or walking quietly along the wooded pathways. The forest, the simple dwellings and the total peace made a deep impression on me. I felt intuitively "This is home. This is where I will find what I've been looking for."

I had been studying with another spiritual teacher for one year and I wasn't sure how I would integrate his teachings with Ananda. Would I have to leave? Does one change gurus after taking initiation from another? Was Yogananda *my* guru? Ananda was everything I had ever hoped to find yet I had to have answers to these questions. Not long afterwards I talked with one of the members here who told me that all true gurus work together for the welfare of the disciple. If I truly felt Yogananda was my guru and Ananda the place where he had brought me to find God, then all would surely work itself out. What a load lifted from my shoulders! I became aware of the vastness of this teaching and the subtle ways in which the devotee learns of the unconditional love of God.

The first summer here was exciting, filled with many new adventures and much learning. We lived with our two pre-teens, Dwayne and Melissa, in a large tent at the Seclusion Retreat where new people came to study and get a feel of the vibration and daily life of this new and unfolding community. The challenge for me was learning how to balance community and family life. In saying "yes" to Ananda I was entering into a whole new world of spiritual community, spiritual marriage and spiritual "step-motherhood." How was I to balance all these and give to everyone the best that I was able? We were all learning and growing so quickly, while an inner joy was welling up in me that brought new life and creativity into every aspect of my day. It was a time in Ananda's history when very few families had taken the plunge to truly dedicate their lives to this path. Just how *do* you do this? How do you stay focused and calm and creative while serving your family and meditating? We all still face these questions daily but at that time the guidelines and examples weren't as prevalent and clear. Vidura and I had to make some tough decisions immediately if we were going to be a dynamic addition to this greater family.

There were only a few families living at the "farm" in 1974—our newest land acquisition, six miles up the road. In September it was time to move as we had a family and needed to find a job for me, get the children in school and find housing. I felt like I was being sent to Siberia! I didn't know if I could keep up my spiritual practices on my own; at the Seclusion Retreat we meditated, ate and worked all together in a very tight-knit family. It was also an awkward time for householders because almost everyone was in the monastery and were more withdrawn. My personality was more outward, friendly and "community-oriented." I also needed and wanted to be able to give quality time to my personal family. I wasn't sure where I fit in.

Should I tone my natural personality down? Would I be able to give sufficiently to the larger family? What was trying to happen for us?

Just about that time, I remember a talk Swami Kriyananda gave, telling us all that the time had come when we needed to reach out to people more, to look them in the eyes when we spoke to them (the monastic way traditionally is to keep oneself more closed within, even to the point of keeping one's eyes averted so as not to lose one's inner focus), to serve newcomers with more joy and openness. Were my prayers being answered so soon? We knew we couldn't make ends meet on the wages Ananda was able to give us at that time so Vidura kept up the construction work he had before coming to Ananda and worked on and off in Reno, Oakland, Sacramento and even Alaska for nine years before he was able to be at Ananda full-time. Meanwhile I found that I, too, had a way I could serve. If there was a strong monastic life, couldn't we also have a strong householder aspect to our work? I worked within the community serving in the macramé business, as print shop manager, school secretary and shipping books for Ananda Publications. Our children went to the Ananda School, a one-room schoolhouse serving children ages 5-12 in eight different grades.

It was this first summer that the macramé business opened which employed many of the moms with younger children, enabling them to work at home and still contribute to the community at large. I soon got a job working there on staff. I was thrilled and thus began the first job making up my 24-year career known as Ananda! Being paid $2/hour made our salaries the highest at the village and we gladly worked hard for that privilege. I remember walking to work one day in late autumn listening to the birds and the wind in the trees and seeing the colors on the trees, feeling the dust under my bare feet and thinking that I was in heaven. I loved my work, my children were happily meeting friends and building tree houses, my husband was helping to put a new roof on the temple—what could be better than that? That winter as I was putting together the strings and beads for a macramé plant hanger, I felt a light soft something on my hand and looked up to see snow drifting into the shop through the holes in the roof! I laughed realizing that Divine Mother was wanting to share in my happiness.

About two months later I was to be given one of Her tests. I received a phone call from Seva, the community manager at that time, asking if I would be willing to act as manager of the print shop. Not quite believing my ears, I told her that I was most happy in my present job and, even though I appreciated the offer, I would rather stay where I was. Besides, I had never even been in a print shop and knew nothing about machines and cost estimates, etc. She listened, asking me to reconsider and we hung up.

I felt a little baffled by the whole thing, but didn't give it much more thought until the next day when she called back, this time telling me that she had consulted with Swamiji and he was delighted with the idea of my moving up the hill to take over the handling of his books! Stunned, I reiterated my position, but this time sought advice from my boss who looked at me saying only with his eyes that this was a decision I needed to make on my own.

I went home confused, not liking the unsettling feeling descending upon my little kingdom of peace and joy. Why was my world being turned upside down? Why did I have to change? I knew that many of my business associates liked the work I did. I knew it wasn't because I was not doing a good job. Why did I feel uneasy about this? Something was pulling at my heart and something was terribly wrong. I meditated for many hours, at times crying to Divine Mother to give me guidance beyond my personal likes and dislikes. Was the test for me to stand up for what I wanted, to be strong in myself and not always think I had to do everything other people wanted me to?

or was it to let go of all thought of personal desires and do what was best for the community as a whole?

The worldly consciousness does not demand that we go inside ourselves to determine what is the best action in a spiritual sense. There's a fine line between understanding what comes from our own will and what is God's will. In this case, the lesson may actually be to stand up for oneself. But there could be another reason: to give up all into the infinite consciousness and will. What are the reasons we don't want to change? Money? Personal taste? To impress others? The outward happiness of it all? Not thinking of others' realities? When I look back on some of the things I've regretted most in my life, it's usually those times that I didn't think about the ramifications of my actions on everyone involved, or I wasn't thinking about what I needed to do to grow spiritually or to help others to do the same.

Finding God has a lot to do with listening deeply within your own heart and listening to His will for you. Surrender to God's will takes courage and the ability to step outside our own desires. That's one of the main lessons I came here to learn. When I was at the macramé shop, my lesson was to listen to others, because sometimes people who are spiritually more mature may also know what's best for your spiritual development.

At the end of that meditation, as I was holding up the two choices into Divine Mother's arms, a feeling of great joy and freedom flooded my being as I visualized letting go of my life into Her care completely. They really needed me at the print shop. I could feel that. As my mind became calm I could see things more clearly and my peace began to return. Later on that day I called Seva, accepted the new position and jumped into a world so totally foreign to me that I knew the only way I and everyone else would benefit at all from my being there was to give it all unto Her care. Wasn't it Hers anyway? I really had no choice. But She had to smack me hard for me to understand the greater picture. The great tangible blessing that came out of it for me was printing Swamiji's books on a small mimeograph machine. Somehow I finally did connect with that printing machine. I remember well one Christmas Eve as Melissa and I printed *Stories of Mukunda*, Swami's Christmas gift to everyone. It was a chance for me to look back on the year and reflect on the blessings that I had received seemingly from nowhere but, in fact, from everywhere. Where we are being led step-by-step is known only to God, but He gives us signs all along the way if we can be open to Him.

That test was right for me at that time. But it's different for each individual. The dharmic thing to do may depend on the situation. I remember one morning years later Kriyananda called at the school office to ask if I would take over the management of our new store, Earth Song, in town. I said, "Swamiji, I can do it, but I really think I'm needed here right now." He said, "Fine." By this time I had been at Ananda eight years or so and could sense a little better what was needed for both myself and for those I worked for.

One thing I've grown to appreciate on this spiritual path is being given the chance to grow, and to learn what is dharmic from the inside, and then to act on that. If I didn't take the job at the print shop, they would've let it go, and I probably would have eventually learned my lesson in another way. And I would have been just fine. But I learned a lot about myself from going inside and listening deeply. It's lessons like these that help us grow toward our goal of Self-realization.

Even though I was a householder and had two children, in the first years at Ananda I felt a pull to be part of the monastery. That's where the energy was in those days. It looked like such an idyllic life. You get up, your time's your own, you serve all day long, go home, meditate. It just seemed like a life of blissful visions and no hassles. One day I was talking to a dear friend of mine who was in the monastery.

I was telling her about the struggles I was having juggling so many balls and she wisely commented, "You know Durga, it's the same struggle for all of us no matter where we live. Yours may be on a more outward level, but we are struggling in much the same ways. It only looks different. God knows where your growth lies and you have given him the permission to train you in the best possible way." Once again, my questions were being answered and my soul felt the freedom to continue my journey just where He had placed me.

Being out here in the country is more conducive to being quiet and listening. I've always loved the wilderness feel of Ananda. Spending time outside in nature brings me closer to Spirit. I know many people liked it when we finally got indoor plumbing, but I fought against having an indoor toilet in my own house. Not because I don't like them, but because I could sense a change that would take us away from the simpler life if we weren't careful.

Everything was carried out at a much slower and more relaxed pace. When we had big snowstorms for days on end, we wouldn't have electricity. It was so peaceful, and the joy we experienced, so contagious! We came out of our individual houses to play together making snowmen and angels, building forts and throwing snowballs, sledding down Sunset meadow hill and laughing gleefully as the snow fell. If you were lucky enough to have a wood stove in your home, you could expect company on cold winter evenings. So quiet and unassuming. Sometimes I try to imagine what it would be like if the entire country could learn to slow down, to be more concerned with its own inner growth and care for those around it than gaining more land, more money, more power. Just imagine people coming together to live as friends rather than as opponents.

And, of course, people can do this anywhere if their consciousness is clear. We have different dharmas to live: some to work in the cities; some to create relaxing retreats; some to build schools and communities; some to nurture the dying and infirm. Whatever the calling, it is important to remember what Mother Teresa said when someone asked her why she chose to work with the dying in Calcutta. She told them that *she* didn't choose it, but rather God did. And that if He had chosen another work for her, she would have gladly done that instead. God's will for each of us is individual and perfect. It is imperative to listen for it in the depths of your inner being.

Each night, as my Spirit roams
In spheres of slumber vast,
I become a hermit and renounce
My title, body-form, possessions, creeds—
Breaking the self-erected prison walls
Of flesh and earthly limitations...

Paramhansa Yogananda
Whispers from Eternity, 1949 edition

Acknowledgments

To all the souls who agreed to be interviewed for this book and opened their hearts to difficult questions, my deepest gratitude—may we all learn and benefit from your insights into the spiritual life. And to all the Ananda community members who gave so selflessly to make this a true cooperative effort: to Cathy Parojinog for her gracious editorial work and her wise guidance; to Lila Hoogendyk for enthusiastically helping with manuscript production and for her angelic disposition; to Renee Glenn for intuitively creating the beautiful cover design; to Seva Wiberg, Julie Morgan, Kim Aho and Mickey Obezo for patiently transcribing hundreds of hours of interviews; to Peter Schuppe for taking on the difficult task of typesetting and producing the interior book; to Nirmala Schuppe for jumping in at the last minute to help with interior photo design; to Cathy Steenstra for her willingness to publish and guide the book through a difficult birth; to Gyandevi Fuller, for her kind help with photography; to Trip Clark for photography; and to all anonymous individuals who have contributed to the Ananda photo archives over the years; to Wayne Green for the cover photo; and to Nakula and Rama—for your endless love and support, I thank you.

Glossary

Ahimsa— "nonharming or nonviolence." One of the moral observances of Patanjali's Yoga Sutras. The practice of abstaining from harming others physically, mentally, or verbally, at all times.

Akashic Records— The records of all things past, present and to come, written in the ether. Some psychics and seers proclaim the ability to access these dimensions.

Ananda— "bliss." Both joy and transcendental bliss; conscious ecstasy.

Ananda Village— (Ananda World Brotherhood Village) The first intentional spiritual community dedicated to fulfilling the vision of Paramhansa Yogananda for spiritual cooperative living, founded in 1968 by Swami Kriyananda.

Asanas— "postures." Typically the physical yoga postures.

Aum— (OM) The all-pervading sound testifying to the Divine Presence in every atom of creation. Sacred monosyllable symbolizing God; the oldest and most venerated of all Hindu (Vedic) mantras, also employed in Buddhism.

Bhagavad Gita— "Song of the Lord." A portion of the Mahabharata. The Hindu Bible: sacred sayings of Lord Krishna.

Bhakti— Devotion. A bhakta yogi practices devotion as a path to God.

Brahmacharya— The model of life of the Vedic student, brahmacharya essentially stands for the ideal of chastity and self-discipline.

Buddhist— The spiritual tradition of Buddhism was founded by Gautama the Buddha. Buddhism stems from the Vedas, and thus can be understood as an elaborate yogic tradition.

Chakras— "wheels." The seven centers of energy located in the astral body with corresponding sounds, colors and astrological meaning.

Devotee— One who is devoted. A worshiper of devotion (bhakti). An aspirant who seeks to acknowledge dependence on a higher power.

Dharma— "Rightness" or "virtue." The moral order, as opposed to adharma.

Disciple— Pupil.

Divine Mother— God manifested as the feminine, mother aspect.

Dwapara Yuga— The third of the four cosmic ages of Hindu lore and the age in which we are presently living, according to Sri Yukteswar, who explains the universal evolution of consciousness, energy, and matter in *The Holy Science*.

Gayatri Mantra— Considered the most sacred mantra of the Vedas, and is chanted each morning and evening as a prayer for wisdom and illumination.

Guru— "destroyer of darkness." The spiritual preceptor who leads the disciple to God. Members of Ananda are disciples of Paramhansa Yogananda. The guru-disciple relationship is thought to extend beyond this lifetime.

Gyana (Jnana) Yoga— "union through wisdom." A gyana yogi practices wisdom as a path to God.

Hatha Yoga— Yoga associated with physical postures. Its objective is to transform the body into a worthy vehicle for Self-realization. Also used as a preparation for deeper meditation.

Hinduism— Dominant culture of India. "Hinduism" describes an amorphous mass of ideas, practices, institutions, and attitudes with a shared history based on the Vedas.

Householder— Married person or a parent responsible for raising children. Yoga is not exclusively for ascetics who retire to the forest or mountain cave. Householders can obtain success in yoga through diligent practice.

Householder Monastics— Married persons or a parent responsible for raising children, who are able to fulfill their worldly responsibilities while devoting their life fully to God. In *Autobiography of a Yogi*, Lahiri Mahasaya was the ideal model of the householder monastic.

Kali Yuga— "The Dark Age." The fourth of four cosmic ages of Hindu lore.

Karma— "action or fate." The moral force of one's intentions, thoughts and behavior. In this sense, karma often corresponds to fate, as determined by the quality of one's being in past lives and the present life. Whatever is experienced in the world—all that springs from karma.

Karma Yogi— A devotee of karma yoga, the yoga of selfless service. One who offers all the fruits of one's actions to God.

Kirtan— Group chanting and singing praises to God, or one's chosen deity.

Kriyananda— Swami Kriyananda (J. Donald Walters), the founder of Ananda Village and Ananda Yoga™ for Higher Awareness.

Kriya Yoga— A meditation technique using mental focusing and breath control; the highest meditation technique taught by Paramhansa Yogananda. Babaji (the deathless yogi) is said to be the father of Kriya Yoga. He passed this technique to his disciple Lahiri Mahasaya; who gave the technique to Sri Yukteswar, the guru of Paramhansa Yogananda.

Lahiri Mahasaya— The guru of Sri Yukteswar, Lahiri was a great Kriya Yoga master and householder monastic.

Mahabharata— One of India's two great national epics composed in Sanskrit, written by the great sage Byasa. Replete with references to Yoga. The Pandavas had been cheated out of their kingdom and were seeking to win it back. They succeeded in doing so with the assistance of Lord Krishna, who is Prince Arjuna's teacher.

Maha Mudra — "The great mudra." A yogic technique.

Mahamrityunjaya Mantra — One of the great mantras chanted as part of the Vedic fire ceremony for freedom from all bondage. The energy released radiates peace and healing throughout the world. Also used for warding off death and difficulties.

Master — A name of respect for one's guru, who is master of himself. In this book "Master" refers to Paramhansa Yogananda.

Meditation — Concentration on God or one of God's qualities. Deep awareness and lucidity accomplished through breathing and concentration techniques.

Nirbikalpa Samadhi — The highest state of divine union where the devotee can move freely in the world and perform duties without any loss of God-realization.

Nishkam Karma — Not being attached to the fruits of one's actions.

Raja Yoga — "Royal Yoga." Classical yoga that includes higher spiritual practices.

Ramayana — "Life of Rama." A tragic love story of folk wisdom complete with allegories, heroes, demons, battles between good and evil.

Reincarnation — The teaching that a person has more that one lifetime is common to most schools of Indian thought. It is part of the Vedic belief system. The ultimate purpose of yoga is to escape this never ending cycle of births and deaths and to reawaken to one's identity as the transcendental Self.

Renunciate — "Renouncer." Inner sacrifice. Relinquishing of the fruit of all one's actions. Renouncing one's worldly ambitions to live a life fully for God.

Sadhana— "spiritual practices." At Ananda Village, sadhana is traditionally composed of Energization Exercises and yoga postures followed by chanting and meditation, practiced at morning, noon and evening times.

Sadhu— A saintly person who may or may not be a practitioner of yoga.

Samadhi— A superconscious state of ecstasy in which the yogi perceives the identity of soul and Spirit.

Samskar— "tendency." In Yoga this word has psychological significance. It stands for the indelible imprints in the subconscious left behind by our daily experiences from past actions or past lives.

Sanatan Dharma— "The Eternal Religion." The indigineous name for Hinduism. The goal of this belief is the upliftment of human consciousness and the expansion of our self-identity through love, that we embrace all life and all reality as our own.

Sannyasi— Portrayed in the *Bhagavad Gita* as the person who neither hates nor desires anything. The yogi becomes immune to the duality of life through the practice of yoga, which includes an element of sensory inhibition, and through meditation, which supports mental detachment.

Satsang— The practice of gathering as devotees for chanting, prayer, meditation and worship. Contact in this way is purifying and uplifting and stimulates the spiritual process.

Shakti— "power." The dynamic or creative principle of existence, envisioned as being feminine and personified as Shakti, the divine consort of Shiva.

Spiritual Path— Spiritual life is almost universally represented as a path that leads from a state of spiritual ignorance to wisdom or enlightenment.

SRF— Self-Realization Fellowship.

Sri Yukteswar— Yogananda's guru; a great "gyana yogi" avatar. He was also a Vedic astrologer and author of *The Holy Science*.

Swami — A common title of respect for a spiritual personage. A swami is understood to be master of himself rather than over other people.

Tapasya — An endurance of extremes and abandoning of desires that can sometimes lead to states of perfection.

TM — Transcendental Meditation.

Vedas — Four profound scriptures of Hinduism. Divinely revealed from age to age, the Vedas possess timeless wisdom.

Yoga — "Union." Indian tradition of spiritual disciplines comprising different approaches to Self-realization.

Yogananda — Paramhansa Yogananda, "Incarnation of Love." The guru of devotees living at Ananda and author of *Autobiography of a Yogi*.

Yuga — "great eons." A cycle or subperiod of creation. Each yuga is composed of 12,000 divine years.

References:

Feuerstein, Georg, PH.D. *The Shambhala Encylopedia of Yoga*, Shambala Publications, 1997.

Frawley, David. *From the River of Heaven, Hindu and Vedic Knowledge for the Modern Age*, Passage Press, 1990.

Walters, J. Donald (Swami Kriyananda), *The Path*, Crystal Clarity, Publishers, 1977; *The Hindu Way of Awakening*, Crystal Clarity, Publishers, 1998.

Yogananda, Paramhansa, *Autobiography of a Yogi*, (Reprint of the 1946 First Edition by The Philosophical Library, Inc.) Crystal Clarity, Publishers, 1994; *Whispers from Eternity*, Self-Realization Fellowship, 1949.

A Selection of Books
by Crystal Clarity, Publishers

The Hindu Way of Awakening: Its Revelation, Its Symbols
by Swami Kriyananda
trade paperback • $14.95 • ISBN: 1-56589-745-5

Meditation for Starters
by J. Donald Walters
trade paperback • $9.95 • ISBN: 1-56589-079-5

Ananda Yoga™ for Higher Awareness
by J. Donald Walters
trade paperback • $10.95 • ISBN: 1-56589-078-7

The Path: One Man's Quest on the Only Path There Is
by J. Donald Walters
trade paperback • $14.95 • ISBN: 1-56589-733-1

Art As a Hidden Message
by J. Donald Walters
trade paperback • $10.95 • ISBN: 1-56589-741-2

Autobiography of a Yogi (the 1946 original edition)
by Paramhansa Yogananda
trade paperback • $14.95 • ISBN: 1-56589-108-2

The Essence of Self-Realization:
The Wisdom of Paramhansa Yogananda
edited by Kriyananda (J. Donald Walters)
trade paperback • $9.95 • ISBN: 0-916124-29-0

Ananda Course in Self-Realization: Part 1 - Lessons in Meditation
by John Novak
spiral bound with 2 cassettes • $24.95

Ananda Course in Self-Realization: Part II - The Art & Science of Yoga
by Swami Kriyananda
ring binder • 600 pages with 4 cassettes • $79.95

Secrets of Meditation
by J. Donald Walters
gift paperback • $6.95 • ISBN: 1-56589-739-0

How To Meditate
by John Novak
trade paperback • $7.95 • ISBN: 1-56589-716-1

Intentional Communities: How to Start Them, and Why
by J. Donald Walters
trade paperback • $7.95 • ISBN: 0-916124-51-7

Affirmations for Self-Healing
by J. Donald Walters
trade paperback • $8.95 • SBN: 1-878265-40-7

Education for Life: Preparing Children to Meet the Challenges
by J. Donald Walters
trade paperback • $10.95 • ISBN: 1-56589-740-4

Audio/Video Selections from Clarity Sound & Light

Autobiography of a Yogi (1946 Original Edition)
by Paramhansa Yogananda. Read by J. Donald Walters (Swami
Kriyananda) a direct disciple.
audio book • six cassettes • selected chapters
10 hours • $29.95 • ISBN: 1-56589-109-0

Ananda Yoga™ for Higher Awareness with Adam Bornstein
video • 72 minutes • $19.95 • ISBN: 0-916124-34-7

Meditation for Starters by J. Donald Walters
talk/guided meditation • 60 minutes • CD $15.95 • Cassette $9.95

Mantra by Kriyananda
vocal chanting • 70 minutes • CD $15.95 • Cassette $9.95

Kriyananda Chants Yogananda by Swami Kriyananda
vocal chanting • 70 minutes • CD $15.95 • Cassette $9.95

I, Omar by J. Donald Walters
instrumental • 61 minutes • CD $15.95 • Cassette $9.95

The Mystic Harp by Derek Bell
instrumental • 70 minutes • CD $15.95 • Cassette $9.95

A Celtic Evening With Derek Bell
live concert • 70 minutes • CD $15.95 • Cassette $9.95

Himalayan Nights by Agni
instrumental • 59 minutes • CD $15.95 • Cassette $9.95

Other Ananda Resources

The Expanding Light

Ananda's guest facility, The Expanding Light, offers a varied, year-round schedule of classes and workshops on topics such as meditation, yoga postures, healing, relationships, spiritualizing your daily life, and more. You may also come for a relaxed, personal retreat, participating in ongoing activities as much or as little as you wish. The beautiful serene mountain setting, supportive staff, and delicious vegetarian food provide an ideal environment for a truly meaningful, spiritual vacation.
For a catalog of programs or information call: 1-800-346-5350.

Ananda Kriya Yoga Ministry

Kriya Yoga is the most advanced meditation technique taught by Paramhansa Yogananda. It greatly accelerates one's progress toward Self-realization and is the heart of the spiritual practices for disciples of Paramhansa Yogananda.

The Ananda Kriya ministry offers support to those who wish to learn Kriya Yoga and to those who have learned it already, through the Ananda Course in Self-realization, and regular contact through Kriya retreats, meditations, phone calls and letters. For more information, please call 530-478-7560 ext. 7024

Ananda Healing Prayer Ministry

We are happy to pray for any prayer requests that we receive. We will keep your request on our Healing Prayer List for one month, at which point you can renew your request if there is still a need for continued healing. This service is freely given to any who ask for it. May you be deeply blessed.
Please call us at 530-478-7561, ext. 7028, or write:

Ananda Ministry
14618 Tyler-FooteRoad
NevadaCity, CA 95959-9316 U.S.A.

Website: http://www.ananda.org